WALTER
RAUSCHENBUSCH

WALTER RAUSCHENBUSCH
AMERICAN REFORMER

Paul M. Minus

MACMILLAN PUBLISHING COMPANY
New York
Collier Macmillan Publishers
London

Copyright © 1988 by Macmillan Publishing Company
A Division of Macmillan, Inc.

Macmillan Publishing Company
866 Third Avenue, New York, NY 10022

Collier Macmillan Canada, Inc.

Library of Congress Catalog Card No.: 88-344

Printed in the United States of America

printing number
1 2 3 4 5 6 7 8 9 10

Library of Congress Cataloging-in-Publication Data
Minus, Paul M.
  Walter Rauschenbusch, American reformer / Paul M. Minus.
    p.   cm.
  Bibliography: p.
  Includes index.
  ISBN 0–02–896470–5
  1. Rauschenbusch, Walter, 1861–1918. 2. Baptists—United States—
Clergy—Biography. 3. Theologians—United States—Biography.
I. Title.
BX6495.R3M56   1988
286'.1'0924—dc 19
  [B]   88-344
                                                                      CIP

Dedicated to the memory of
Susan DeWitt Minus
1966–1981

"To such belongs the Kingdom . . ."

CONTENTS

❯❯❯❯ PREFACE ❮❮❮❮

Only a few years after Walter Rauschenbusch died in 1918, his widow began hearing from people who were interested in writing a biography of him. Initially Pauline Rauschenbusch had reservations about approving the project. For one thing, she knew her husband had discouraged the idea. For another, with characteristic modesty she doubted that his life had been sufficiently eventful to warrant such attention; after all, Walter Rauschenbusch had been a pastor and a teacher, not a conspicuous leader in the historic dramas that attract the world's attention and provide the usual backdrop for illustrious lives.

Fortunately, however, as she talked with friends, her doubts gave way to the conviction that a sympathetic telling of Walter Rauschenbusch's life story could extend his influence to circles he otherwise might never touch. She realized also that his gentle hand had significantly shaped religious and secular developments in the latter part of one of the most extraordinary transitional periods in American history—the years between the Civil War and the First World War—and she concluded that posterity had a legitimate interest in knowing about her husband.

The task of writing the biography fell to D. R. Sharpe, who had been one of Rauschenbusch's student secretaries, and in 1942 his important volume appeared. But others before and after Sharpe also felt the lure of Rauschenbusch and attempted to measure the man and his impact. Most agreed that Rauschenbusch's writings brimmed with a religious force that was rare in his time or in any time. "He continued to speak the language of the prophets and St. Paul," ob-

served theologian H. Richard Niebuhr.[1] Rauschenbusch addressed his
message to people caught in a period when familiar ways were col-
lapsing everywhere. Industrialization, urbanization, immigration,
secularization, imperialism, and war were ending one era and starting
another. Above all else, Walter Rauschenbusch wanted to move the
church into its God-intended role of bringing biblical wisdom to the
building of an America in which there truly would be liberty and
justice for all.

At first, people resisted Rauschenbusch and his message, but during the heyday of Progressivism he gave voice to a great movement
of conscience, and for a season he enjoyed a national acclaim rarely
accorded seminary professors. Near the end of his life, however, the
courageous position he took on the Great War brought rebuke, and
Rauschenbusch died a sad man. His name fell under another cloud
during the middle decades of the twentieth century, when "neoor-
thodox" theologians declared his optimism excessive and certain
doctrines deficient. In more recent years, however, fresh interest has
arisen in Rauschenbusch. It was anticipated by Martin Luther King,
Jr., who acknowledged in 1960 that when he read Rauschenbusch's
Christianity and the Social Crisis a decade earlier it "left an indelible
imprint on my thinking." King added that despite several theological
shortcomings, Rauschenbusch "gave to American Protestantism a
sense of social responsibility that it should never lose."[2]

More than any other person, Rauschenbusch was responsible for
moving the churches to a new sense of social mission, but in some
respects his thought is dated and belongs to another era. Most notably,
he assumed the presence of a largely Christian culture ("Christendom"). But it is also true that key problems he addressed many years
ago continue to plague us today and that much of what he proposed
then remains compelling and instructive. There is something more
to be learned from his insistence that God's redemptive purpose for
the human family reaches to individuals and institutions alike, that
adoration of God and obedience to Christ must issue in sacrificial
service for disadvantaged neighbors everywhere, that the person concerned with saving souls must be concerned also with changing the
economic and social conditions that blight souls, and that both church
and nation must be reformed to make them properly responsive to
the divine will.

My own discovery of Rauschenbusch led eventually to the decision
that I must undertake a fresh study of him. I saw, however, that the
man's swath was so wide and his legacy so rich that I would have to
focus my effort carefully. Four possibilities beckoned. There was need
for an investigation of his thought—its origins, evolution, inner con-

nections, and impact. The time was ripe, too, for a new effort to understand the whole "social awakening" in which Rauschenbusch played such a key role. Moreover, it was important to reflect from a Rauschenbuschian perspective upon current issues facing the church and the nation. Although I have touched the first two realms in this book (and the third elsewhere), none of them has been my major concern; they continue to deserve attention, and it would please me greatly if some readers are prompted to test those waters.

The focus of my work is upon the life of Walter Rauschenbusch. The Sharpe biography continues to be useful, but it is clear that, after nearly half a century, new data and new questions call for a new biography. I have been fascinated, stirred, and instructed by Rauschenbusch, and I have attempted so to present and evoke his life that others will sense its quiet power. I believe people of all persuasions—those sympathetic with his commitments and those not—will find themselves enriched by taking this remarkable man into the circle of their acquaintances.

My introduction to Rauschenbusch occurred in 1955 in a course on American intellectual history taught by Professor Ralph Gabriel. Other Yale scholars subsequently nurtured my budding interest in Rauschenbusch and the Social Gospel. Roland Bainton remembered hearing him deliver the Nathaniel William Taylor Lectures in 1917 and continued to represent many of the same social convictions. Kenneth Scott Latourette embraced much of Rauschenbusch's Evangelical-Baptist perspective. H. Richard Niebuhr weighed his thought and appreciated it, but judged it too colored by the culture of the time. Sydney E. Ahlstrom helped me comprehend Rauschenbusch's place in the whole sweep of American religious history. To these good teachers—all now departed—I am more grateful than I can say.

The decision to begin work on a new Rauschenbusch biography was made in 1979. My enthusiasm for the project in the years since has been sustained by a number of events and people. Steps taken by the American Baptist Historical Society in the 1970s to gather nearly all the Rauschenbusch papers (including many never seen by Sharpe and other researchers) into a single Rauschenbusch Family Collection in Rochester, New York, have greatly facilitated scholars' access to the Rauschenbusch story. William Brackney and Susan Eltscher were models of cooperation during the months I spent in Rochester working through some 107 linear feet (approximately 151,500 pages) of Rauschenbusch papers in the American Baptist–Samuel Colgate Historical Library. I also studied Rauschenbusch materials at the North American Baptist Seminary in Sioux Falls, South Dakota (successor to the German department of Rochester

Theological Seminary); Hamburg Baptist Theological Seminary, Marburg University, and Gütersloh Gymnasium in the Federal Republic of Germany; the Rockefeller Archive Center in North Tarrytown, New York; the Valley Stream Baptist Church in Valley Stream, New York (successor to the Second German Baptist Church); Cornell University; and Yale University.

I was able to travel to these places and otherwise pursue my Rauschenbusch agenda because the faculty, administration, and trustees of the Methodist Theological School in Ohio generously allowed me time off from my teaching duties. A one-year fellowship from the National Endowment for the Humanities gave substantial financial support, and the staffs of the Library of Congress and the Colgate Rochester Divinity School / Bexley Hall / Crozer Theological Seminary provided repeated kindnesses. The difficult German script of numerous sermons and letters became intelligible to me through the translating skills of Ilse Meyer, George Dunger, and Wilhelm Braun. Several friends and relatives of Walter Rauschenbusch (including his three surviving children) shared their time and memories. A number of others offered valuable information and counsel over the years. Seven friends—Christoph Bresina, Donald Gorrell, Robert Handy, Gail Hovey, Norman Kansfield, Austin Kerr, and Reinhold Kerstan—have gone beyond the call of duty by reading the entire manuscript and making helpful suggestions. For all this kindness and assistance, I express my sincere appreciation.

Finally a word about my family. Better than others, my wife and sons know the alternations of spirit through which I have passed in these years of life with Rauschenbusch. They have supported me lovingly and resourcefully, and I shall always be grateful. I am pleased to dedicate this biography of a great man to the memory of a great person within my family circle who did not live to see it completed: my daughter, Susan DeWitt Minus.

CHAPTER 1

SON OF AUGUST RAUSCHENBUSCH

The autumn of 1861 brought a happy change of fortune for August Rauschenbusch. The program for German-speaking students he headed at the Rochester Theological Seminary in western New York had its largest enrollment ever and appeared to be stabilizing. Earlier in the year, he had moved with his wife, Caroline, and two daughters from a rented house into their own home. In Rochester's immigrant community he was beginning to be treated with the deference professors in Germany traditionally enjoyed. On the national scene, though he took no pleasure in the war with the Confederacy, he felt grim satisfaction in knowing that the terrible evil of slavery was under attack.

On 4 October 1861, a stirring event occurred. For months August Rauschenbusch had prayed that the child Caroline was carrying would be a boy. Three years earlier his only son had died, and there was no male heir to continue the Rauschenbusch name and traditions in America.

Years later August Rauschenbusch told Walter about that October afternoon in Rochester. At first he resented the "flippant remarks" of the doctor attending Caroline and retreated to the yard to chop wood. Then, at four o'clock, "Frau Auchter came with the cry, 'Mr. Rauschenbusch, come, for you have a little son!' That was music to my ears." As August reflected on the new arrival and pondered the infant's future, he committed him to God's keeping with the prayer "Walt' Herr, über diesem Kinde" (Rule, Lord, over this child) and in his prayer found the newborn's name: Walther. Two days later the happy father wrote his brother in Germany about the birth and confessed the hope that "God will make a Christian and a preacher out of him, a Rauschenbusch and a man of deeds."[1]

Eventually the world knew the boy as Walter Rauschenbusch, but until his early forties he preferred the German form of the name given him at birth. He knew his father had deliberately chosen German names for all the Rauschenbusch children and did not want them Americanized. He knew too that his father had raised them to prize their German identity and follow his lead by working among German immigrants in America. This child was special to August Rauschenbusch, who poured into his son the best he had to give. Throughout his life Walter was proud to be the son of the great patriarch of the German Baptists in North America. No one influenced him so much. But there also was a quiet, abiding sadness linked to the memories of life with his father.

August Rauschenbusch was a formidable man—a rare combination of intellect, fervor, and energy. Born in Germany in 1816, he came from a prominent Westphalian family and was the sixth in an unbroken line of university-trained Lutheran pastors. His "long and strenuous" education was capped by four years of university study in Berlin and Bonn. In Berlin he was tempted by the theological rationalism vigorously espoused by some of his professors, and for a period the young theologue rejected such traditional touchstones of orthodoxy as the belief that Moses was the author of the first five books of the Bible. But in January 1836 he underwent a dramatic conversion and adopted a conservative religious stance that remained essentially unchanged the rest of his life.

August Rauschenbusch's turnabout was precipitated by contact with German Protestants involved in an Awakening closely resembling the revival then under way in American Protestantism. These fervent believers recovered the insistence of an earlier generation of German Pietists that Christianity centers in the individual's conversion experience, disciplined obedience to Christ, and unquestioning acceptance of the Bible as the rule of belief and conduct. Many of the neo-Pietists also sought aggressively to reshape the church and the world according to their vision of biblical truth. In this spirit August Rauschenbusch threw himself into his first pastorate, which was in the same Lutheran church at Altena that his own father had served for many years. There he boldly denounced the sins of the parishioners, met for prayer and Bible study with the small group of people he considered true believers, and campaigned on behalf of foreign missions and temperance.

After four stormy years as a reforming pastor, Rauschenbusch felt called to America as a missionary, and by October 1846 he was spreading religious tracts among German immigrants on the Missouri frontier. The following autumn he moved to New York City to direct the American Tract Society's national program for German immigrants. There he lived with a Baptist family, whose convictions about baptism soon attracted him. Intense study led August Rauschenbusch to agree that the New Testament authorizes baptism for the converted only, that it is a sign of dying and rising with Christ, of giving up worldly ways in order to follow the Lord. He concluded that infant baptism is wrong and that its practice over the centuries by Catholics and Protestants alike had obscured the true meaning of church membership and fostered worldliness in the church. The point was emblazoned on his soul, and in later years, though he maintained unusually friendly relations with Christians of other traditions, August Rauschenbusch never tired of arguing that on this key matter non-Baptists had departed dangerously from Christian truth.

To the chagrin of his Lutheran family in Germany, Rauschenbusch decided that as a regenerated Christian he must be baptized according to the New Testament model. That event occurred in May 1850, by immersion in the Mississippi River. Walter Rauschenbusch later wrote proudly of his father's baptism: "It was a step that cost him dear; it cut his family to the quick; it completely alienated many of his friends; it rendered his entire future uncertain; but he followed the truth." Following the truth, regardless of cost, became a hallmark of the elder Rauschenbusch's life, and generations of Baptist students in Rochester were to admire him for it, but none more than his son.[2]

After several years in New York and Germany, Rauschenbusch returned to the Missouri frontier in 1854 as a Baptist missionary preacher. With him was his bride, Caroline, whom he had taught as a young confirmand in Altena. His frequent travels and wise counsel made him a respected leader among the small band of German Baptists scattered across North America and brought him to the attention of Baptist educators in Rochester, New York. When an invitation to join the faculty of the young Rochester Theological Seminary arrived in 1855, he knew it was the wrong time to leave Missouri. German immigrants, he said, were being dragged down by "worldliness and indifference, or led away by soul-destroying errors" of Roman Catholicism, and his preaching to them was beginning to bear fruit. On Independence Day of that year he baptized seven people and with them formed the German Baptist Church on Pin Oak Creek. On Sundays the new congregation met for worship on the Rauschenbusch farm, and on weekdays Rauschenbusch taught children from the area in his home.[3]

The constitution August Rauschenbusch prepared for the Pin Oak Creek congregation revealed his fundamental convictions. This body of believers, he wrote in the preamble, is "a union of souls who have surrendered themselves to the Lord Jesus and entered into a bond of Christian brotherhood for the purpose of seeking how best to follow him." Christian discipleship entails constant spiritual warfare against the evils of the world, especially against America's most monstrous evil—slavery. That institution, declared the first article of the constitution, is "wholly adverse" to divine teaching; hence slaveholders were excluded from membership in the church, and fraternizing was forbidden with any Baptist church that allowed slaveholders to become members.[4]

Many German immigrants in America at this time shared the passion for freedom that had swept through Germany earlier, but August Rauschenbusch's love of freedom and detestation of slavery were unusually strong. According to Walter Rauschenbusch, his father's conviction was so strong that he considered crossing to the Illinois side of the Mississippi River in order to be baptized on free soil by a pastor who shared his position. As it turned out, he persuaded an antislavery friend from New Jersey to perform the baptism. August Rauschenbusch's rejection of slavery was accompanied by a rare ability to see the issue from the higher ground of a theological perspective that avoided self-righteousness and encouraged reconciliation. A few years later, as the Civil War raged, Rauschenbusch urged German Baptists (virtually all of whom were in the northern states) to recognize that responsibility for the conflict did not rest upon slaveholders in the South alone: "The war is the judgment of God upon us all, both North and South. The North has given silent approval to slavery and has been enriched by it. Let us therefore confess our sins and pray that God may have mercy on our land." Walter Rauschenbusch later remembered his father's position against slavery and took his own stand against another massive denial of freedom, and the father's analysis of the Civil War was echoed by the son half a century later in the midst of another war.[5]

August Rauschenbusch's flock recognized that their pastor was a resourceful, hardworking man, but they also knew he had eccentricities they must abide. One Missourian later recalled his nervousness: "We had to stop all the clocks in our house when he came. We had to lock the dog up and put all the chickens up. There couldn't be any noise." There also was a sternness in their pastor that could become severe. But despite such difficulties, warm bonds developed between pastor and congregation, and they hoped to keep him. With the Pin Oak Creek Church membership growing, and with the Rauschenbusch family expanding (Frida was born in September 1855; Winfrid in April 1857), August Rauschenbusch seemed destined for a long ministry in Missouri.[6]

But events that would take August Rauschenbusch in another direction were unfolding. The Rochester Theological Seminary had been established in 1850 as a postgraduate school to prepare ministers for Baptist churches in New York and nearby states as well as for mission posts in America and overseas. Devout, learned ministers were needed to sustain and direct the prodigious revival that had surged through American Protestantism since early in the nineteenth century. During the years of the Second Great Awakening, a mighty stream of missionaries flowed across America and beyond, multitudes joined churches, numerous associations arose to stamp American life with Christian values, a common Evangelical conception of Christianity emerged, and Baptists became the second largest denominational family in the land.[7]

At midcentury a European observer noted that the United States was "by far the most religious and Christian country in the world," but few American Protestant leaders were content with what had been achieved. They believed that Christianity was still gaining strength and that opportunities for further advance were immense. In 1855 Zenas Freeman, the industrious corresponding secretary of Rochester Theological Seminary, voiced a conviction that spread widely in the decades ahead and permeated the school he loved: Ministers must be raised up who will "aim at nothing less than the conversion of the world to Christ."[8]

Freeman and his colleagues knew that August Rauschenbusch shared their vision and possessed the gifts necessary to make the school a force in the evangelization of German immigrants. They wanted him to train German Baptist ministers to preach among German immigrants in their native tongue and seek them for the Baptist fold. By 1855, after nearly a decade of effort, eight Baptist congregations existed among the Germans. Seminary leaders knew these new Baptists respected Rauschenbusch, and they believed that with proper planning and support his work in Rochester would hasten the winning of the immigrants.

Protestants throughout the United States felt a growing uneasiness about the Germans. Earlier generations had been assimilated with relative ease, but now unprecedented numbers were arriving, and many of them insisted upon perpetuating their foreign ways. In 1852 a Baptist official warned the seminary's governing board that these "strangers scattered over our land" brought with them such contaminants as Romanism, infidelity, and rationalism. If the newcomers could be won to Evangelical Christianity, they would become formidable allies in the struggle to make America a truly Christian nation and a light to all the nations, but if they were not won, the forces of darkness would be measurably strengthened.[9]

The beginnings of a German program at Rochester Theological Seminary occurred in 1852 with the help of part-time instructors, but the results were disappointing. Leaders of the school saw the need for a learned and pious teacher who could devote himself full-time to the German students. August Rauschenbusch, they knew, embodied the best of German Pietism, was at home in American Evangelicalism, and seemed ideally suited to pass on his blending of Pietism and Evangelicalism to future German Baptist ministers. Seminary leaders persisted in their overtures to him to establish and direct a German Department at the school, and they were rewarded by his decision to journey to Rochester in the summer of 1857 to consider the position.

August Rauschenbusch liked what he found in Rochester. Gardening long had been his favorite avocation, and the city was a flourishing horticultural center, offering a dazzling array of fruit trees, shrubs, and flowers. The seminary's faculty of three had a conservative theological outlook that harmonized with his own. Its library boasted the 4,600-volume collection of the eminent German historian Johann August Neander, Rauschenbusch's favorite teacher in Berlin. The seminary shared a building with the University of Rochester, which also had been founded in 1850 under Baptist auspices. The intellectual life could not match that of German universities, but the local university offered an environment that was certainly more in tune with his temperament and training than the Missouri frontier.

A sizable minority among Rochester's population of 45,000 were German immigrants. One of the city's churches, First German Baptist, had been established among the immigrants several years earlier. Rochester's fifty churches reflected the entire spectrum of Christianity's denominational diversity and together were a strong influence in the community. Many had been established during the flurry of revival that swept across western New York during the preceding quarter-century, and some still glowed from the spiritual fire lit the previous year by revivalist Charles G. Finney. Church members rallied in large numbers to voluntary societies that supported causes dear to Rauschenbusch, such as missions, temperance, and Sabbath schools, and some supported the more radical movements championed by local reformers Susan B. Anthony and Frederick Douglass.[10]

Shortly before his visit to Rochester, the American Tract Society had invited August Rauschenbusch to resume the work he had left in New York City five years earlier, at an annual salary double the $600 offered by the seminary. But salary did not rank high in his scale of values. The critical factor in his decision, his son Walter wrote later, was the need of the German students. They were "sheep without a shepherd, young minds without a teacher," and August Rauschenbusch felt called by God to become their shepherd and teacher. He agreed that after another year at Pin Oak Creek Church he would take on the new responsibility.

During the summer of 1858 the Rauschenbusches made their way circuitously to Rochester. August went to New York City, while Caroline and the two children visited German Baptist friends in Berlin, Ontario. There tragedy struck. Sixteen-month-old Winfrid was stricken during an outbreak of dysentery, and on 28 August he died. Deeply wounded by this blow, the grieving parents continued their journey to a new life in Rochester. They carried with them a pot of soil from Winfrid's grave, which they kept throughout their thirty years in Rochester. Eventually the son born to them there would name his own firstborn after the brother he never knew.[11]

August Rauschenbusch's first year as a professor at Rochester Theological Seminary was inauspicious. Only six students enrolled in the German Department, and the school failed to pay his full salary. At the end of the academic year, some suggested that he close the German Department and seek another position. Rochester and the nation were in the midst of an economic slump, and gathering clouds portended an even graver crisis. It was extremely difficult to raise funds for the school. Seminaries were still a relatively new mode of preparing clergy, and Rochester had been only the third Baptist seminary established in the United States. Many Baptists (including German Baptists) doubted that men destined for the ministry should be specially educated for it. If God called them, would God not equip them for their work in the same ways that had been fruitful in years past? Fortunately for the school, not all Baptists reasoned this way, but even among those who were sympathetic to the cause of theological education, fund raisers for Rochester Seminary had to compete for contributions with the University of Rochester as well as with the Baptist seminary and college at Hamilton, some 140 miles away in central New York.[12]

These were weighty considerations for August Rauschenbusch, but he refused to be diverted from his mission in Rochester. Caroline expected another baby (Emma arrived in August 1859), and besides leaving his family in the lurch, the proposed closing of the German Department would constitute a breach of faith with the handful of students already enrolled. Surely God would not desert this enterprise. It was, he insisted characteristically, a time for faith, courage, and self-sacrifice.

Financial difficulties were to continue for the German Department throughout August Rauschenbusch's tenure there, but prospects for it and for the Rauschenbusches slowly brightened. Thanks to August's travels and advocacy of theological education among German Baptists, the number and quality of students began to rise. A son and a house came in 1861, and two years later Rauschenbusch received an honorary Doctor of Divinity degree from the University of Rochester. A measure of financial stability was achieved the following year with the gift of a $20,000 endowment for the German Department. By the end of the war, August Rauschenbusch was firmly in place at Rochester Theological Seminary.[13]

In 1900 Walter Rauschenbusch presented his wife, Pauline, with an expansive, lighthearted account of the first eight years of his life. He intended it to be the beginning of a "biography . . . written only for you, with the garrulity and love of trifles which will be welcome to your fondness, however foolish it might seem to others." Regrettably, only a first installment of 8,500 words was written. He began with a playful look at his beginnings:

> My memory seems to have been imperfect even at that early age, for I remember nothing of the first year or two. I seem to have been rather a good-looking child; at least Mother used to tell with pride what a fine baby I was. . . . My head seems to have been abnormally big, so that some doctor cautioned Mother that I might have water on the brain. He must have been an unusually discerning man. Said too, that if I lived, I would be a smart man.

> Mother says I was a contented child, with a satisfactory capacity for finding my own fancies sufficient company. I could potter around with my play-things a long time and be quite happy. One anecdote has often been repeated as prophetic of a theological bent in a line with my ancestry. Father had been reading the 14th Psalm at family worship: "Fools say in their hearts that there is no God," etc. Afterwards I had been playing with my blocks and had constructed a cross, and then Mother heard me say to myself, "But there is a God." Another time, when I was asked, "What do you want to become?" I replied, "John the Baptist," which was especially gratifying to all good Baptists.[14]

Most of Walter Rauschenbusch's childhood memories came from four years spent in Germany. In 1865 August Rauschenbusch sent his family to the fatherland because he knew how fragile were the ties connecting immigrants' children with family and traditions across the Atlantic, and he wanted to make those ties strong and lasting for his own children. Caroline, Frida, Emma, and Walter spent the first year in Neuwied and the last three years in Barmen. Both cities were in a region that August had loved as a young man, and both were under the control of the rapidly ascending Prussian kingdom.

Because German had been the language spoken routinely in the Rochester home, Walter Rauschenbusch had little difficulty adjusting to the new setting. In Neuwied he had playmates other than his sisters for the first time. To his delight he was invited to join other boys drilling on a market square in imitation of the Prussian troops who had passed through town fresh from victory. Here Walter also committed his first remembered misdeed. One day the four-year-old was allowed to go on an excursion with Emma and her classmates, and he proudly carried an American flag. When the time came for the children to return to school, his mother told Walter to come home with her, whereupon the boy replied that Emma's teacher had asked him to march back with the older children because he had the flag. Caroline quickly discovered that Walter had fabricated the story, and he "went home in disgrace." Later Walter reflected that it had only just occurred to him "that this first memorable sin of my life was for the sake of the American flag. I confess, however, that it was not so much as a symbol of my country that I cared for it, as because it gave my little person a sense of distinction."

In Barmen the family lived in a rented apartment over a bakery close to the Wupper River. On Sundays they worshiped in a nearby Baptist church, and on weekdays the three children attended the same school. In this time of intense bitterness between Protestants and Roman Catholics in Germany, Walter Rauschenbusch was swept into the rivalry between his Protestant school and a nearby Catholic school. Each group of children taunted the other with a song. "I do not remember the Catholic war-hymn, but ours ended with 'fried in butter, stirred with flour, led to the devil.' I think we really felt that these children were bad and dangerous, quite different from us, who were good and altogether on the way to righteousness."

During their Barmen years the Rauschenbusches frequently visited family and friends. Especially pleasurable for Walter were trips to see Rauschenbusch relatives a short distance away in Elberfeld, a major industrial center in the Wupper valley. There his grandmother, his father's sister Lina Döring, and her daughter Maria Döring shared a comfortable home. The two older women were widows, the younger one was unmarried. Because Grandmother Rauschenbusch was deaf, she carried a slate board on which people wrote for her; Walter delighted in demonstrating his ability to form German letters. The Elberfeld Rauschenbusches and Dörings were an affluent, prominent family. Their Lutheran sensibilities had been wounded when August became a Baptist, but feelings of family solidarity ran deep, and lasting ties were knit between Rochester and Elberfeld.

August Rauschenbusch joined his wife and children only in the fourth year of their time abroad. The summer of 1868 brought Walter such pleasures as playing in the Rhine and hiking in the Black Forest with his father. Once when August was helping the six-year-old boy dress after a swimming lesson, "he gave me my first warning on sexual morality. It was not needed for several years yet, but it did me no harm." For much of the family's final year in Barmen, August Rauschenbusch was away researching Anabaptist history in pursuit of German antecedents of the Baptist movement. Walter recalled his father's return once to baptize thirteen-year-old Frida, whose "seriousness and absence of childhood folly," Walter believed, were especially gratifying to his father. At this time the boy felt less close to Frida than to Emma, who was a "little termagant," quick to insist on her own rights. "What sort of a boy I was myself, or what impression I made on others, I can only imagine. I think on the whole I was physically satisfactory, made an impression of intellectual promise, and was thought a good little boy." August and Caroline Rauschenbusch were proud of their son.

On 21 July 1869 the five Rauschenbusches left Hamburg on the steamship *Cambria* and two weeks later arrived in New York harbor. August could be pleased at the children's awareness of their roots. Walter had become as fluent in the language and as comfortable in German ways as any of his bright Barmen playmates. The door to Germany was open to him, and he would pass through it often in the future.

When August Rauschenbusch and his family returned to Rochester, he bought a house at 10 Arnold Park, only two blocks from the splendid new quarters of Rochester Theological Seminary. This elegant home was more in keeping with the dignity of a German professor than previous quarters the family had occupied. Arnold Park had been recently developed on the city's fashionable east side, and the street was noted for its sugar maples and spruce firs. The yard of the new home soon was filled with fruit trees, grapevines, a vegetable garden, a berry patch and a row of beehives. This yard was a special delight to the elder Rauschenbusch, because many years before he had discovered that tending plants and trees was a tonic to body and spirit. Young Walter often worked there with his father; he wrote his aunt that he was "helping Papa a great deal in the garden, pulling weeds and doing other things," and he boasted that they had received "more than four dollars for a bushel-and-a-half of cherries."[15]

August Rauschenbusch's desire that his son learn to enjoy the outdoors, coupled with the wish that he work for a living, led him to send the boy during the summers to farms owned by German immigrant friends. Walter Rauschenbusch's first rural experience occurred in Connecticut in 1872. The ten-year-old wrote his Aunt Lina of his adventures: "I often milked myself a glass of milk, and while it was still steaming I drank it. . . . When we came home from work, we threw off our clothes and jumped into the cold water of the brook, and I was very happy." Part of the following summer was spent with farm friends in Ontario. The years of his rural experience as a teenager occurred in Lycoming County, Pennsylvania. Later Walter Rauschenbusch recalled the enjoyable simplicity of life there: "On market days we took butter, eggs, and berries to Williamsport and sold them to the housewives on the street curb, or we went from house to house offering what we had. The old farmer liked to have me along because multiplying pounds by cents was a confusing operation for which a city boy came in handy." The summers were happy times for young Walter. The "city boy" learned to mix easily with the "old farmer" and folk like him. In subsequent years Walter Rauschenbusch enjoyed the company of such people and shared many of their values, especially the convictions that hard work is the mark of a good person and that people are entitled to the fruits of their labor. So rich was Walter's youthful farm experience that he later arranged comparable opportunities for his own sons.[16]

Except for the summers, father and son were together often during the 1870s. This pleased August Rauschenbusch. In 1873 he wrote his sister Maria Ehrhardt in Alsace that Walter "is the best of my children, has a very lovable and sensitive mind, and gives me much joy." Earlier he thought Walter would enter the ministry, becoming the seventh in line of Rauschenbusches to do so, but the lad's "nervousness" appeared to stand in the way. His father now hoped he would become a naturalist or gardener, though the boy said he wanted to be an architect. August conceded that this would be a "very rewarding profession" because of all the building under way in prosperous America, and added that he would not object if this were his son's decision.[17]

In later years, when Walter Rauschenbusch looked back upon his youth, he realized how much of his father's outlook had been transferred to him: "He educated me by sharing his own interests with me. . . . Without the physical and mental vigor that he put into my body, and without the sense of duty and of God which contact with him imparted, my life would have been far poorer and feebler." During the 1870s, as his father's prominence grew in the city and among German Baptists across the nation, Walter became more aware of the intensity and breadth of his religious convictions. On weekends and holidays students often came to 10 Arnold Park for dinner, and the three Rauschenbusch children eagerly joined in the conversation. At times, too, father and son ate with students in the school's dining room, and Walter attended German classes at the seminary.[18]

Walter Rauschenbusch discovered that his father was an unusually able teacher, with a talent for clear expression and a wide range of knowledge in the classical and theological disciplines. Because Professor Rauschenbusch believed it was important for his students to move beyond the narrow cultural and educational experience that most of them had brought to Rochester, he developed and taught both a liberal arts curriculum and a theological curriculum. He also wanted students to feel at ease outside their familiar religious culture, so he regularly took them on field trips to institutions such as prisons and nurseries to learn how they operated.

August Rauschenbusch's desire to stretch the horizons of his students and son reflected his breeding in a five-generation-old family tradition of cultured university graduates. A dimension of political awareness not customary among Lutheran clergy had been added by his father's service as a military chaplain in the War of Liberation against Napoleon and by an expectation over the next several decades that ministers of the state church must help build a strong fatherland under the godly rule of the Prussian king. For August Rauschenbusch this unusually broadened field of interest blended easily with his conviction that God's gracious will reaches to every realm of life—from the inner depths of conscience to the multifarious events of history. His beloved teacher Neander had called the sphere of this all-encompassing divine intention and activity the "Kingdom of God." This term was used widely and diversely by German intellectuals and activists throughout the nineteenth century, it had been prominent in the American Protestant tradition, and it was on the lips of many Americans during the nineteenth century. August Rauschenbusch spoke often of God's Kingdom. He believed that freedom and moral deeds were key marks of its presence, but he had neither the time nor the temperament to explore its meaning and implications. This task eventually became a major pursuit of his son Walter.[19]

A formal education was high on August Rauschenbusch's requirements for Walter. "He kept me at school," Walter later wrote, "till I was twenty-four." His enrollment in a private German school and two public schools was followed by three years at the Rochester Free Academy. Students at the local high school chose a classical, scientific, or business curriculum, and Walter elected the classical. In these years he formed close friendships with many of the students, notably Ed Hanna, Munson Ford, and Katherine Davis. During their final year at the academy Walter, Hanna, and Ford helped form the Pi Phi fraternity, launched to make its members better speakers and writers.[20]

In a two-page high school essay (the earliest of his extant thematic writings), Walter Rauschenbusch proudly affirmed the land of his birth and assailed England, reflecting a tinge of the hostility toward England that many Germans felt in these years. American "liberality and love of freedom," he argued, contrast sharply with English "greed and selfishness." The two nations may well go to war again, and if they do, the United States, now "one of the great powers of the earth," surely will emerge victorious.

At commencement exercises on 27 June 1879, twenty-two Free Academy graduates made short orations. To Ed Hanna fell the honor of giving the valedictory address; Walter Rauschenbusch was the salutatorian. Walter declaimed on the topic of Greek religion, and a local newspaper observed, "The young gentleman delivered his oration in a very clear, impressive manner, and it showed a thorough knowledge of the subject." The newspaper report did not mention a humorous note introduced into the solemn proceedings. Members of the class had conspired to produce a brochure parodying the events of the long June morning. The ceremony was renamed "Benny's Grand Baby Show of the Twenty-two Educated Infants from the Rochester Foundling Asylum," and an introduction of each student orator, allegedly by Principal Nehemiah Benedict, was included. The statement about Walter Rauschenbusch demonstrated the youthful irreverence of his classmates as well as their respect for him: "The phenomenal baby, noted for the size of his feet, muscular control of his right ear, and his moral principles respecting lager and dancing. He is my especial pet and is designed to the ministry. Good boy. Smart boy."[21]

Most of the information we have about the life of Walter Rauschenbusch in the 1860s and 1870s suggests that those were happy years for him, but some signs point to a barely concealed anguish. Later he told several of his own children that he wanted their childhood to be happier than his had been and that he did not want to be like his father. But he kept to himself the details of his painful memories.[22]

Letters that came to light only in the 1970s reveal that his home was torn by marital bitterness. In 1854 August Rauschenbusch's mother had come to fear her son's proposed marriage to Caroline Rump and warned him against it. Caroline was twelve years younger than he, she had little familiarity with the cultured professional circles that the Rauschenbusches frequented, and the two of them scarcely knew each other. Perhaps August's mother also recognized that her son's chronic irritability and religious zeal would make him a difficult husband for any woman and that life in a foreign land would put additional burdens upon their union. But her counsel went unheeded, and by the 1860s serious strains had developed in the marriage. Usually they were hidden from the view of outsiders, although friends occasionally saw and wondered. Augustus Hopkins Strong, president of Rochester Theological Seminary, wrote privately of the conflict: "Poor Mrs. Rauschenbusch learned early that absolute submission was for her the only way of peace. This submission was not natural to her. There grew up a shocking alienation between them." The main reason August Rauschenbusch wanted to go to Europe when he retired, Strong added, was to get away from his wife.[23]

Letters from August to his sister Maria during the 1870s reveal the existence of a chasm greater even than Strong had suspected. Unfortunately there are no letters from Caroline that tell her side. In 1871 August reported that never had his married life been so troubled as it was during the previous winter and spring. Since then a "kind of reconciliation" had taken place, which pleased him, especially for the sake of the children. But he saw no prospect of a lasting change: "I am still of the opinion that she is no Christian. Her supposed conversion twenty-eight years ago and her spiritual renewal eighteen-and-a-half years ago were not genuine." Moreover, he feared, "She is not entirely well mentally, otherwise she could not have thought such foolishness of me as that I was keeping a mistress in some isolated part of town."[24]

Two years later August expressed anxiety about Caroline's tormenting of their daughters. Emma had told him "she had lost most of her respect" for her mother. Caroline, he said, objected to his intention to send Frida to college, desiring instead that Frida do housework until she married. Walter, he added, "suffers much less under her." August now was desperate, and he asked his sister to join him in a grim pact.

At times, when I consider myself to be growing old and superfluous, I wish that God might deliver me from the pain of this earthly life, especially from my marital sufferings. But then I think that I must live in order to protect my children from their evil mother. . . . I would like to tell you openly, dear Maria, I ask God to liberate my children and me from her by removing her from this earth. I would not pray for this if I believed it possible that she could experience conversion, but I consider this impossible. I believe she is neurotic. You have no idea how full she is of malice and falseness—she increasingly is becoming a liar. It will be dear to me if you intercede with me in prayer.[25]

Later that year, while both Frida and Emma were away (the older girl had begun a two-year course at Granville College in Ohio), August wrote Maria that Caroline was unwilling to prepare lunch for Walter and him. Consequently he and his son ate with the German students. "If Walter were not here, I could not tolerate Mother's bad temper. . . . People wonder and questions are being asked." They can see, he explained, that she does not care for the welfare of her husband and son.[26]

The couple's stormy parenting inevitably created difficulty for the children, some of it patent, as in the case of the girls' relationships with suitors. The older daughter, Frida, met many of the German students, and eventually Georg Fetzer won her fond attention. When Fetzer began walking her home from church, August told him of his displeasure and cautioned Frida that the young man came from a poor, uneducated family. The two were not deterred, and August gave his blessing to Frida when she followed Fetzer to Germany in 1877 to marry him. She and her husband soon became pillars of the struggling Baptist denomination in Germany.

Emma was less fortunate. At age eighteen she became engaged to a German Baptist pastor in Buffalo. Her father concluded that the young man was not fit for his daughter and told Emma he would never be welcome in the Rauschenbusch home. Emma reluctantly agreed to break the engagement. Later August reconsidered and gave him permission to renew the courtship, but by now he had lost interest. It was many years before Emma married, and even longer before she and her father found peace with one another.[27]

The effect of his parents' alienation upon Walter is less evident. As a young child he became aware of their quarreling and was grieved by it. One of the earliest memories shared with his wife in 1900 came from the period before the family's trip to Germany. He recalled: "I come in from the back yard into the kitchen. Father is leaning on a table and Mother is at the other side of the room. I see by their faces that they are angry and I feel afraid and distressed. They tell me to go into the other room." In all that he wrote over the years, this was the only look Walter permitted an outsider at his embattled home life. The autobiography he began for his wife never progressed beyond 1869. Moreover, his extensive biographical writing about his father gave not even a hint of marital conflict. A heavy curtain was drawn over this most tormented part of Walter Rauschenbusch's life. It was as if a painful wound had never healed and must be protected from touch. Here lie the origins of his lifelong reticence about revealing his innermost thoughts about himself.

This lad, possessing what August Rauschenbusch rightly called a "sensitive mind," was pained by the contradiction between his parents' public profession of a religion of love and their private lovelessness toward one another. Walter believed that his father was chiefly culpable, and he rose to the defense of his mother. "I stood up against my father when he spoke against my mother," Walter reminded Emma many years later. But as exasperated as he was with his father, Walter admired him for his good qualities, continued to love him, and sought an end to the hostilities. This experience doubtless fostered a major personality pattern of his adult years: He protected the weak from the strong, the victim from the aggressor, and he did so without rancor, in ways intended to end the wrong and establish peace between adversaries.[28]

A fateful turn in Walter Rauschenbusch's religious development occurred in the late 1870s. Throughout childhood he had attended Sunday school and church with his family and participated in family prayers and Bible discussions at home. His behavior as a schoolboy appears normally to have been exemplary, but it was not always so. In 1913 he recalled the period when as a youngster he "ran with a gang; for a time I tried very hard to become their leader in swearing, but I never could. I think, however, that other people who observed me thought I was on the road to the devil." One friend remembered his being "quite unruly and seemingly far removed from any thought of the Christian life." Another recalled that his father once whipped him for spreading "unbelief" among the boys in his Sunday school class; the chastised lad threatened to run away from home, but his mother prevented it.[29]

These recollections of youthful misbehavior doubtless bespeak a reaction by Walter against his father and the strains in his home life. They may have been painted in deliberately somber hues to make greater the contrast with the light that soon came. Anticipating and remembering one's conversion experience was a key part of Walter Rauschenbusch's Pietist-Evangelical inheritance. The event probably occurred at the age of seventeen. He later wrote a friend that it was preceded "by a long struggle extending through several years" and, more immediately, he told his daughter, by a bobsled accident and a protracted convalescence. It was followed by his profession of faith and baptism at the First German Baptist Church in Rochester on 16 March 1879.[30]

Only once, in 1913, did Walter Rauschenbusch publicly relate his conversion experience, doing so in language that evoked the parable of the prodigal son.

> And then, physically, came the time of awakening for me, when young manhood was coming on and I began to feel the stirring of human ambition within me; and what I said to myself was: "I want to become a man; I want to be respected; and if I go on like this, I cannot have the respect of men." This was my way of saying: "I am out in the far country, and I want to get home to my country, and I don't want to tend the hogs any longer." And so I came to my Father, and I began to pray for help and got it. And I got my own religious experience.

In retrospect he viewed the experience with gratitude and a touch of skepticism.

> Now, that religious experience was a very true one, although I have no doubt there was a great deal in it that was foolish, that I had to get away from, and that was untrue. And yet, such as it was, it was of everlasting value to me. It turned me permanently, and I thank God with all my heart for it. It was a tender, mysterious experience. It influenced my soul down to its depths.

Vocational consequences followed quickly from his conversion: "Very soon the idea came to me that I ought to be a preacher, and help to save souls. I wanted to go out as a foreign missionary—I wanted to do hard work for God."[31]

Walter Rauschenbusch never retreated from his commitment to be a preacher, to save souls, and to do hard work for God. All this he wanted to do in the style of his father—serving the Lord by seeking arduously to make his own life, the church, and the world conform to the divine will. Such was the direction of his life for the next forty years. The intellectual framework of his commitment, however, was pliable, and in the years ahead he was exposed to people and ideas that caused him to question much of the religious outlook learned in his childhood and youth. How much of his inheritance was "true" and should be retained? How much was "foolish" and should be rejected? Because he had received most of his early religion from his father, the struggle for his own religious ground was entwined with his struggle to achieve a personal identity free from his father's domination.

"Life is nothing but a series of emancipations," Walter once told his daughter Winifred. Intellectual and personal emancipation did come to him, but it was not gained easily.[32]

✹✹✹ CHAPTER 2 ✹✹✹

PRIMUS OMNIUM

By the time Walter Rauschenbusch graduated from the Free Academy, he was preparing to leave Rochester for the next phase of his schooling. The German educational system was the envy of the Western world, and August Rauschenbusch wanted his seventeen-year-old son placed in the hands of German educators. He had enrolled Walter at the Evangelische Gymnasium zu Gütersloh, a private secondary school in Westphalia, noted for its teaching of the humanities in a conservative religious atmosphere. On the second day of July 1879, Walter left Rochester with his father, who was going to Germany for a year-long sabbatical leave. Fifteen days later the two Rauschenbusches reached Gütersloh.[1]

Momentous events had occurred since the family's departure from Germany ten years earlier. Under King William I and Chancellor Otto von Bismarck, Prussia had defeated France and had become the dominant force in the new German Reich. The industrialization, urbanization, and militarization of German life had accelerated. Government restrictions had tightened against the feared Roman Catholic church and Social Democratic party. Rich coal deposits had made the Rauschenbusches' beloved Westphalia one of Prussia's key industrial provinces. The Reich was now a major power in Europe, and some dreamed of even greater might and glory.

Gütersloh remained untouched by the clamor of the time. The major rail line between Cologne and Berlin ran along the edge of town, but few trains stopped. It was a tranquil, undistinguished spot, rating only a few lines in Baedeker's guidebook for visitors to northern Germany. Most of Gütersloh's 4,500 inhabitants earned their living by raising hogs, making sausages, smoking hams, and boarding students. Walter Rauschenbusch complained to high school classmate Munson Ford (who had enrolled at the University of Rochester) that Gütersloh was dirty, had no sidewalks, and emitted "a great variety of smells, odors, stinks, and stenches." Later he would love "this dear little town," but initially it disappointed him.[2]

August Rauschenbusch had chosen this school for his son because he believed in its educational philosophy and its mission in the new Germany. The Gütersloh Gymnasium was established in 1851 by Westphalian leaders of the Awakening who shared King Frederick William IV's abhorrence of the "wicked doctrines of a modern and frivolous secular wisdom" that inspired the unsuccessful revolution of 1848. They believed with their king that a prime way to counter the novel notions of liberty, equality, and fraternity was to produce young men in whom the Western humanistic tradition was yoked with a Christian perspective unalloyed by modernist error. The school's graduates would help restore a Christian Germany united behind a pious monarch. In their souls, declared an early leader of the school, would be a durable union of "love for God, love for king and fatherland, and love for science and art."

The town seemed to be the perfect site for such a school. Its isolation promised to keep students safely distant from evil influences, and its inhabitants—imbued with the spirit of the Awakening—welcomed the opportunity to help shape the young boarders entrusted to their keeping.[3]

The first task facing the Rauschenbusches and the school's administration was to determine the grade level at which Walter would begin. Differences between the American and German educational systems complicated the question. A gymnasium prepared boys for university study through a rigorous nine-year program in the humanities; they usually began at age nine and left at eighteen. Most students his age already were nearing graduation, but Walter's knowledge of Greek and Latin lagged several years behind theirs, and he had not even begun French and Hebrew. The director of the gymnasium decided that in six weeks the American must report for a placement examination to determine the level at which he would enter.

Young Rauschenbusch hoped to start in the *Untersekunda*, the level four years from graduation; this would allow him to finish at the same time as Ford and other friends who were attending American colleges. He anticipated that his four-year gymnasium program would count as the equivalent of an American college education and that he could therefore begin his graduate theological education with students his own age. A cousin who taught in the gymnasium at Dortmund doubted that Walter was ready for the *Untersekunda*, but he agreed to help with preparations for the examination. The next weeks were a time of intense cramming: "I translated German into Greek, Latin, and French all day long." When Walter presented himself on 8 September to be tested, school officials announced that he did not have to take the exam, but could enroll in the *Untersekunda* immediately on a trial basis. If he performed satisfactorily for three months, he would be allowed to remain there. "I nearly stood on my head," he exclaimed to Ford.[4]

Rauschenbusch's elation was short-lived. On the third day of classes a teacher scolded him for gazing out the window; such disrespect for authority would not be tolerated in a Prussian school. On his first Greek translation he performed "horribly." Walter now saw that he must apply himself as never before. He was in classes Monday through Saturday, four to six hours a day, and hard at work in his room most of the remaining time. A notebook from 1879 shows that his study began at 6:35 A.M. and continued throughout the day with periods designated for religion, Latin, mathematics, French, Greek, history, geography, and Hebrew. It was clear that a highly disciplined life was necessary for academic success.

Gradually the intense effort bore fruit. "Matters were rather critical at first," he reported, "but by dint of working like an American" his class rank rose. He was proud when one of his teachers, announcing Walter's improved standing, called him "the energetic American." By the end of the school year he had risen to sixth in his class of forty.[5]

Over the next three years Rauschenbusch's mental agility and analytical powers grew under the prodding of his instructors. He read widely in the masterpieces of Greek, Latin, biblical, German, and French literature and frequently wrote essays on the style and thought of such authors as Homer, Cicero, Saint Paul, Goethe, and Lessing. He confessed to a friend that often the essays were begun in the late afternoon and completed in the early morning hours of the day they were due—"good preparation," he hoped, for writing he would do in the future.[6]

Usually the essays sparkled, and Walter's teachers rewarded him with high grades. By the end of the second year he had gained the top rank in his class. That distinction continued the next year, and at the end of it Rauschenbusch received the supreme honor the school could bestow: selection as the student body's Primus Omnium. This position went to the student who on the eve of his final year was judged by the faculty to possess superior intellectual and personal qualities. When Walter learned in March 1882 that he had been chosen, he wrote Munson Ford that he was now "first man of the establishment. . . . I am blooming like a wild rose."

Several duties went with the honor. During his final year, Rauschenbusch presided over weekly meetings of the two upper classes, brought the students' points of view to teachers and administrators, and led formal marches of uniformed students through the streets of Gütersloh. For the others the marching was preparation for the military service required of young German males. For Walter it contributed to the erect frame and crisp gait that remained with him in later years.[7]

His delight at earning academic distinction was accompanied by an intellectual pleasure that grew during the Gütersloh years, for he found beyond the toilsome coursework a realm of enjoyable mental adventure that came partly from meeting great minds. In 1882 he wrote of his thrill at discovering Socrates' "quickness and acuteness of reasoning," and he confessed he was "very much in love" with Plato and Sophocles as well as with the giants of German literature. Intellectual pleasure came also from the exercise of his linguistic and creative skills. Walter Rauschenbusch especially enjoyed writing poetry. In spare moments he composed poems in German, English, Latin, Greek, and Hebrew that were occasionally sent as gifts to family members. Most of the poems were undistinguished (as his father candidly observed), but writing them gave him enjoyment and contributed to a deftness with words that became a major asset in his adult years. In addition, Rauschenbusch's mastery of several languages gave him direct access to intellectual and cultural worlds unknown to most Americans. In later years he was especially attentive to developments in Germany, but his writings also showed an unusual awareness and appreciation of a variety of histories and cultures beyond his own.[8]

Rauschenbusch now recognized that his mental gifts must be brought fully into play in his work as a minister. A poem written in 1880 contrasts the rewards of being a farmer to those that awaited him as a Christian intellectual. It concludes:

No! Ne'er would I surrender
The joys of intellect.
The lofty walks of knowledge,
Ne'er would I them reject.

The "lofty walks" not only brought pleasure, they also pointed to a duty. "You see," he explained to a friend, "I believe I owe mankind a full development of all that my brain contains the 'potentia' of."[9]

Life at school in Gütersloh provided opportunity for less-lofty pleasures as well. Early in his student career Walter became a member of the gymnastics club. He was larger than most students, and his sturdy build (about 5 feet 10 inches, 180 pounds) won him a position at the base of a three-level "human pyramid," the speedy formation of which was the climactic event at exhibitions by the club. In wintertime he enjoyed skating on nearby frozen fields. A small harmonium given him by his sister Frida provided an additional source of amusement and nurtured his musical talent.

By the time of his selection as Primus Omnium, Rauschenbusch had won numerous friends among students and townspeople alike. He evinced a wit and a discerning interest in others that attracted friends all his life. Moreover, he stood out as one of the oldest students and as a foreigner actually eloquent in German. Most of the school's three hundred students came from prominent families in Westphalia and the Rhineland. Walter grew particularly close to three of his classmates: George Schaaf, the son of a pastor in Potshausen, near the Dutch border; Ernst Cremer, the son of an eminent Lutheran theologian at the University of Greifswald; and Charles Strong, the son of the president of Rochester Theological Seminary. Walter spent parts of vacations in the homes of both German friends and enjoyed talks with Strong about politics in America.[10]

In a letter to his father, Walter Rauschenbusch commented that the school's heavy academic demands gave students little time to visit in the homes of townspeople and that consequently many grew "very wooden socially." But Walter had no such handicap. He mixed easily with the ordinary people of Gütersloh as well as with its leaders. The home of Heinrich Bertelsmann became a favorite haven for him. Bertelsmann's father had been a founder of the school, and the publishing house he owned had printed a hymnal edited by August Rauschenbusch. Heinrich Bertelsmann was now allied with Professor Hermann Cremer and other Lutherans opposed to the liberal theological currents championed by such innovators as Albrecht Ritschl. Members of the Rauschenbusch family who visited Walter in Gütersloh were hosted by the Bertelsmanns, and in later years when he visited the school they were among the first people he greeted.[11]

Walter's talent for making and keeping friends was amply developed, but with the school open only to males, there was little opportunity for companionship with women his own age. He complained,

"I hardly get a glimpse of young ladies here." His capacity for fantasy, however, did not atrophy, and in a poem written privately he pined,

> *How I long my lips to press*
> *On thy mouth, O sweet caress,*
> *That would all my sorrows chase;*
> *Could I hold thy rosy charms*
> *Fast within my loving arms*
> *Call thee ever mine!*

When the time came for his return to Rochester, he confessed to an American friend that he had been buried so long in the Westphalian town "that I turn all green when a girl only looks at me, which you probably know is the most violent form of blushing," and he admitted that he would need help in reentering "ladies' society."[12]

At the time of his departure from the gymnasium, Rauschenbusch's teachers expressed approval of his religious growth, and hope for his future as "a loyal servant of the church." They had seen him move impressively in channels first marked by his father and reach toward his own religious outlook, and they believed he would successfully transplant his maturing faith in American soil.

The person charged with oversight of student religion was the school's chaplain, D. Theodor Braun. A child of the Awakening, Braun had joined the gymnasium staff in 1859, and by the time of Walter's arrival his teaching of religion and pastoring of boys had won him great respect and affection. More than half of the school's graduates chose to concentrate their university study in theology, and Braun's influence was considered a major reason.[13]

Rauschenbusch grew to love Braun as he did few people. Three decades after he graduated, he wrote, "The Chaplain was a man whom I shall never forget. Slender and frail of stature, he was a man of penetrating intellect and one of the noblest embodiments of religious life in all my experience." Students criticized and mocked other teachers, but not Braun. "He dealt personally with the souls of the men in a brotherly and searching way, and his connection with some of them continued long after they had passed from his official sphere." Here was a model for his own future ministry. Perhaps, too, Walter found in Pastor Braun something of the warmth and affirmation that came only sparingly from his father.

Week after week in Sunday worship, Rauschenbusch heard Braun preach, and the sermons so impressed him that he regularly made copious notes. "I get more out of them this way," he explained to his father, "and besides I hope they will be useful to me later." At cele- brations of the eucharist, Walter marveled at the reverence with which young communicants went to the altar to receive the cup and the host. But the sacrament was open only to Lutherans and to the few members of the Reformed tradition at the school, and he admitted to his father that the exclusion pained him, even though he knew that August Rauschenbusch was among those Baptists who believed it proper for a congregation to practice closed communion.[14]

Braun often talked privately with Walter about his personal life and religious commitment. The chaplain gave him a booklet con- taining one hundred questions to guide readers' scrutiny of their souls. The questions bespoke the Awakening's concern for personal piety, right belief, and good deeds:

> Do you resist the devil and all his works? . . . Are your Sundays devoted to secular amusements or to God's word? . . . Do you believe that Jesus Christ is true God and true man and that he has made a complete offering of himself for your sins? . . . Do you care about all who suffer, both at home and abroad?

Such questions touched Walter deeply, and they contributed to his sharply alternating moods of elation and gloom. In October 1880 he admitted to his father, "Sometimes I have wholehearted contempt for myself," and the following month he added, "I cannot help it that I still dislike myself. . . . A year ago I saw only my good side and did not think that the devil had power over me, but now I definitely know he does." Nevertheless, he knew that the demonic power had not sep- arated him from God: "I thank and love the Lord from the bottom of my heart because he has lowered himself to such a miserable person as myself."[15]

A chief occasion for personal struggle was the question of whether he should drink. His German schoolmates did not share his Baptist scruples about alcohol, and some imbibed to the point of drunkenness. Initially Walter abstained, but in 1881 he explained to his father that he occasionally consumed wine and beer, particularly at social gath- erings, when moderate drinking seemed harmless and convivial. And as Primus Omnium he was expected to propose toasts at such festive occasions as the king's birthday. When other students went too far, however, he believed that he must make a religious witness by ab- staining altogether. Walter assured his father that when he returned to America he would resume a policy of total abstinence. It helped greatly, he told a friend, "to feel the guiding hand of Jesus" as he decided which road to take in such matters.[16]

Walter Rauschenbusch was introduced to German Protestantism's method of addressing larger issues of social morality shortly after his arrival in Germany in 1879. He journeyed to nearby Bielefeld to observe the homes for epileptics directed by Pastor Friederich von Bodelschwingh. Seven years earlier, Bodelschwingh had begun a ministry on behalf of the disadvantaged that made him one of German Protestantism's most beloved figures. Rauschenbusch returned to Bielefeld several times during his years at Gütersloh. After one visit he acknowledged that his life had been shielded from such suffering and that "great and heavy pain" came to him as he gazed upon it.[17]

The teachers at the Gütersloh Gymnasium knew and admired the social ministries of Bodelschwingh and his older cohorts Theodor Fliedner, founder of the deaconess movement at Kaiserswerth, and Johann Wichern, organizer of the Inner Mission. Sensitized to human suffering by the Awakening, these pioneers urged German Protestants to recognize that the church must join the state in addressing the needs of the alarming numbers of people devastated by war, disease, and industrialization. Progressive though they were, however, such religious leaders had no sympathy for socialists' aggressive criticisms of German society and their proposals for far-reaching political and economic change. Attachment to the monarchy and to the traditional hierarchical shape of German society caused most Protestants to shudder at the radicalism of the socialists. Their Lutheran heritage made them prefer to do as they believed Jesus had done: leave political and economic matters to the state and extend a loving hand and an instructive word to the fallen.[18]

The focus of Pastor Braun's classroom teaching was the biblical and historical foundations of Christianity. There was an element of drudgery in it for students; they were required to memorize Luther's Small Catechism, the Augsburg Confession, thirty-two hymns, and dozens of Bible verses. As a latecomer to the school, Rauschenbusch worked intensively his first year to learn what classmates had memorized in earlier years, but memorization came easily, and he quickly mastered this part of his coursework.

The religious depths of the Lutheran Pietist tradition appealed strongly to Rauschenbusch and fit comfortably with the spirituality received in his Rochester home. One of the hymns he learned, "Befiehl du deine Wege," had been written by German Pietist Paul Gerhardt in the seventeenth century, and eventually it became a favorite. Gerhardt's words called for the believer's trustful acceptance of God's all-powerful providence:

Commit whatever grieves thee
Into the gracious hands
Of him who never leaves thee,
Who heav'n and earth commands,
Who points the clouds their courses,
Whom winds and waves obey,
He will direct thy footsteps
And find for thee a way.

In later years Rauschenbusch sang his children to sleep with the hymn, and near the end of his life he acknowledged that it was "the best expression of that faith in the guidance and mercy of God which has sustained me in darkness and loneliness."[19]

Among his favorite courses at the Gütersloh Gymnasium were several in church history and the Bible, and he regretted that the school offered so few hours of instruction in so important a field as religion. His work with Braun on the Letter to the Romans brought a new appreciation of Paul's thought, but for Rauschenbusch the center of the Scriptures lay elsewhere: "The Gospels," he told his Aunt Lina in 1882, are "the best of the entire Bible."[20]

Walter Rauschenbusch treasured the Gospels because they presented the life and teachings of Jesus, and he learned with other students that a central teaching of Jesus had been the Kingdom of God. He learned, too, that *das Reich Gottes* was a favorite term among nineteenth-century Germans, used by neo-Pietists, philosophers, theologians, missionaries, preachers, and humanitarians, all of whom gave it their own meaning. The term had recurred often in Braun's teaching; his assignment to the graduating class in 1880 was to write an examination essay on the theme "What do we mean by the prayer 'Thy Kingdom Come'?" Walter sat under Braun in courses entitled "The History of the Kingdom of God in the Old Testament" and "The History of the Kingdom of God in the New Testament." One of his last essays at the school was on the latter topic, but unfortunately it is not extant.

The chief view of Rauschenbusch's thought on the Kingdom that has survived from this period is a thirty-two-line poem in German sent to his father in September 1882. In it he reflected upon the parable in Matthew's Gospel about the seed that germinates into the Kingdom of Heaven. The major theme is the contrast between that kingdom and the fruit emerging from seeds strewn by human initiative. From them "no green sprig has come forth"; they produce knowledge devoid of "life and strength." But from the divinely planted seed has come "a high and green tree" extending to the entire world. Few nations remain unshaded by this tree. Birds sing happily in its branches. Soon its growth will be finished and Jesus will return. "Come, Lord Jesus, come soon," he concluded.

In another ten years the concept of God's Kingdom dominated Rauschenbusch's thought and activity. His understanding of it evolved greatly, but several characteristic motifs were apparently formed by 1882: The Kingdom of God is a divine gift, it makes a palpable effect upon the world, and it elicits in the Christian a mood of eager expectancy.[21]

The religious development of Rauschenbusch also was affected by visits to Baptist circles scattered around Germany. The initial Baptist congregation in German-speaking lands had been organized in Hamburg in 1834, and since that time the Baptist community had grown to more than 30,000 members. Rauschenbusch's first article in English praised these brave Christians for persisting in their faith despite harassment by government officials and ostracism by members of the state church. It was a stance reminiscent of the Anabaptists, and, following his father's lead, the young Rauschenbusch became fascinated with that sixteenth-century movement. Occasionally he was invited to preach in Baptist churches; his first sermon was delivered at Halle, a stronghold of early Pietism. "The proclaiming of God's word gave me joy," he reported to his father. But he also experienced the precarious legal status of Baptists. At Altenburg he was prohibited from preaching by an official who invoked laws designed to restrict subversive activity by socialists.[22]

The Altenburg experience sharpened Rauschenbusch's aversion to German Lutheranism's linkage of crown and altar. Nevertheless, his appreciation of Lutheranism grew. Prolonged contact with Lutherans, particularly with Gütersloh friends and Elberfeld relatives, taught him that God's grace flows through that channel too, and it fostered an enduring openness on his part to Protestants beyond the Baptist community.

Few Protestants in Germany had the opportunity Walter Rauschenbusch had to become intimately acquainted with both the dominant Lutheran tradition and the minority Baptist tradition. He moved easily between the two religious cultures and found much to respect in each of them. Lutherans knew that God calls them to perform their duty in the world gladly, but Baptists also were right in judging that the world is sinful and must not be allowed to distract them from their true homeland. Different though they were, the two traditions offered important insights, and Rauschenbusch later developed a theological vision that drew from both.

Recognizing good qualities in Roman Catholicism was more difficult for Walter Rauschenbusch. Part of the problem was the deep

gap between Baptists and Catholics in their fundamental understanding of Christianity, but there was more to it than that. Since
the sixteenth century, Westphalia had been an area of bitter acrimony
between Lutherans and Catholics, and Bismarck's *Kulturkampf* against
German Catholics exacerbated the conflict. The younger Rauschenbusch's hostility was symbolized by an incident reported to his father.
When visiting Bonn in 1882, he deliberately refused to remove his
hat when the host passed by during a Catholic public procession. Even
more poignant was the rift that grew between Walter and Rochester
classmate Ed Hanna. After Hanna went to Rome to study for the
priesthood, the two friends agreed to preserve the bonds between them
and covenanted to pray for one another. As each internalized more
of his own religious tradition, however, the divisive power of the three-
century-old split asserted itself. Their correspondence continued, but
Rauschenbusch wrote in 1883, "I always feel as if we did not half
understand each other." To a mutual friend he exclaimed about Hanna, "I wish I could take the Jesuit spectacles off his nose and take
him around the world and make him see life as it is, instead of the
caricatured image his teachers show him."[23]

A characteristic of Rauschenbusch's exchange with Hanna that
also appeared in letters to others was a striking candor about the
personal life of those close to him. It grew partly from what Rauschenbusch was learning about the importance of frankness in examining his own life, and partly from his concern for the well-being
of friends. True friendship, he believed, requires taking the risk of
telling others what they may not want to hear. This Rauschenbusch
did in letters to another high school friend, Joe Gilbert. Rauschenbusch had urged that he examine his soul, and Gilbert was uneasy
about the result: "You ask me in regard to my spiritual condition,
but I do not feel like talking about that now. . . . I want you to pray
for me, Walter, for I sorely need it. Your last letter set me to thinking
more seriously than I had done for some time." And when his sister
Emma decided in 1881 to go to India as a missionary, Rauschenbusch
asked her to examine herself to be sure that the decision was responsive to a divine call rather than to "human feeling." Perhaps he
feared that Emma was moved by a desire to flee their troubled home,
but he came to accept her decision for India as a true missionary
vocation.[24]

Walter Rauschenbusch's four years in Germany brought important
shifts in relationships with his family. Ties to both sisters became

closer. He frequently visited the home of Frida and Georg Fetzer, initially in Volmarstein, where Georg was pastor, and after September 1880 in Hamburg, where his brother-in-law became the first professor at a new Baptist theological seminary. Walter had the joy of meeting his nieces Agnes and Emma, but he also shared the Fetzers' grief at the death of their infant son, Walther. "It is good," he wrote his parents, "to enjoy the love of a sister when I am far from home."[25]

For Emma's twenty-second birthday Walter composed a poem that recalled times of shared happiness and sadness, then affirmed their mutual affection as adults:

> *And supported by their love,*
> *O'er the blinded world they rove,*
> *Man and woman, together strong,*
> *Singing forth their battle-song.*

When he wrote the poem, he did not know that soon he would be reunited with his sister, for Emma's route to India would take her first to Germany. She and Walter went for a month-long trip up the Rhine, into the Swiss Alps, across to Strasbourg, then to Hamburg. The trip was a gift from their father, and Walter wrote him that they had benefited greatly from it and were "both grateful from the bottom of our hearts." After Emma's departure for India, Walter hung a picture of her in his room, alongside the one already there of 10 Arnold Park.[26]

A marked shift occurred in the relationship between father and son. In frequent letters home (fifty-eight to his father, six to his mother), Walter scrupulously reported his activities and often asked his father for advice. Usually he did as his father proposed. But with success at school in Gütersloh bringing self-confidence and independence, Walter more and more disagreed with his father about such matters as travel plans and evaluations of his schoolwork: "You must permit me sometimes to have another opinion."

More telling was the younger Rauschenbusch's intervention in the relationship between his father and mother. Caroline Rauschenbusch accompanied Emma to Germany and wanted to remain there only six months, but August insisted that she stay longer, until Walter returned to America. When Walter discovered his father's dictate he wrote him that his mother should stay no longer than she wanted.

> Look here, Papa: Even if you do not have the happiness with each other that I wish for you from the bottom of my heart, it is better that you be together than stay apart. . . . I wish both of you well in your old

age, and I know that you will find no one who can be such a good, loyal
nurse to you as Mama has often shown herself to be. I still have not
given up the hope that in old age you will grow closer to one another. . . .
You cannot imagine how the quarrels at home have oppressed us children.

The son's counsel prevailed, and Caroline returned the following
month. Walter then wrote his parents that he hoped God would bless
them and become "the third party in their marital bond." This maturing young man had dared to challenge his father and to propose
peace between adversaries he loved greatly. For the moment he had
won, but only time would tell whether it was a lasting victory.[27]

New relationships developed between Walter Rauschenbusch and
members of his father's family as well. There were frequent trips to
Elberfeld to visit the Dörings, in whose home Walter had spent many
happy hours as a boy. Now he was old enough to admire their religious
activism. Aunt Lina's husband had been a distinguished Lutheran
pastor in Elberfeld during the Awakening and had helped guide the
city's outpouring of philanthropic effort. After Pastor Döring's death,
his family maintained the same tradition of service. Walter's cousin
Maria served gallantly as a nurse among wounded Prussian soldiers
and was decorated by the royal family. She and her brother were now
prominent leaders of Elberfeld's aggressive public program for the
needy in the industrialized Wupper valley.[28]

Walter visited other relatives on his father's side. Wilhelm Rauschenbusch, his father's brother, was an affluent lawyer in Hamm
and a member of the king's advisory council. He took a strong interest
in his bright American nephew and periodically gave him welcome
gifts of money. At Uncle Wilhelm's death in 1881, a portion of the
estate went to August Rauschenbusch, and the funds subsidized Walter's remaining years in Europe. There were also frequent visits to
his father's cousin Karl, pastor of the Lutheran church in Herford.
Walter enjoyed the large family farm near Herford, and during a visit
to the *Rauschenbuschhof* in 1883 he studied the family "Chronicles,"
a document tracing Rauschenbusch history from medieval times. He
copied its table of contents and large excerpts from chapters about
recent years.[29]

The Rauschenbusch past fascinated Walter. For centuries the family had owned large tracts of land and was politically prominent in
eastern Westphalia. In the Herford graveyard he discovered that the
usual spelling of the family name before the early nineteenth century
was "Roschenbusch." Family legend told of a Swedish nobleman who
was wounded near Herford during the Thirty Years' War and was

nursed back to health by the daughter of the *Rauschenbuschhof*'s owner; he married the daughter, took the family name, and added his noble blood to the family line. Especially provocative to Walter was what he learned about his seventeenth-century forebear, Esaias Rauschenbusch, and the next five generations of clergy sons. All had been university-trained Lutheran pastors distinguished by learning and piety.[30]

As he studied the family history, Walter wondered about its effect upon him. Reading the biography of his great-grandfather, Hilmar Ernst Rauschenbusch, prompted a report to August Rauschenbusch that the young man was eager to find "a distinctive family character." Careful study of family history, he said, can help one "make a more confident prognosis as to how one will develop in the course of time." Walter did not then predict the direction of his own development, but many years later he acknowledged he had sought to "live up to the traditions of education and religion which had been set for our family by our forefathers." He added that knowledge of these traditions was "one of the strongest safeguards and impulses in my life. It turned me almost automatically into a vocation of service to my fellow men, and served as a kind of supplementary conscience to turn me from the meaner and baser things."

In later years Walter Rauschenbusch wanted his own children to know and prize the family heritage. He named his first son Hilmar Ernst and gave the other children names from the Rauschenbusch past. The family coat of arms, first used in the seventeenth century, was etched on a window in Walter's Rochester home. The Rauschenbusches did not belong to the German nobility, but they had a proud past. In Walter there was a quiet sense of noblesse oblige. At the time of his death a close friend observed that Walter Rauschenbusch was an "aristocrat."[31]

❀❀❀

Rauschenbusch's travels to the homes of relatives fit into a larger design. His father knew Walter shared his wanderlust, and he believed vacationtime travel constituted an important part of the lad's German education, for it would stimulate his mind and senses and create further links with Germany.

The beauties of the Rhine exhilarated the younger Rauschenbusch. During the trip with Emma, he wrote Munson Ford that he was "intensely happy when I can drink in with full draughts the beauty that God has poured with a prodigal hand over this earth of ours," and he regretted that Americans had not learned to "cultivate the per-

ception of the beautiful" as much as Europeans. Comparable excla-
mations came after travel through the Alps and along the Elbe in
Saxon Switzerland.[32]

After graduation in March 1883, Rauschenbusch spent three
months visiting German cultural and academic centers. Numerous
hours in museums, galleries, and concert halls fostered a lasting enjoyment of human artistic achievement. He attended university lectures in Berlin, Leipzig, Halle, Greifswald, and Erlangen and heard
such scholars as Mommsen, Curtius, and Treitschke, who had brought
renown to German higher education, but most of his class time was
spent attending lectures in church history and theology, the two disciplines recommended by his father. There he found himself attracted
more to the tangible issues addressed by historians than to the ab-
stractions of theologians. With August Rauschenbusch, Pastor Braun,
and Professor Cremer acting as his chief advisers in planning this
rapid tour of German academic theology, Walter was steered to conservative stalwarts rather than to liberal scholars who were charting
fresh directions for religious thought. He did not become acquainted
with these German pioneers until the early 1890s, after the main lines
of his theological outlook had developed.

Rauschenbusch did not remain at any of the universities long
enough to undertake serious study or reflection: "I drank in their
words eagerly, soon to forget them in boating-parties, etc., with
friends." He did, however, appreciate the thoroughness of the university professor's academic labor, and he admitted a year later that
he had been tempted to become "a learned theologian and write big
books."

In 1883, at the suggestion of his father, Walter went home by way
of England, where he spent two weeks. England attracted him more
than he had expected, and he regretted that so little time had been
allotted for this unanticipated delight.[33]

As Walter looked homeward, he realized how great his love for
the United States had grown. The four years in Germany provided
him with happy memories, and he would always prize his Gütersloh
education and cherish the land of his ancestors. But it was clear to
him that Germany was their land, not his. Students, teachers, and
townspeople at Gütersloh had received him warmly, but they viewed
him as a foreigner—"the energetic American"—and thereby helped
him discover his real identity. He was an American indeed, and enormously proud of it. At times his longing to be back in the United
States grew intense. He believed he was away at a critical time in
American history, when powerful new forces were shaping the future,
and he confessed his regret at not being present to help preserve "my

fatherland." At times, too, he realized how uncomfortable he felt with the rigid stratification of German society and how much he appreciated the freedom and equality that pervaded much of life in America.

On Independence Day in 1880 and 1881, Walter penned poems about the nation he loved. He sent both to his father, who slightly altered one, then submitted it to a Rochester newspaper. The first words Rochesterians ever read by Walter Rauschenbusch were a celebration of America:

> *My country hail to thee!*
> *Land of the mighty free*
> *Shining afar . . .*
> *Raise high the beacon-light,*
> *Pierce through the world's black night.*
> *Show her the noble sight of liberty.*

August Rauschenbusch had reason to be proud. His son had discovered that liberty was the real strength of America, and he was almost ready to put his budding talent to the task of ensuring that liberty prevailed.[34]

CHAPTER 3

SEMINARIAN

Walter Rauschenbusch had only a short respite between his return to Rochester in late July 1883 and the beginning of seminary. Four years earlier, when he decided to become a minister, he knew he wanted to pursue his graduate theological education at Rochester Theological Seminary, for it was the only school that offered specialized training for men who planned to work among German Baptists in North America. He now looked forward to living again at 10 Arnold Park and helping his aging parents with household chores. There was hope, too, that he might ease the strains in their marriage.

Returning to the American educational system presented a problem. Rochester Seminary accepted his Gütersloh study as the equivalent of a college education and admitted him. But the gymnasium had left gaps normally filled by American colleges, and this made Walter uncomfortable. "In Political Economy, English literature, and such things," he admitted to Munson Ford, "I know perfectly nothing." Moreover, he lacked a university degree, and he did not want to become the first Rauschenbusch since the seventeenth century to enter the ministry without that mark of achievement. The answer to his problem was to enroll in the local university.

The question was how he would handle both the university and the seminary programs. August Rauschenbusch wanted him first to complete advanced courses at the University of Rochester and later to begin seminary study. His son, however, preferred to attend final-year classes at the university and first-year classes at the seminary concurrently. A double load would be taxing, but he believed that during his last year at Gütersloh he had grown "quite lazy," and he welcomed the prospect of academic demands that would "press me down into habits of studiousness." He persuaded his father and authorities at the two schools to accept his proposal, and in September Walter began the dual program.[1]

By 1883 many American colleges were shedding the aggressive Christian outlook of their founders, but the University of Rochester still flew its religious colors proudly. "It is the aim of the Faculty," declared the school's catalog, "in connection with the discipline of the intellect to inculcate a pure morality, and those truths and duties concerning which all Christians are agreed." The university's president, Martin B. Anderson, was a friend of August Rauschenbusch and a figure widely respected in Baptist circles for his advocacy of traditional religious and academic values. Daily required chapel, frequent prayer meetings, and Sunday worship in Rochester churches were standard for the 165 students.[2]

Walter Rauschenbusch found few familiar faces at the university. Charles Strong was there, but other close friends from Free Academy days had graduated in June. A busy schedule gave him little time for campus activities that might have enlarged his circle of college friends, but he did impress some with his industry and talent. One student later remembered that Rauschenbusch "became an object of scholarly awe to the rest of us," and he was elected to the Delta Upsilon fraternity, though it remained on the edges of his student career.

Discrepancies in university records from the period suggest that administrators were perplexed about his unusual program. One set of records lists his name on the rolls of nine courses, another lists him in thirteen courses, but they agree he received a grade in only one—a perfect 10 in physiology. His teachers saw enough of his mental prowess to conclude that he deserved the school's endorsement, and in 1885 the University of Rochester awarded him an A.B. degree.[3]

The course in physiology was taught by Harrison E. Webster, who became the university's first professor of geology and natural history at the time Rauschenbusch matriculated. Webster received his undergraduate education at Union College, fought in the Civil War, did advanced study at Yale's Sheffield Scientific School, and by 1883 was an authority on marine invertebrates. During the winter term Rauschenbusch reported to Munson Ford that he walked daily to the university "to hear Professor Webster ramble on about brachiopods and the riddles of life in his breezy and geniusy way." Webster's interests ranged widely, and he enjoyed conversing with students about issues of the mind and heart that mattered to them.

Rauschenbusch and Webster spent long hours together over the next three years, and a strong tie developed. In the 1890s, after Webster became president of Union College, Rauschenbusch performed the marriage ceremonies for two of his friend's children, and at Webster's funeral in 1906 he delivered the eulogy. There was in him, said Rauschenbusch, a remarkable Socrates-like intellectual vigor. "One chief cause for his mental suppleness was the utter lack of dogmatic ballast in his mind. He had strong opinions, . . . but he always held them open for discussion." Webster was an "utterly fearless" thinker, and to those students drawn to him, he imparted the "best gifts of an intensely human heart and of a very active, keen and versatile mind."

During Walter Rauschenbusch's three years in Rochester, Webster's role was comparable to Braun's at Gütersloh. He was a valued older friend who both listened sympathetically to his student and pointed him toward new horizons. Rauschenbusch undoubtedly remembered his own experience when he testified that Webster had been "a real pastor" to his brighter students as they began to question customary certitudes: "He gave them assurance in turning their back on obsolete traditions" and helped them find their way to a deeper commitment to "God and the moral law."[4]

In two realms where Christians often let "dogmatic ballast" shape their reaction to epochal changes in American life, Webster showed Rauschenbusch appealing alternatives. One of them was the churches' response to the emergence of an urbanized and industrialized nation. Factories were multiplying, immigration was accelerating, cities were expanding, wealth was piling up for a few, urban poverty was gripping more and more, tensions were mounting between owners and workers, and traditional religious symbols were losing their power to guide the American people. Most Christian leaders (including Rochester Seminary professors) were either unmoved by this tangle of problems some now called "the social question" or content to address it through traditional ethical exhortations and familiar revivalistic techniques. Webster talked with Rauschenbusch especially about the economic dimensions of these issues and commended Henry George's provocative new analysis to him. This, Walter Rauschenbusch recalled later, was his "first awakening of interest" in matters that came to occupy him profoundly.[5]

The other realm of Webster's influence rose from his intimate knowledge of the new evolutionary science. Many considered it a dangerous threat to Christianity, but Webster did not. Instead, he worked to bring Darwinism into a harmonious relationship with Christian faith. Calling himself a "Christian evolutionist," Webster believed that God's presence pervades the entire creation, that God's bestowal of a moral nature distinguishes *Homo sapiens* from lower forms of life, that courageous questing for truth is the engine of human progress, and that unselfish love is the supreme human act. During Walter Rauschenbusch's search for his own theological ground in seminary, Webster stood nearby as a reminder of the high calling to seek truth unflinchingly and to welcome it as a friend wherever it appeared.[6]

Two weeks after he began his study at the seminary, Rauschenbusch reported that he found it "grandly interesting." He knew more about the coursework than most entering students, and he was pleased that his instructors would take time to talk with him after class. The courses he took in the three-year program were the ones prescribed for students in the English Department: four semesters of Hebrew Old Testament, five semesters of Greek New Testament, four of church history, six of homiletics, five of elocution, and six of theology.

By 1883 the Rochester Theological Seminary held an important place within the rapidly growing Baptist denomination. Alumni filled hundreds of pulpits across the nation, many were missionaries overseas, and some occupied prominent administrative and educational posts. The school's enrollment of eighty-seven students was the third largest among the eight Baptist seminaries in the United States, and its faculty of ten was the largest. The growth of German Baptists had been so great, and August Rauschenbusch's promotion of an educated ministry had been so successful, that forty-one of the Rochester students were in the German Department (though several, like Walter, did the bulk of their work in the English Department). Among Baptists, Rochester was admired for its allegiance to the old faith and its resistance to new winds of doctrine. In 1885 an outside examining committee reported that "in these days of so-called liberal thought and new departures" it had found at Rochester Seminary that the "supreme authority of the Scriptures, in matters of religious faith and practice, is devoutly recognized, and . . . a Biblical scheme of doctrine is taught." It was a reassuring, albeit unsurprising, word to the constituency.[7]

Baptists, together with most American Christians, believed they had ample reason to fear "liberal thought and new departures." A Pandora's box had been opened by German scholars who brought to Scripture the same critical methods used in analyzing other ancient literature. That scholarship, coupled with new scientific and philosophical currents, called into question numerous traditional beliefs. Was the Genesis account of Creation true? Had Moses written it? Did human life result from God's gracious act or from a savage struggle for survival? If Genesis is not trustworthy, what can one believe about other parts of the Bible? About the Virgin Birth? The Resurrection? On and on came the questions. Not for centuries had Christian orthodoxy fallen under such a withering attack and Christians faced such theological bewilderment.

Walter Rauschenbusch first heard the sounds of battle in his Bible courses. The school's Old Testament professor, Howard Osgood, was one of America's most conservative biblical scholars. Rauschenbusch discovered that this learned Southerner was "deeply read in the literature of criticism, but never yielded an inch to it." Professor Osgood charged that Germans who practice higher criticism impose their own notions about God upon Scripture instead of clarifying what is taught there. Because sound interpreters start by recognizing that Jesus "taught only what the Father taught him," argued Osgood, they recognize that the Lord's words about the Old Testament are authoritative for Christians. Osgood believed he could use this standard to show that the Genesis account of Creation is true; that Moses was the author of the Pentateuch; that the Scriptures are infallible ("Every word came from God and was freighted with the intent of God"); and that Jesus' essential purpose was to fulfill Old Testament prophecies about the coming of a Messiah.

Rauschenbusch's work with Osgood won high marks, but his competence in Old Testament studies expanded only in such areas as Palestinian archaeology and Hebrew grammar. He could not accept Osgood's basic approach to Scripture, though he appreciated what his father's good friend had done to develop the school's collection of Anabaptist source materials. For three years Osgood made no public issue of Rauschenbusch's failure to embrace his views, but shortly after graduation he felt duty-bound to register disappointment at his student's lapse from orthodoxy.[8]

The high point of Walter Rauschenbusch's first-year work in biblical studies was his course on "The Life of Christ." This, he reported, "I enjoy as I don't remember enjoying any study." His New Testament instructor, William Arnold Stevens, was the least conservative member of the Rochester faculty. Earlier, Stevens had published a critical edition of the orations of Lysias, and he brought to his New Testament scholarship the same methods of analysis employed in the investigation of classical Greek literature. The Bible, he said, is not revelation but the "record of a revelation," bearing limitations that are associated unavoidably with all human language and communication. Therefore, one should not regard the Bible "as composed of infallible or errorless documents, or as being or expressive of absolute truth."

At times Rauschenbusch disagreed with certain of Stevens's interpretations, but he accepted his instructor's approach to Scripture and held him in high regard for the thoroughness and honesty he displayed. "He taught us an important code of ethics, the ethics of the man whose business in life is to think and to seek the truth."

Walter Rauschenbusch wrote his first seminary essay for Professor Stevens. In a study entitled "The Synagogue: Its Construction, Worship, and Relation to New Testament History," he depicted the architectural and liturgical patterns of the synagogues in which Jesus preached. His view of Jesus' teaching stressed its continuity with the prophets of Israel. Instead of "fanciful interpretations or learned doctrinal and casuistic discussion, he opened up the spirit of God's word, . . . having like the prophets of old, not only the right but also the power to stir the hearts of men." Jesus' link with the prophets became a central theme in Rauschenbusch's mature theological position.[9]

During his first-year study with Professor Stevens, Walter Rauschenbusch plunged into what he later termed "the travail of a religious unsettlement." He had come to the seminary, he said, having "no outlook except the common evangelicalism." In that view little notice was taken of discrepancies in the New Testament accounts of Jesus' life; all Scripture was true, all was binding on Christians' thought and behavior. But in Stevens's class Rauschenbusch became acutely aware of conflicting materials in the Gospels. He later reported that this discovery came not "by reading skeptical books but by making a very close study of the Synoptic passages." Some claimed one thing about Jesus' actions, while parallel passages in another Gospel claimed something else. The consequences of this discovery were far-reaching: "My inherited ideas about the inerrancy of the Bible became untenable. I determined to follow the facts as divine, and let my man-made theories go if they conflicted." He would proceed in the same spirit as Harrison Webster and other scientific seekers of truth, who had abandoned outdated explanations of natural phenomena in favor of an inductive pursuit of more adequate explanations.

The way Walter Rauschenbusch resolved his "unsettlement" aligned him with a growing band of liberal religious thinkers who forged what Rochester Seminary professors disdainfully called the New Theology. These pioneers in the United States and Europe believed the time had come for a restatement of ancient Christian truth that took full account of new truths that God was teaching humanity. The New Theology was suspect in conservative circles like Rochester Seminary, and Rauschenbusch knew that those who held the old doctrines dear—including his father—would be mortified if he moved in this new direction. His primary task in the remaining years at seminary was to assess how far he could travel this road. He wrote later, "It cost me a hard struggle."[10]

His interest in theological reconstruction was furthered by study of Christian history under Professor Benjamin True, whose major interest was post-Reformation English Christianity, from which the American Baptist movement had sprung. One of True's few published works surveyed recent developments in the Church of England and showed familiarity with such pioneering thinkers as Samuel Taylor Coleridge and Frederick Denison Maurice.

Two papers that Rauschenbusch wrote for True explored issues raised by controversial earlier dissenters—the Donatists and the Waldensians. A third paper, which reviewed a book about suppression of heresy by the Roman Catholic church, later appeared in the *Baptist Quarterly Review;* it was Walter Rauschenbusch's first essay in a scholarly journal.

Benjamin True was intently interested in the ground-breaking work of Johann August Neander and he assigned portions of the German scholar's six-volume *History* for his students to read. From his father and Pastor Braun, Rauschenbusch already had learned something of Neander's outlook; now he was intrigued by closer study of his contentions that in Jesus Christ a divine power had entered human history, had generated beneficent change across the centuries, and would finally triumph over all that resisted it. In this view, history was less a chronicling of the past than a discerning of God's purposive work in the human drama.[11]

Walter Rauschenbusch's interest in English church life was furthered by Thomas Harwood Pattison, the seminary's professor of homiletics and pastoral theology. Having lived in England most of his life, Pattison knew more about English Christianity than the other Rochester professors. He spoke appreciatively of Anglicans noted for their preaching, and he sparked in Rauschenbusch such interest in Frederick W. Robertson that he decided to learn more about the Anglican priest.

Pattison's lectures on preaching were carefully recorded and preserved by Rauschenbusch. Every sermon, Pattison taught, should have only one theme, which should be taken from a biblical text and should be explicated in simple, direct speech. Each preacher must choose the style of delivery that best suits his personality and talents. Some speak best with a manuscript before them, others do best extemporaneously, still others by memorizing. Pattison encouraged his students to consider adopting his own practice—the "composite method"—which he noted had been Robertson's. Here the sermon is written out, practiced several times, and delivered without a manuscript. Rauschenbusch liked this method and made it his own.[12]

Augustus Hopkins Strong, the school's president and professor of biblical theology, taught all Rochester Seminary courses in theology. Strong had come to the two positions in 1872, and he retained them until retirement in 1912. Over those four decades he knew Walter as a boy, taught him as a student, and eventually became his colleague and superior. More than any other, Strong was the theologian through whom Walter Rauschenbusch carried on a dialogue with traditional Protestant thought.

A patrician who found fund raising distasteful, Strong nevertheless moved effectively among wealthy Baptists, believing like most Americans that their money was a reward for such virtues as foresight and self-denial, and reminding them of the obligation to use their wealth to advance Christian causes. Especially responsive to Strong's appeals were two Baptist laymen, John Trevor and John D. Rockefeller. Strong had known Rockefeller during the years both lived in Cleveland, and he persuaded the fabled multimillionaire to serve first as a vice-chairman, then in 1886 as chairman, of the body responsible for financial support of the seminary.

Like President Ezekiel Robinson before him, Strong vigorously affirmed the Baptist tradition of free intellectual inquiry. His own openness to new currents led later to a more liberal outlook, but during Rauschenbusch's years as a seminarian, Strong was a rock in the conservative camp. Professor Strong took as his theological task a systematic charting of the biblical ground in which the Christian message is rooted. A Calvinist with a mind disposed to orderliness, he found revealed in Scripture "a magnificent and organic scheme of doctrine." His first published explication of Christian doctrine, *Lectures on Theology*, appeared in 1876 and was Rauschenbusch's textbook for three years. In his *Lectures*, Strong proceeded like the seventeenth-century architects of Protestant scholasticism. The whole range of Christian doctrines was presented in seven parts, from prolegomena to eschatology, with each heading divided and subdivided into component parts, alternative positions summarized, and reasons given for choosing the position that Strong thought best accorded with Scripture. Key tenets in Strong's system were the holiness of God, human depravity, Christ's substitutionary death, the election of some for salvation, the baptism and gathering of the elect into the church, the final sanctification of the elect, and the final destruction of the wicked. Pervading the entire presentation was Strong's assumption that God's truth can be known purely, without dilution by human minds and historical contingencies, and that the theologian's task is to strive for just such knowledge.[13]

For Strong's courses Rauschenbusch wrote two papers that provide glimpses of his theological journey. The first, from his middler year, was a study of the thought of the third-century theologian Sabellius. Here Rauschenbusch roundly declared the futility of such speculative pursuits as that ventured by Sabellius: "What is this attempt to define in a metaphysical way the deepest mysteries in the nature of the almighty God doing for us? Are we meant to know these things or are we treading on forbidden ground?" Far better, he concluded, to leave wrangling about such matters to the past and to help people today love God and obey the divine will. In harmony with the mainstream of the American theological tradition, Rauschenbusch had no interest in theology's more philosophical endeavors, and he rarely sought enlightenment from those who did.

During his third year of seminary, Rauschenbusch prepared a major essay for Professor Strong entitled "The Bushnellian Theory of the Atonement." Earlier in the century Horace Bushnell had been a Congregational minister in Hartford, Connecticut, and his writings constituted the first major formulation of the New Theology by an American. Strong regarded Bushnell's view of the atonement as "faulty by defect," but Rauschenbusch disagreed. He noted that Bushnell, along with English contemporaries Maurice and Robertson, had recovered Jesus' own teaching about the meaning of his life and death. Bushnell rightly saw that Jesus had come to reveal God's eternal love for all people and to win them to new life. So intense was Jesus' love for others that he took their suffering upon his heart, like parents with wayward children. His love persisted even when they turned against him and crucified him. In the suffering love of Jesus, humanity can see the love of the God who sent him. Those who truly see are moved to open themselves to Christ's empowering presence and to love as he loved.

Rauschenbusch's explanation of Bushnell's position was accompanied by important objections and affirmations. He admitted that there might be some truth in the traditional view of a substitutionary atonement, but for several reasons he doubted its adequacy: It was not taught by Jesus; it makes salvation dependent upon a trinitarian transaction that is remote from human experience; and it implies a concept of divine justice that is repugnant to human sensitivity. Bushnell's view, on the other hand, issues from the Gospels, is immediately intelligible, and provides great comfort for persons struggling against sin. Rauschenbusch added that although elements of the substitutionary atonement theory reflect certain New Testament passages (especially in the Letter to the Hebrews), Christians are not obligated to accept a scriptural statement "if it does not by its own right appeal to us as truth." Nevertheless, he conceded that he would keep an open mind and give careful attention to the passages in question. To his paper Rauschenbusch appended a note saying that Strong had judged it "subversive of scriptural authority" and that its theological errors had prompted several corrective lectures to the class.[14]

Rauschenbusch's assault upon such staples of orthodoxy as biblical inerrancy and the substitutionary atonement was fed by his reading of authors who had explored alternative positions. It was important, he told a friend, "to have time for side-reading." His fluency in several languages gave him access to a broad range of literature, and his talent for discipline helped him make time for extra reading. Most of these "teachers" were Englishmen; like many of his American contemporaries venturing upon new roads, Rauschenbusch found the blending of old and new by English innovators more attractive than the work of counterparts in Germany, who seemed less appreciative of tradition and its continuing power in the church. Late in his first year at Rochester, he began keeping a notebook, a "Collectaneum" of excerpts mined from numerous writings, and by the end of his theological education he had filled most of its fifty-eight pages. Short, provocative statements were copied from such authors as Frederick W. Robertson, Robert Browning, Blaise Pascal, Phillips Brooks, Friedrich Tholuck, William Wordsworth, Samuel Taylor Coleridge, James Russell Lowell, and Thomas Carlyle.

Especially striking are the statements by Robertson. A few months after graduation, Rauschenbusch acknowledged his indebtedness to the Englishman; to Robertson, he told a cousin, "I owe more than to any other writer." Many years later he recalled that from Robertson he had "absorbed the idea of the law of the cross as the obligatory and distinctive thing in Christianity." Parts of the Anglican clergyman's journey resembled that of Rauschenbusch. In the 1840s Robertson had moved from the religious conservatism of his youth to a more liberal outlook. Study at Oxford and in Germany was followed by ministry in a working-class parish at Brighton for seven years, until his death in 1853 at the age of thirty-seven. Publication of his papers twelve years later brought a rapid spread of Robertson's influence in England and the United States.[15]

Rauschenbusch read intently the eight-hundred-page collection of Robertson's writings edited by Stopford E. Brooke. Among the ten excerpts he copied, several forcefully addressed his condition, reinforcing his commitment to follow Jesus Christ in every circumstance, but freeing the commitment from its orthodox encasement:

> Sever yourself from all parties and maxims, servant only to the truth; the way of reaching the truth is by obeying the truth you know.

It is something to feel the deep, deep conviction which has never failed me in the darkest moods, that Christ had the key to the mysteries of life and that they are not insoluble; also that the spirit of the Cross is the condition which will put anyone in possession of the same key: Take my yoke upon you, and ye shall find rest for your souls.

I hold that the attempt to rest Christianity upon miracles and fulfillments of prophecy is essentially the vilest rationalism; as if the trained intellect of a lawyer which can investigate evidence were that to which is trusted the soul's salvation.

To the question, Who is my neighbor? I reply as my Master did by the example that He gave: "the alien and the heretic."

Words by Brooke about the Anglican priest were Rauschenbusch's final Robertson entry: "Living above the world, he did his work in the world. Ardently pursuing after liberty of thought, he never forgot the wise reticence of English conservatism. He preserved amid a fashionable town the old virtues of chivalry. In a very lonely and much tried life he was never false or fearful." Brooke's words strangely anticipated the life Rauschenbusch was to lead, especially as a preacher to workers and their families during the next decade. In those years Robertson's name was invoked more than any other in Rauschenbusch's sermons, and the figure of the Englishman remained an inspiring presence in his consciousness.[16]

Classes and outside reading were not the only sources of stimulation for Rauschenbusch. Each year the seminary invited people active in the church beyond Rochester to address students and faculty. Two guests brought provocative messages that planted seeds in Walter's mind. At the 1884 graduation exercises the speaker was John E. Clough, director of the famed Baptist mission to the Telugus in India, where Emma Rauschenbusch toiled. Clough fascinated his audience with the story of the recent "mass movement" of outcastes to Christianity and urged the young men to join him in India to continue the tasks of evangelism and nurture. Eleven months later, Rochester students heard a stirring account of a closer mission field. An Episcopal clergyman, W. S. Rainsford, related his transformation of St. George's Church on New York City's East Side into a center providing recreation and education for working-class families crowded into the area. Only by such innovations, he contended, will the church reach the surging masses of city dwellers. In America's large cities the church will "win her greatest victory or suffer her most disastrous defeat." Rainsford was heard and applauded, but none of Rauschenbusch's professors believed that the nation's rapid urbanization raised issues that were critical enough to merit major classroom attention. Later, after only a few weeks living in the midst of those issues, he was appalled by the faculty's insensitivity.[17]

During summer vacations in 1884 and 1885, Rauschenbusch worked in Louisville, Kentucky, as interim pastor of a small German Baptist congregation that had been wracked by dissension. For two months he visited members in their homes, listened to their backbiting stories, organized the youth, and preached twice on Sundays and twice at midweek services. In his first sermon he admonished members of the congregation to love one another in the same way Jesus had loved. Otherwise, he said, their lovelessness would make Christianity unattractive to outsiders and turn them away from Jesus.

When he left Louisville at the end of the summer, he looked back upon a fruitful experience. The size of the congregation had nearly doubled, and reconciliation had been achieved. "I rejoiced in a number of conversions, I saw the members again united by their common affection for their common Master, I saw them deeply affected when I said farewell to them at the little social they gave me, and I was satisfied." This success, he believed, must be attributed to God, not to him: "I am but the instrument in his hand."[18]

The work in Louisville had exhausted him, and as the next summer approached his parents urged that he spend the vacation months in a more relaxing way on a farm. But because the Louisville church did not yet have a pastor and the people wanted him to return, he decided to go back.

The decision to return to Louisville grew from religious commitments now moving toward definitive form. Rauschenbusch explained to Munson Ford that the temporary pastorate in Louisville gave him "a chance to do something for others" and that such selfless action is fundamental to Christianity. "Unselfishness and self-sacrifice seem to me the idea of Christ's life and therefore the expression of God's character. In proportion as they become the dominant facts of our own life, are we conformed to his image." Recognition of this truth, he maintained, constituted a turning point for him. "I tell you I am just beginning to believe in the gospel of the Lord Jesus Christ, not exactly in the shape in which the average parson proclaims it as the infallible truth of the Most High, but in a shape that suits my needs, that I have gradually constructed for myself in studying the person and teachings of Christ, and which is still in rapid process of construction."

The hallmark of his new position was the importance of living like

Christ, not of believing a prescribed doctrine about Christ. The person who travels this road, Rauschenbusch continued in his correspondence with Ford, who "begins to live a Christ-like life . . . will find that tho' there is no cross for him to be nailed to, he will die piecemeal by self-sacrifice just as Christ did even before his crucifixion and then he is at one with Christ and placed by God into the same category."[19] Walter Rauschenbusch never surrendered this piety centered upon imitation of Christ's suffering love, but he knew that piety alone is not enough, that it must be joined to a theological vision capable of informing his role in the entire drama of redemption. With his views on Scripture, atonement, and the imitation of Christ firmly in place, a substantial start toward such a vision had already been made, but its full articulation did not occur until well after he had completed his formal theological education.

--***

The three years Walter Rauschenbusch lived at 10 Arnold Park brought a new loneliness. The sisters and friends who had been closest to him were far away—Frida, Schaaf, and Cremer in Germany, Emma in India, Ford in Illinois. His parents were at hand, but they had no sympathy for the direction of his religious journey. Although he was careful not to parade his new views, they were noticed, and some of the people close to him worried. New friends at the seminary did not provide the full measure of affection and affirmation he craved. Occasionally his ties with his Aunt Lina brought comfort: "You write me so full of love," he exclaimed once, "and you have no idea how good this makes me feel. I am so pleased that there are good people who continue to see enough good in me to still love me." Times of self-doubt and loneliness recurred, however, and he had to address this uncomfortable new fact of his life.

Largely because of his relationship with Webster and Stevens, a partial resolution was reached by the end of his final year of seminary. At graduation exercises in May 1886, Rauschenbusch was one of six seniors chosen to deliver addresses. He and Arthur Ramaker, who also was destined for ministry among German Baptists, had finished at the top of their class. Rauschenbusch spoke on "The Ethics of Thinking." He said that those whose calling in life is to think must exercise caution, for "he who deals with thought handles fire." But even more must they avoid the excessive caution that leads one to withhold truth that is capable of shaking people from comfortable, accustomed ways. Those who bear such truth must be prepared for the "awful loneliness" of seeing truth others have not yet seen. They must utter the truth entrusted to them with confidence that it is from God and that God will bring it to fruition. For them to keep silent would be a denial of God. To speak is faithfulness to God.[20]

Rauschenbusch was clear about which of these paths he wanted to take, and he hoped that when his moment of testing came he would be found with the faithful.

Augustus Hopkins Strong and other professors at Rochester Seminary must have become concerned at seeing Walter Rauschenbusch move from beneath their wings. He did not bear the usual Rochester stamp, and they were not sure what stamp he would eventually bear, for there was a still fluid mix of the old and the new in him. But they also were proud of him; he was a bright, articulate, and winsome servant of Christ. No one seemed surprised when two years later the school paid him the compliment of inviting him back as a teacher in the German department.

━━━ CHAPTER 4 ━━━

PASTOR

A major question facing seniors at Rochester Seminary was where they would begin their ministries after graduation. Several friends had encouraged Rauschenbusch to consider an English-speaking church, but to no avail, for he was firmly committed to remaining on the German track his father intended for him. The German Baptist community in the United States and Canada now numbered 12,500 members and 147 churches, and during the winter of 1886 six of the churches were seeking new pastors. In February young Rauschenbusch received an offer from the First German Baptist Church in Springfield, Illinois, but he was only mildly attracted and felt the church was asking for a speedier acceptance than he could responsibly give.[1]

Another invitation soon followed. Members of the Second German Baptist Church on New York City's West Side feared that their chances of luring Walter Rauschenbusch were slim, for they guessed that this gifted son of the venerable Professor Rauschenbusch would find little about their city or church to attract him. In their eyes New York was a modern-day "Nineveh." The church lay just beyond the northern edge of Hell's Kitchen, one of the city's most notorious districts, where gangs of hoodlums roamed with near impunity, and only a few blocks west of the Tenderloin, where prostitutes and gamblers prospered. All over the city, people lived crowded together in squalid conditions that made them easy prey for disease and a host of temptations, including the city's nine thousand licensed saloons and untold numbers of unlicensed ones. Police and city government appeared powerless, or too corrupted, to make things better.

49

The arrival of boat after boat of immigrants had swollen New York's population to 1.5 million, making it the largest city in the nation and the second largest in the world. Nearly 400,000 German immigrants lived there. The growth of population had long ago outpaced the growth of Protestant churches, and only 5 percent of the people belonged to New York's four hundred Protestant churches. Five Baptist churches ministered to German immigrants, but like the churches generally, they reached only a handful.

The Germans had experienced the same social and psychic dislocation as other immigrants when they moved from traditional rural settings into the American metropolis, and they longed for better wages and a better life. A severe economic slump the last few years had made matters worse. No wonder the strident voices of Johann Most and other German socialists reached so many attentive ears among the German immigrants; no wonder, too, such large numbers of workers heeded the call of Samuel Gompers and other labor leaders to strike. The people of Second Church worried about all this, for though most of the immigrants in their neighborhood came from conservative areas of northern Germany and did not support the radicals, who could tell what might lie ahead, particularly in the wake of the recent Haymarket violence in Chicago. Any new pastor was bound to find his ministrations intruded upon by the passions of a troubled time.[2]

The church stood in a particularly depressing section of West 45th Street, near Tenth Avenue, surrounded by crowded tenements and noisy factories. The building was old and ugly, the minister's basement apartment tiny and damp. After thirty years of effort, the congregation numbered only 125. Most were factory laborers who lived and worked in the neighborhood, one of the most densely populated sections of the city. Previous pastors had left the congregation fractured and dispirited. The last pastor, an elderly man, had been content with a holding action.

To undertake so dismal a task the church could offer Rauschenbusch an annual salary of only $600. He immediately accepted, and the congregation was amazed. One member wrote that his decision was "a miracle before our eyes." Later, as they grew to know and love their young pastor, they understood why he had come to them. Besides placing him in the city that had been important in his father's pilgrimage, this pastorate offered him an opportunity to act upon his deepest convictions. He would live in near-poverty, deny himself, and minister like Christ to the poor and abused. He would be a missioner to the city that more than any other was shaping America's future. His moment to do "hard work for God" was at hand.[3]

Walter Rauschenbusch arrived in New York City on the first day of June 1886. A delegation of church leaders met his train and escorted him to the West 50th Street home of one of the few members with space enough for a guest. Soon pastor and congregation agreed that, instead of living at the church, he would rent an apartment nearby, for which he would receive a $300 annual allowance.

On Sunday, he preached his inaugural sermon on Jesus' words "Thy Kingdom come." Even this little flock, he said, has a place in God's grand design, for it exists to speed the coming of God's Kingdom and the return of Christ. The spread of Christianity around the world in recent decades signals that the consummation of the Kingdom is closer than ever before, but until it occurs, this company of believers must labor mightily to bring the justice and love that God wills for humanity into its own ranks, as well as into the life of the city.

This exhilarating vision was presented with energy and enthusiasm, and the people warmed to the message and the messenger. Over the next several weeks Rauschenbusch visited all members in their homes, preached at Sunday morning and evening services, led prayer meetings two nights a week, and met with youth members another night. By the end of June, attendance was up, wounds were healing, and plans were under way to paint the building. Clearly he was making a mark.[4]

But a cloud had followed Rauschenbusch from Rochester. The previous year he had noticed a decline in his ability to hear, and the condition worsened alarmingly after arriving in New York. He consulted a doctor, who immediately ordered a regimen of treatments requiring ten office visits and minor surgery. At the end of June he warned the young pastor that there was a "neurological defect" and that his hearing might not improve. Knowing that his grandmother had been deaf and that his Aunt Maria suffered from an ear disorder, he feared that his time as a pastor might be limited.[5]

Because the month of pastoral toil and ear treatments had drained him, the church gave Rauschenbusch a two-month vacation. Most of the time was spent with a seminary classmate at his rural parsonage in the Allegheny Mountains. He now had time to reflect upon his first month as a pastor. It had confirmed his belief, he wrote Munson Ford, that he could help people most by "bringing them into living and personal relations with our Lord Jesus Christ." He realized, too, that he liked his work as a pastor even more than he had expected. "I enjoyed everything because in everything I did I felt I was achieving something good." He had plunged into a world that was vastly different from the protected, artificial world of the seminary. In New York a person "feels the waves of human life all around, as it really is, not as it ought to be according to the *decretum absolutum* of an old theology." It was a heady, instructive experience. "I have not read anything except newspapers, and yet, I have learned more than in a long time before."[6]

A letter in mid-August interrupted his vacation calm. An executive of the Baptist Mission Union informed him that a new president was urgently needed for the Telugu Theological Seminary in India and asked whether he would be interested. Rauschenbusch was tempted. A contagious missionary enthusiasm was sweeping through his generation of American Evangelicals, and he remembered vividly Dr. John Clough's account of the Telugu Mission. Moreover, he was thrilled at the thought of working near his sister in one of the most innovative and successful Baptist outposts anywhere. But his New York pastorate was a mission too, and he did not want to leave it. His hearing problem put a question mark over everything, and he decided to answer cautiously that he was willing to have his name considered, whereupon the Mission Union promptly solicited appraisals of his qualifications.

A few weeks later Rauschenbusch was told that numerous letters of commendation had been received, but he also was advised that unnamed respondents who praised his ability nevertheless believed that he should continue as a pastor "for a few years in order to acquire experience and the settled convictions which come with it." A subsequent letter, on 29 September, reported the bittersweet news that the Mission Union had decided not to pursue his appointment to the position in India.

The matter seemed to be closed, but a later letter brought a clarification and a feeler. The executive secretary of the Mission Union, J. N. Murdock, told Rauschenbusch that he had been dropped from consideration earlier "in consequence of certain representations suspecting your view of the Divine Authority of the Old Testament." Murdock did not disclose the source of these "representations," but Rochester Seminary insiders subsequently revealed that Professor Osgood had been responsible for the Mission Union's cooling toward Rauschenbusch. Murdock went on to say that his agency had high regard for Rauschenbusch and wished to reopen discussions about overseas service. The young pastor's answer was courteous but brief. He continued to be interested in foreign missions but now was immersed in his New York pastorate: "I know what is to be done and how it can be done. . . . I do not feel at liberty to leave this work to which I have put my hand."[7]

With the question of India behind him, Rauschenbusch began to prepare in earnest for the examination required of candidates for ordination. As the date of the examination approached, his parents

wondered whether the examining council would discover his uncon-
ventional theological views and reject him. August Rauschenbusch
guessed it would not, for he knew that his son was discrete about
such matters, and he believed the council would not probe into the
Old Testament realm, where Walter's "doubts and deviant attitudes"
centered. Caroline, though, was unsure and nervously appealed to
her son to conform to the orthodoxy of the Baptist mainstream. This
he would not do, but he sought to comfort his mother by writing that
the pursuit of truth was taking him along the same path trod by all
faithful Christians, including his parents. Never did he make a more
earnest declaration of faith and independence:

> I have no desire more serious than to perceive and believe in the
> whole truth of Jesus Christ and the entire Word of God. . . .
>
> This is all the consolation I am able to offer you. I believe in the gospel
> of Jesus Christ with all my heart. What this gospel is, everyone has to
> decide for himself, in the face of his God. I am now stepping into Papa's
> and your footsteps. When you left the great and venerable Lutheran
> Church in order to join the small and despised Baptist Church, you too
> invoked the right to interpret the Scriptures according to your own
> conscience; now, I am doing the same.
>
> I am looking forward to the council undisturbed. Whatever its decision
> may be, I shall be satisfied.

There is no indication how August or Caroline Rauschenbusch responded to their son's letter. Whatever they thought about him, Walter
Rauschenbusch believed that he was yoked to them at the deepest
level of their shared faith and that differences regarding such matters
as Old Testament interpretation were powerless to shatter that union.[8]

The Second German Baptist Church invited representatives of
other Baptist churches in the area to gather in council "to consider
the advisability of setting apart Brother Walter Rauschenbusch, pastor elect, to the work of the gospel ministry." Sixty-one people from
twenty-five churches met on 14 October for the examination. They
were impressed by the candidate and voted unanimously to advise
Second Church to ordain him. Later in the day, one of the examiners
wrote that he had never met a candidate who was so well qualified
for ordination. One week later, on 21 October 1886, Walter Rauschenbusch was ordained.[9]

A final hurdle had to be cleared before he could settle into his
work. Immediately following the ordination, he journeyed to Rochester in order to bring his mother back to New York City to live with
him. After all the years of bitterness—and despite their son's efforts—

August and Caroline had decided to separate. A pleasant public face could be put upon the step: Caroline was helping her bachelor son cope with his trying new circumstances. After she moved into Walter's apartment, contact between the estranged couple became rare. When August Rauschenbusch decided in 1888 to retire from teaching and return to Germany, he visited Walter and Caroline just before sailing. The younger Rauschenbusch noted in a diary that his father's "parting from Mama was sad. He only shook hands with her." A few minutes later Walter "found her quite convulsed in the little room."

For two more years Caroline shared an apartment with her son. The relationship between the two was cordial though at times strained. They agreed it was the best option available for Caroline. In 1890, however, she returned to Germany to live with her husband near the home of their daughter Frida in Hamburg. Family members later believed that Baptist friends had been scandalized by the prolonged separation and had privately entreated them to live under the same roof again.[10]

Until 1891, when he returned to Europe for ten months, Walter Rauschenbusch's chief activity was shepherding the people of the Second German Baptist Church. All were immigrants or children of immigrants and shared the anxieties and aspirations of the unchurched multitudes around them. Rauschenbusch discovered that many who came to America with high hopes were now dejected: "They find no work. Their wings of ambition are clipped. They grow shiftless. They mutter discontent against God and men." Socialists found fertile ground among the discontented. A smaller number of the immigrants had fared well and was enjoying the scramble for wealth: "They live better than ever before and feel the delight of having money and of being able to get things. They join in the mad race for gaining the whole world, no matter whether they lose their soul or not." For them the American dream of rags to riches seemed vindicated, but Rauschenbusch had doubts.[11]

He believed that the main help he could offer both groups was to do what Christian clergy had done for nearly two millennia: tell them about God's redemptive deeds and seek their response of faith, hope, and love. The focal point of this ministry was his Sunday preaching—one sermon in the morning and another in the evening. Following Professor Pattison's counsel, the young pastor chose a biblical text, explained the author's meaning, and drew implications for the congregation. The main themes of each sermon were sketched in sturdy notebooks that he carefully preserved. They reveal Professor Osgood's lingering negative influence, for only 15 percent of the texts came from the Old Testament. The Gospels of John and Matthew were Rauschenbusch's favorite sources, together supplying over one-quarter of the sermon texts.[12]

Rauschenbusch had absorbed Pattison's advice that sermons be pitched at a level comprehensible to all. Aware that most of his congregation had meager educations and no interest in erudite expositions, he labored to express himself in plain, forceful language. He wanted to make "the gospel simple," he told one of his friends, "so that slow-moving brains can understand." His message those first years in New York resembled what one would have heard from most other recent seminary graduates in Baptist churches across the United States. It was a Calvinist version of the gospel, modified by a Pietist-Evangelical heritage in the direction of Arminianism, with only a touch of his nascent theological liberalism apparent. There was still no sign of the social outlook that soon became so important for him. His own later assessment was apt: "My idea then was to save souls in the ordinarily accepted religious sense."[13]

The central theme of his sermons was the human journey from sin to salvation. Week after week he explained that this journey begins with a person's acknowledgment that selfishness corrupts the mind and the heart. So devastating are the consequences of sin that only God can save one from it. God does this through Christ, not only by forgiving sinners but also by removing their sin, giving them new life, and receiving them after death into eternal rest.

The road to salvation, he continued, is perilous. Evil lurks all around, and Christian travelers must help one another resist its allure. But the journey is also exhilarating. God's Spirit helps earnest travelers stay close to Christ, who leads them in the struggle, empowers them to love as God loves, and thereby makes them holy.

From the beginning of his pastorate, Rauschenbusch taught that believers also participate in a corporate journey from sin to salvation. The world itself is moving from evil toward a divinely appointed transformation. The mood of his sermons on this subject alternated. Some manifested millennialist optimism about the global spread of Christianity and the gospel's penetration of society; other sermons reflected a more sober assessment of the world's resistance to the faith and of the conflict between God and Satan. In both types he urged individual Christians to contribute to the advancement of God's Kingdom. They aid God's cause by surrendering themselves to Christ, by seeking others for him, and by urging everyone to obey the laws of the Kingdom.

Not until 1889 did Rauschenbusch begin occasionally to call his congregation's attention to the need to change economic and social patterns. The "salvation of society," he said, has too long been neglected by the church; "the best way to get the self ready for heaven," he added, "is to get the world ready for God." But his growing awareness of the importance of a Christian social mission received less-frequent expression in his pulpit than in other settings. He realized that members of his congregation were far removed from centers of power and consequently could do little to right social wrongs. Moreover, in keeping with the German Baptist ethos, they wanted to hear—and they wanted the unevangelized masses on the West Side to hear—preaching that called individuals from sin by offering them "the old faith" of their spiritual forebears.[14]

Walter Rauschenbusch had heard the Evangelical message of individual salvation from his childhood, and he believed its essential claims wholeheartedly. But he realized that a busy pastor could stop drinking from the spiritual fountain to which he led others. To avoid this professional hazard, he knew that he must heed the charge he had delivered at a friend's ordination: "Be not so busy in the Master's service that you have no time to be in the Master's presence." A key way he sought this "presence" early in his ministry was attendance at summer revivals. One experience in 1887 was unrewarding, but in August 1888 he spent a memorable ten days at a conference in Northfield, Massachusetts, sponsored by the famous revivalist Dwight L. Moody. He had heard Moody in Rochester four years earlier and now was lifted by his sermons, by the forested beauty of the Berkshires, and by the warm Evangelical commitment of those present. In his diary he wrote, "I gave myself to God unreservedly and had a rich blessing," and in a scrapbook he began keeping that year he pasted newspaper transcriptions of Moody's sermons as well as accounts of the conference.[15]

An integral part of Moody's meetings was the spirited singing led by Ira D. Sankey. Like numerous other Protestants, Rauschenbusch found his faith invigorated by hymns that had emerged from American and British revivalism over the last century, and he coveted for his congregation and other German-language churches an opportunity to sing the hymns in their native tongue. Several months after the Northfield revival, he and another New York pastor published a booklet of German translations they had made of twenty-four "gospel hymns" originally compiled and published by Sankey. The booklets were quickly sold, and Rauschenbusch realized that a larger collection of translated hymns would be welcomed by German-Americans. At his initiative, he and Sankey collaborated on a new hymnal containing

218 hymns previously published by Sankey. Rauschenbusch translated half of them himself, including such favorites as "I Need Thee Every Hour," "What a Friend We Have in Jesus," "Rescue the Perishing," and "Onward Christian Soldiers." The others he assigned to friends. The new hymnal, *Evangeliums-Lieder*, appeared in 1891 and sold well. Rauschenbusch was pleased to receive nearly $1,000 for his labors.

In subsequent years he worked with Sankey and his son to publish several German hymnals. Some 137 hymns were rendered into singable German by Rauschenbusch. It was a remarkable literary and musical feat. To some later it appeared incongruous that this champion of social Christianity had done so much to encourage the widespread use of old-fashioned gospel hymns. Rauschenbusch did feel uneasy about the theology of many of the hymns, for they typically obscured the social dimensions of sin and salvation. But he believed that they were correct in praising the God who saves people from sin, and he was glad to help Christians celebrate their deliverance and declare their discipleship.[16]

Rauschenbusch enjoyed other opportunities for contact with men and women beyond his congregation. As pastor, a key responsibility was to link Second Church with the wider community of Baptists in North America. This entailed attendance at occasional national and regional meetings of the German Baptist fellowship, along with weekly sessions of all Baptist pastors and annual meetings of all Baptist churches in metropolitan New York. In each of these realms his talent was recognized and he was appointed to a variety of committees, especially those dealing with missionary and educational issues.

In the weekly gatherings of Baptist ministers he met two men who became close friends and valued colleagues. Leighton Williams was appointed pastor of the Amity Baptist Church on West 54th Street the same year Rauschenbusch arrived in New York, and Nathaniel Schmidt was called to the First Swedish Baptist Church on East 20th Street the year after. Williams, a graduate of Columbia College, had practiced law for ten years before becoming a minister. His father, William R. Williams, had been a prominent pastor in New York and played a key role in the formation of Rochester Seminary. Schmidt studied at Stockholm University and Madison Theological Seminary in Hamilton, New York, before coming to his pastorate. Williams later recalled that a "warm friendship" between the three young men quickly developed, "cemented by a close similarity of ideas and regular weekly meetings. Our theological views were much the same and we were still more united in our social opinions." For each the relationship proved to be an invaluable testing ground for ideas about

how to cope with the formidable mission fields in which they labored.[17]

Schmidt's return to Madison Seminary as a professor in September
1888 ended the weekly sessions, but the trio now began a lively correspondence and met whenever possible. Their most fruitful gatherings were at the Williams family's 400-acre summer home called
Plas Llecheiddior, located on a hilltop sixty miles north of New York
near Marlborough on the Hudson River. The three men first met there
in August 1888 and returned often in succeeding years. The impact
of the friendship upon Rauschenbusch was evident in a comment he
wrote in the Williams guestbook in September 1890: "Only an afternoon and evening, yet enough talk to turn over the world and enough
love to make any heart happy." It was an association reminiscent of
those enjoyed by Francis, Ignatius, Wesley, and other Christian pioneers early in their ministries.

In 1889 Williams suggested that the three men establish a band
like that proposed by his father more than fifty years earlier. It would
be a "true society of Jesus" linking like-minded Protestants in disciplined obedience to Christ. The idea intrigued his friends, and
though it did not lead to exactly what the elder Williams had envis-
aged, it helped yoke the trio until a later time, when they became the
nucleus of a consequential new organization.[18]

❈❈❈

Increasingly "Brother Rauschenbusch" grew to love his flock and
to relish his ministry on West 45th Street. He lived among the people
as one who consoled, admonished, baptized, married, and buried. Especially did he welcome the times with young men his own age.
Rauschenbusch organized a class for them on Sunday mornings,
taught it, and enjoyed wide-ranging discussion of "all sorts of practical, ethical, and religious questions in an entirely uninhibited way."
Members of the class and his entire congregation reciprocated Walter's
love. In July 1888 one of them voiced their affection. She wrote she
had been strengthened by his Sunday message and wanted him to
know "there are many silent prayers going to heaven for you; many
here have grown stronger in faith these last two years. We hope God
will let us have you a long time yet in our Church."[19]

As the church experienced new life, its ranks began to swell. By
1888, membership reached 187 and enrollees in Sunday school numbered 358. Attendance at Sunday and midweek services also grew, as
did giving for benevolences; the church's average gift per member
made it the thirteenth of the forty-nine churches in the Southern New

York Baptist Association. Other Baptists in New York took note of the reviving church and of Walter Rauschenbusch—called its "excellent pastor" by the leading Baptist periodical in the area.

Walter Rauschenbusch's success also attracted the attention of his teachers at Rochester Seminary. In the spring of 1888, when August Rauschenbusch decided to retire and return to Germany, the school invited his son to replace him. It was a flattering proposal, but the younger Rauschenbusch knew he must continue the New York ministry. He explained to German Baptist friends that he was reluctant to return to the "hothouse atmosphere of a learned institution," as much because of his own needs as those of the church: "I still need the contact with the people, simple work modeled after my Master's, if my inner life is to keep on growing." Moreover, he believed the congregation had reached a major turning point and needed his leadership still.[20]

It was evident to Rauschenbusch that the upturn of Second Church posed a problem. The building could no longer comfortably hold the increased numbers, much less the additional people who might come in the future. Some had wanted to move to larger facilities as early as 1886, but the issue had been shelved. Now it could no longer be avoided. Serious discussion about a new building began in the summer of 1888, and early in 1889 the process of relocation was set in motion. The congregation sold its building on West 45th Street, bought two adjoining lots on West 43rd near 9th Avenue, and commissioned architectural drawings for a more spacious and attractive church. All this was done, Rauschenbusch said, "without any assurance of outside help." He admitted that anxiety ran high, because the amount needed was $27,000—a sizable sum for a congregation of working-class people.[21]

As chairman of the building committee, Rauschenbusch spent long hours on the project and proved to be an adept fund raiser. After members contributed $7,000, he decided to ask John D. Rockefeller for funds. Rockefeller's philanthropy was well known, and although his business practices as head of Standard Oil had come under fire, Rauschenbusch saw no reason to shun him. He was a major backer of Rochester Theological Seminary and father-in-law of Rauschenbusch's friend Charles Strong. Rockefeller had taken an interest in Rauschenbusch while he was still a seminarian and had given him a graduation gift of $100 that financed his vacation in the summer of 1886. Rauschenbusch met Rockefeller at Charles and Bessie's wedding in March 1889, broached the issue of Rockefeller help two months later, and discussed the matter in Rockefeller's home in November. The multimillionaire agreed to contribute $8,000, on condition that the church raise the remainder. The Baptist City Mission gave the needed amount, Rockefeller's gift arrived, construction began, and the new building was dedicated on 30 March 1890.[22]

In the end, Rauschenbusch felt ambivalent about the accomplishment. He told his congregation that their lovely new building could either become a "workshop" for doing "great work for the Master" or lure them into "pride, indolence, quarrels, selfishness, and the attractions of worldliness." He knew that large, plush churches were particularly tempted to compromise their spiritual mission in pursuit of alien goals prescribed by a culture obsessed with wealth. Increasingly, too, he realized that the lowly position of German Baptists, beyond the main currents of American Protestantism, helped protect them from the culture's strong coloration of religion. Now he wondered whether the congregation's proud achievement, marking it as another American success story, would become its undoing. A year after the dedication of the new building, he noted in his diary that despite increases of numbers and activities he had misgivings: "Spiritually I am not sure that either the church or I have profited by the building, and it is questionable to me now whether the game was worth the candle."[23]

Walter Rauschenbusch worried about the enticements of "worldliness," but he knew better and feared more the terrible chains of poverty. Day after day he moved among people whose lives were buffeted and drained by conditions over which they had no control. Three-quarters of New York's population lived in tenements; as many as two dozen families pressed into the dimly lit, foul-smelling, five-story buildings. Tenement life was especially brutal to children. In one section of the city it was reported that 68 percent of the deaths that occurred were among children age five and under. Rauschenbusch felt nothing more keenly: "Oh, the children's funerals! They gripped my heart—that was one of the things I always went away thinking about—why did the children have to die?" For him there was no theological sense in the answer that many pious people gave, that the children died because God willed it.

Poverty also caught adults in its horrible grip. Rauschenbusch reported to Maria Döring that within one week he was visited by three young men whose university studies had been interrupted by the death of the uncle who supported them. Without work, they now were reduced to begging for shoes and food. "The world is hard and without feeling," he confessed to Maria. "Here I see so much of this that my heart bleeds for the victims."[24]

Anguish arose not only because so many suffered so much. It was clear to him that their suffering came because the world was "without feeling"—comfortable people made peace with others' poverty and ignored their own complicity in causing it. Less than a mile away dozens of millionaires flaunted their wealth in ornate homes. In this Gilded Age prosperous Americans invoked such names as Smith, Malthus, and Spencer to support their contention that inexorable laws decree that a society cannot progress without hardship for some of its members, that the best of all worlds is emerging from the marvel of capitalism. A further rationale for accepting the status quo was added by reminders from the American religious tradition that God's hand governs everything that happens and must not be questioned, that the poor suffer because of their vice, that their plight has the good effect of prompting charity among the affluent, and that Christians should aim more to prepare immortal souls for heaven than to rescue mortal bodies from affliction.

Day after day Rauschenbusch saw firsthand the conditions his congregation and their neighbors endured, and the experience burned into his soul the conviction that poverty and its causes must somehow be overcome. In 1889 he told a Baptist audience that for three years he had lived among the poor "and by reason of the pity and sympathy which the Lord Jesus Christ has implanted in my heart, I have not been able to look on the things I see about me unmoved, or without thinking on the causes of those sad appearances." Initially, however, he felt unable to cope. "I had no idea of social questions," he admitted later. Attempting to apply his "previous religious ideas to the conditions I found, I discovered that they didn't fit." The Pietist-Evangelical tradition had cultivated instincts that told him something was wrong, but neither Gütersloh nor Rochester had given him conceptual tools for analyzing and correcting the problem.[25]

His floundering was short-lived. At the very moment he was ripe for their message, two Christian laymen—both pioneering economists—entered Rauschenbusch's life with the declarations that poverty is not inevitable, that it can be eliminated, and that God summons Christians to a mighty battle against it.

The first of these teachers was Henry George. In October 1886 the crusading journalist launched his campaign for mayor of New York as the reform candidate of a coalition of labor unions and socialists. Two years earlier Rauschenbusch had begun his participation in the American political process through vigorous support of Grover Cleveland's candidacy for President. At the same time he had learned about Henry George from Harrison Webster, and he now welcomed the chance to learn more. On the second day of October, Rauschenbusch joined other New Yorkers at a rally for George. Any doubts he may

have had about supporting him were dispelled when Father Edward
McGlynn, a fervent Catholic backer of George, invoked words from
the Lord's Prayer at the beginning of his speech. Walter later wrote
that he remembered "how Father McGlynn, speaking at Cooper Union,
. . . recited the words, 'Thy Kingdom come! Thy will be done on earth,'
and as the great audience realized for the first time the social significance of the holy words, it lifted them off their seats with a shout
of joy." Here was a different kind of commentary on Jesus' prayer for
the Kingdom, and Rauschenbusch was stirred.

George lost the mayoral race, but he made an indelible mark on
young Rauschenbusch, who years later acknowledged George's contribution: "I owe my own first awakening to the world of social problems to the agitation of Henry George in 1886 and wish here to record
my lifelong debt to this single-minded apostle of a great truth." As
he heard George speak and read his writings, he was captured by the
man's prophetic fire and vision. George knew the deprivation that
was the daily lot of wage earners, and he believed this "industrial
slavery" resulted from violation of "the eternal laws of the universe."
The Creator God intended the land and its bounty to be used to support all people, but a system of injustice allowing some people to
monopolize these resources and charge exorbitantly for them had
arisen, thereby bringing unearned wealth to themselves and poverty
to others.[26]

George attacked economic theories that condoned the injustice and
called for corrective intervention by the state. The key step would be
institution of a tax on all land according to its full rental value and
use of the proceeds to fund a vigorous public program of care for the
needy. A host of benefits would issue from this "single tax." It would
free land now held for speculation, stimulate construction, create new
housing and employment for workers, lower rents, and invigorate industry.

Some thought George was a socialist, but though there was an
affinity with aspects of socialist theory, he believed strongly in the
benefits of competition and rejected what he considered socialism's
excessive curtailment of individual liberty. For George no revolutionary measures were necessary for moving to a just and humane
society. Progress would be made by correcting abuses of the capitalist
system through such application of fundamental democratic and religious values that eventually no person would be denied the opportunity to lead a full life.[27]

Rauschenbusch learned much from George, but the more he observed and studied, the more he realized that a Georgist analysis did
not account for all aspects of the social question and that George's

remedies would not accomplish everything that was needed. Richard
Ely, an innovative economist whom Rauschenbusch met through their
mutual friend Leighton Williams (Ely's classmate at Columbia), offered other tools for analysis and change. An Episcopal layman and
professor of political economy at Johns Hopkins University, Ely believed as much as George that Christians must view the American
capitalist system critically and seek its reform. His thought was
shaped by study in Germany with academic economists who, like colleagues in other university disciplines, looked to history for guidance.
Their study led them to reject the claims of English economists that
immutable universal laws cause some to enjoy wealth and others to
suffer misery. That regrettable pattern, they insisted, is the consequence of peculiar historical circumstances, and it can be changed,
because people are free to shape the economic order according to their
distinctive conditions and values.

For Ely this was a liberating message to be spread as far as possible.
In numerous articles and books, in his classroom, in public lectures,
and in the American Economic Association, which he organized in
1885, Ely urged that American economic patterns be reformed to ensure that no person's material well-being is denied. He challenged
prevailing economic theory by arguing that the state should intervene
to promote properly competitive trade and the rights of the downtrodden. Moreover, government should own such natural monopolies
as gas and water utilities, but not intrude in realms where private
ownership is just and productive. He warned capitalists that workers
are unfairly treated and that, unless remedies soon were found,
America would be rocked by violence.[28]

More than George, Ely attempted to move the churches to a positive role in social and economic reform. He was deeply influenced
by F. D. Maurice and other English Christians who several decades
earlier had rejected laissez-faire capitalism as incompatible with
Christianity and sketched an alternative they called Christian Socialism. With them Ely believed that the West was passing through
an epochal "social crisis" and that the church was neglecting its responsibility to shape a new socioeconomic order. In a widely read
book, *Social Aspects of Christianity* (one chapter of which Rauschenbusch heard presented to a meeting of Baptist ministers in 1888), Ely
argued that in recent centuries Christians taught only a "one-sided
half-gospel" of individual salvation and forgot biblical religion's passion for social righteousness. The churches now must recover the
complete teaching of Christ. "What we need is the whole truth, and
that includes a social as well as an individual Gospel. . . . The Gospel
of Christ is both individual and social. It proclaims individual and

social regeneration, individual and social salvation." Like Maurice, Ely believed that no enduring recovery of social mission could occur without a parallel recovery of the authentic biblical message.

Ely counseled that as Christians take their places in the movement for social reform they must expect change to come gradually and on many fronts. No single, dramatic step would bring the millennium. All the changes needed were fundamentally religious, inasmuch as all would fulfill the Lord's command to love one's neighbor: "It is as truly a religious work to pass good laws, as it is to preach sermons; as holy a work to lead a crusade against filth, vice, and disease in slums of cities, and to seek the abolition of the disgraceful tenement-houses of American cities, as it is to send missionaries to the heathen."[29]

Rauschenbusch read Ely as avidly as he did George, but he absorbed more of his Episcopal mentor's fusion of religion, ethics, and economics. In 1891, when he recommended books to help German Baptists understand their social mission, three were by George and three were by Ely. About Richard Ely he wrote that he was "a personal friend of mine, a simple and serious man, a convinced Christian and one of the top experts on national economy." Through Ely, Rauschenbusch realized the commitment he must make to lifelong study if he were to contribute significantly to social reconstruction. Centuries of neglect, Ely contended, make it difficult for Christians to know how to proceed in this crucial work. The complexity and importance of the questions call for "hard study, pursued with devotion for years." Rauschenbusch now believed that God called him to this task, and Ely remained a major guide over the years.[30]

Armed with conceptual weapons supplied chiefly by George and Ely, Rauschenbusch ventured forth as a reformer eighteen months after arriving in New York. His initial efforts sought to persuade affluent Americans to look beyond self-serving explanations of poverty and respond constructively to the widespread presence of social injustice. The first cautious blow was a paper about Henry George read privately to Rochester friends in December 1887. He urged them to heed the "wails of the mangled and the crushed" and to work for a new society. Next, his first reformist article appeared in a national Baptist publication. It told of a "little bullet-headed tailor" denied permission by his employer to go to the bedside of his dying daughter and asked readers to look "beneath the glitter" of life and discover the vast sea of misery there. The article was signed "A New York Pastor." Rauschenbusch later acknowledged that he had "felt scared and sick with fear" at early turning points of his social ministry, but this was the only occasion he declined to sign his work. In the years ahead he would continue to believe this gentle "muckraking" was an important part of his ministry. The affluent must be made to see the human costs of the economic system that gave them their wealth.[31]

In 1889 Rauschenbusch escaped sufficiently from the demands of his church's building project to undertake a vigorous program of reading and writing in which he explored the connections between religion and the social question. The major issue engaging him was how the church could close the widening gap between itself and the urban masses. The issue presented itself as two questions: How far can Christians go toward embracing the aspirations of workers, especially those expressed in socialism, and how can Christians be made to care about the social revolution under way in their country?

The most fateful conclusion he reached from his study was that he must endorse socialism. Sympathy for a socialist vision of society had been growing slowly over the last three years. Several months after he came to New York, Maria Döring had given him a biography of F. D. Maurice, which he read intently. He knew that Leighton Williams and several New York Episcopal clergymen had responded warmly to Maurice's advocacy of Christian Socialism, and he too felt attracted by it. In May 1889, when Rauschenbusch and Williams attended Baptist meetings in Boston, they made contact with the Society of Christian Socialists, established there only the previous month by W. D. P. Bliss, an Episcopal priest. Its president was O. P. Gifford, a Baptist preacher and friend of Williams and Rauschenbusch. The Society championed no particular brand of socialism, though its members were cool toward Marxist radicalism. Gifford, Bliss, and the others said they wanted "to show that the aim of socialism is embraced in the aim of Christianity" and "to awaken members of Christian churches to the fact that the teachings of Jesus Christ lead directly to some specific form or forms of socialism." Rauschenbusch's contacts with this small band convinced him that they took seriously the plight of workers and the need for a fresh Christian response to it. He was ready to join them.[32]

In August 1889, when the *Christian Inquirer*, a national Baptist newspaper published in New York, criticized Edward Bellamy's *Looking Backward* as a socialist pipe dream that ignored human depravity, Rauschenbusch leaped to Bellamy's defense. As always with his stance toward socialism, he was more affirmative of the fundamental direction of Bellamy's utopian thought than of particulars. He argued that the socialist vision inspiring the author had become too powerful a force in England and Germany to be dismissed so cavalierly. Socialism has won the hearts and minds of people who see it as the way to fulfill their noblest dreams. It feeds their hope for a future akin to the one for which Christians should aspire. "If there are men who think that 'Thy Kingdom Come' are not idle words but that they can do something to make it come, let us cheer them on. There is none too much of faith and hope in the world." Such visionaries can be important allies for Christians.

Two further public endorsements of socialist ideas occurred in November 1889. That month Leighton Williams accompanied Rauschenbusch to Toronto for a meeting of the Baptist Congress, an association of professors and pastors who had gathered annually since 1883 to discuss theological and ethical issues. Rauschenbusch wrote in his diary that at Toronto the two men "made the most open declaration of our economic faith that we had so far made." In a session on monopolies, Rauschenbusch endorsed Henry George's proposal that privately owned natural monopolies be taken over by the state, but he disagreed with George's claim that repeal of laws creating artificial monopolies would permanently restore healthy competition. Rauschenbusch argued that it was futile to think competition could be reinstituted in such realms, for as the Italian patriot Mazzini had insisted, the forces of modernity tend irreversibly toward association and concentration. He agreed with the socialists that every monopoly should be assumed by the state so that the advantages of concentration would accrue to all instead of a few.[33]

Also in November 1889 the first issue of a modest paper edited by Rauschenbusch, Williams, and two other Baptists appeared. *For the Right* was intended for workers in New York and resembled a paper published by Maurice and two associates in 1845 for London workers. At the suggestion of Rauschenbusch the paper's name was taken from the English title of a recent novel by the German author Karl Emil Franzos. Its aim, explained the editors, was to discuss questions affecting workers "from the standpoint of christian-socialism." They said the paper served no party or association and would not propose new theories. Instead it intended to reflect "the needs, the aspirations, the longings of the tens of thousands of wage-earners who are sighing for better things; and to point out, if possible, not only the wrongs that men suffer, but the methods by which these wrongs may be removed."

Over the next sixteen months Rauschenbusch wrote twenty-one articles for the paper. All showed the crisp, engaging style that was becoming characteristic of his writing. The articles fell into two groups. In one he sought to win workers' commitment to gradual, nonviolent methods of social change. Their aspirations for better wages and living conditions, he assured them, are supported by Christian teaching, even if not yet by most Christian churches. Jesus himself was a worker, and God is for them—therefore they can know that eventually their hopes will be realized and right will prevail. Until that time, they must shun those who advocate violent change, for "ideas are more powerful than dynamite, and a thousand times more helpful." The way ahead for workers is to clarify their aims, organize, spread their message, reason with their employers, and make full use of the ballot box.

In the other set of articles, Rauschenbusch endorsed a variety of objectives sought by workers in New York. His list of particulars included an eight-hour workday, the single tax, municipal ownership of utilities, a city-owned underground rapid transit system, ballot reform, and socialization of the railroads.

The paper lasted until March 1891. From the beginning the editors could give it only part of their time. One of them, Elizabeth Post, became disturbed at the economic radicalness of her partners and withdrew. Early in 1891 Rauschenbusch's departure for Europe ended his involvement. Fewer than two hundred subscriptions were sold, and debts mounted. Shortly before the paper's demise, a reporter for the *New York Times* noted that *For the Right* took a "radical yet Christian" stance. He rightly saw that it was a rare combination of perspectives, but for most affluent Christians who bothered to read the paper, it was too "radical," and for distressed workers eager for corrective action it was too "Christian." In retrospect Rauschenbusch believed the failed venture had been useful, at least to its directors. He wrote in his diary that although it had caused "the moneyed men to feel a little shy about us," it had served as a rallying point for a handful of Baptist pioneers in New York and had given them an opportunity to experiment with "the methods of agitation."[34]

In 1889 Rauschenbusch also began formulating a theological basis for social mission that he hoped would stimulate Christians to become more involved in reform. For several years trailblazers such as Episcopalians Ely and Bliss and Congregationalists Washington Gladden and Josiah Strong had sought to turn the churches toward these issues, but it was a mammoth task and their message had moved few. Rauschenbusch later testified to the resistance he encountered within Baptist circles:

> The older brethren told us that the true function of the ministry was not to "serve tables" but to save the immortal souls of men. One told me that these were "mere questions of mine and thine," and had nothing to do with the gospel. A young missionary going to Africa to an early death implored me almost with tears to dismiss these social questions and give myself to Christian work. Such appeals were painfully upsetting. All our inherited ideas, all theological literature, all the practices of church life, seemed to be against us.

But Rauschenbusch believed firmly that God's hand was in the movement for social justice, and he knew that a key task for himself was
to discover how to restate the Christian message in ways that made
God's summons to a social mission plain and inescapable.[35]

At the 1889 session of the Baptist Congress, Rauschenbusch enun-
ciated important new theological themes. He stated that there are
two main objectives of Christianity, one widely recognized and the
other not. Christians agree that the church must seek to change the
lives of individuals. "But I claim that that is only one-half of the object
of Christianity, that the other half is to bring in the Kingdom of God,
and that the efforts of the Christian Church ought to be directed in
a like measure to the accomplishment of that last object." It is not
adequate, he explained, to wait for changed individuals eventually
to correct social wrongs. The church must now mount a direct corporate attack upon "the wrongs of human society and the unjust laws
of the community to bring about righteousness." As social reform is
accomplished, a good society will generate beneficent influences that
help the church in its effort to make good individuals.

All the institutions of the world, he continued, ultimately will be
transformed and absorbed into God's Kingdom. Until that time the
church must both denounce injustice and seek to extend the ways of
the Kingdom in the world. This mission requires special concern for
the state. Like other Baptists, Rauschenbusch insisted that the or-
ganizational patterns of church and state be kept separate. But, in-
voking the names of Anglicans F. D. Maurice and Thomas Arnold, he
added that the church must not hesitate to prod the state to accept
its God-given role. "The State must be built on righteousness. Its very
purpose is to exercise righteousness among men." It does so with the
aid of prophetic souls whose task is to herald the coming of God's
Kingdom. Such persons "see the things that shall be in the future,
but which are not yet." Through them the church announces "those
things in the ears of the State; it must declare that truth which is not
yet recognized; it must perform that duty which has not yet been
performed; and if necessary it must suffer in doing so." Here was a
higher doctrine of the church, and even more of the state, than most
American Protestants had heard. Both, said Rauschenbusch, play in-
dispensable roles in furthering God's Kingdom. This position was to
endure in his thought as a central legacy from the Anglican tradition.[36]

A more comprehensive theological reformulation occurred in a series of weekly Sunday school lessons that Rauschenbusch wrote over
a two-year period for the *Christian Inquirer*. Begun in December 1888,
each of the eighty-seven lessons ran to about two thousand words and
exposited an assigned portion of Scripture. Especially in his yearlong

commentary on the Gospel of Luke, Rauschenbusch showed that a social mission springs from the heart of Christianity.

The theme of conflict recurred throughout the lessons. In the Bible, he said, one discovers the meaning of the struggles in which the world is engaged. The world rebels against God and follows Mammon, who urges his followers to indulge themselves and forget others. God has responded by sending Jesus to lead a "revolutionary movement" whose purpose was "to turn things upside down, . . . to substitute love for selfishness as the basis of human society. It worked toward the reign of absolute justice on earth." In the end God's rule will be established and the Kingdom will prevail. Meanwhile, the task of Christians is to obey Christ as he asserts God's will in every realm of life. This is admittedly difficult, for the law of Christ is demanding. Nevertheless, he is Lord, and the way of Christians is "radical obedience" to his commands.[37]

As he wrote the lessons, Rauschenbusch made little use of Bible commentaries, for they were steeped in the old orthodoxy and seemed irrelevant to contemporary issues. At this time, however, he discovered Leo Tolstoi and read him with great interest. In one of the lessons, Rauschenbusch noted Tolstoi's lament that the church has softened Christ's commands in the Sermon on the Mount, and he agreed with the Russian seer that those commands are intended for Christians today fully as much as they were for the first-century church. Christians especially must recover and heed Christ's teaching about the acquisition and use of money. "There is nothing," wrote Rauschenbusch, "about which the Christian church is so silent and about which it has so far departed from the teachings of its Master as about all that concerns wealth." He saw that, measured by the standards of Jesus and God's Kingdom, on this critical issue the church had stumbled as badly as the world. Each needed reform.[38]

Several years would pass before Rauschenbusch could undertake the double-pronged program of reform of church and world to which he increasingly felt himself called. In 1889 President Strong had renewed the invitation to teach at Rochester Seminary, but Rauschenbusch again declined. Late the following year the question of leaving Second Church returned from an unexpected quarter. He recorded the dreadful development in his diary: "My hearing which had steadily decreased since I first discovered its failing in 1885 took a sudden drop downward, so that I could hear only what was spoken directly to me and very near to me. I saw then that I should have to resign my position."

In January 1891 a shaken Walter Rauschenbusch announced his resignation and explained to the congregation that he planned to go abroad for a year of study and then begin a literary career. Church leaders quickly responded that they wanted him to retain the position, spend up to a year in Europe as a sabbatical with pay, and resume his pastoral duties when he returned. In his absence they would hire an interim minister, whom they would retain if Rauschenbusch wanted help when he returned.

It was an extraordinary expression of love and appreciation. He wrote: "Their affection surprised and held me. I also realized that the church gave me a position for effective work such as I could scarcely find elsewhere." He gratefully accepted the church's proposal and in March 1891 sailed to Europe for the third time.[39]

✖▶▶▶ CHAPTER 5 ◀◀◀✖

SEEKER

Walter Rauschenbusch's eagerness to return to Europe had mounted during the winter. Much of what he needed at this stage of his life seemed to await him there. For the last several years he had plunged deeper and deeper into the social question, but the demands of his pastorate had given him little opportunity for systematic reading and writing. What better place than German libraries for such scholarly leisure? He also wanted to observe firsthand the reform movements that appeared to be so instructive to Americans like himself just starting on the road European pioneers had taken earlier. Along with this light for the mind, however, there was something more personal he sought. He had heard of the progress Germans had made in treating deafness, and he hoped against hope that his hearing could be restored.

Emma also was at a critical juncture, and she accompanied her brother across the Atlantic. Five taxing years as a teaching missionary in India had been followed by an extended furlough in the United States, including two years as a student at Wellesley College in Massachusetts. Now she was eager for rest and for opportunities to read in European libraries.

Their first destination was England. Rauschenbusch's appreciation for the land of Maurice and Robertson had risen markedly since his days at the Rochester Free Academy when he denounced England as dangerously expansionist. For the last several years he had perused English socialist literature and was excited by the call of Sidney Webb and other Fabian Socialist leaders for a gradual evolution of English society that extended the blessings of liberty into the economic realm; through education and legislation—not the violence of the radicals—

workers' misery would be ended and their opportunity for full participation in English life ensured. Rauschenbusch had written in 1889 that socialist ranks include "men whose minds are lofty, whose lives are pure, whose hearts are hot with the love of mankind." Now he would see for himself what they had accomplished.[1]

The initial week in England brought shock and disappointment. The port city of Liverpool contained masses of people who were poorer than any Emma had seen in India or Walter had seen in New York. "We were both horrified at the looks of the people," he wrote in his diary. Particularly dreadful were the children—"such old looking, wrinkled children . . . bodies 12 years old and souls 100." Some said the children's appearance was induced deliberately by gin in order to make their begging more effective.

From Liverpool they went to Birmingham, where they discovered another world. "I have traversed the city in various directions to the outskirts," Rauschenbusch wrote, "but have nowhere found that awful, loathsome poverty which flutters in rags and scowls in the faces of the people of Liverpool." He learned that earlier in the century industrialization had brought a rapid growth of population and poverty to Birmingham, but in the 1870s a remarkable change occurred. Under Lord Mayor Joseph Chamberlain the city government initiated an aggressive program of reform, taking over the water and gas systems, renovating a major slum district, building parks and libraries, giving the suffrage in local elections to women, and providing free meals to schoolchildren. Now Birmingham was reputed to have the best educational system in England and to be the best-governed city in the world.

Rauschenbusch marveled at this glowing instance of "municipal socialism," and in the first of several reports written about his European discoveries he encouraged new American cities to "do by foresight what Birmingham did by hindsight." Here was evidence for him of the truth of Sidney Webb's contention that municipal reform was socialism's major contribution to progress.[2]

Next on the American pair's schedule was six weeks in London. It turned out to be a fateful time for Emma. She became fascinated by Mary Wollstonecraft, an eighteenth-century English advocate of women's rights. Four years later Emma would complete a dissertation on Wollstonecraft and become one of the first women to receive a doctorate from the University of Bern. In London she and Walter also visited frequently with John Clough, her supervisor in India, who had stopped in England on his way back to the United States. In 1894 John and Emma would be married.[3]

For Rauschenbusch the English capital gave access to a variety of reformist activities. He spent many hours reading the periodical literature of groups arrayed against poverty. Most were new, for though sensitive souls had warned of the perils of industrialization earlier in the century and some remedial steps had been taken, it was not until the 1880s, during an extended economic slump, that important organizations arose to fight poverty. The group that Rauschenbusch observed most closely was the Salvation Army. Under the direction of its founder, General William Booth, the Army sent men and women recruited from the working classes to seek souls for Christ in the bleakest urban areas. In 1890 Booth had announced a new strategy in his book entitled *In Darkest England:* Since poverty impeded people's acceptance of Christianity, the Salvation Army would devote itself to helping the poor escape poverty and thereby prepare them for religious conversion. Shortly after the book appeared, Rauschenbusch applauded Booth's proposals for "soul saving and society saving," and now he was eager to see those proposals implemented. He visited the Army's food depots, shelters, and international headquarters. After hearing Booth speak, he noted that the general "looks more like the typical Yankee deacon than like an Englishman." Later that year, he probably had Booth and the Salvation Army in mind when he wrote that charitable efforts to relieve poverty are good as far as they go, but that they are inadequate because they address only the symptoms of pauperism, not its causes.[4]

Rauschenbusch also attended a conference at Toynbee Hall, a settlement house in the impoverished Whitechapel district of East London. It had been established a few years earlier as a memorial to Arnold Toynbee, a young Oxford economist who, prior to his death in 1883, spent vacations among London's poor. A dozen Oxford men lived at Toynbee Hall and sought through their educational and civic activities to provide uplift for residents of the area. Although Rauschenbusch did not comment on what he saw, it too probably impressed him as a palliative measure to be appreciated for the good it did but faulted for failing to attempt a greater good.

Rauschenbusch responded most enthusiastically to what he observed in Hyde Park on the first Sunday of May in 1891. While well-dressed Londoners attended respectable churches and chapels, a great throng of ill-clothed workers flocked to hear leaders of competing socialist factions preach their gospels from crude platforms in the open air. Among the speakers was Eleanor Marx-Aveling, the daughter of Karl Marx, who with her husband had translated Marx's *Das Kapital* into English. Now she spoke in behalf of the Marxist-oriented Social Democratic Federation. Rauschenbusch was more impressed by two of the nation's major labor union leaders, John Burns and Tom Mann.

"Burns," he wrote admiringly, "is the man who for weeks got up every morning at four, harangued the starving dockers, infused courage into them, persuaded them not to use violence, and then went off to his shop to earn his living." He also noted that "Tom Mann is the fellow who heard that in a certain trade chemicals were used, dangerous to health. He got himself employed and worked until his hands were raw and bleeding that he might help the men by knowing the business." It was the kind of hard work and self-sacrificing leadership that always moved Rauschenbusch. That morning he asked an American friend with him in Hyde Park, "Where would Christ be if he were in London?" He agreed with the friend's answer, "Here, talking to the multitudes on the social question"—doing so, Rauschenbusch undoubtedly believed, much in the winsome style of Burns and Mann.[5]

Earlier Rauschenbusch had admired the initiatives taken by the Christian Socialist movement in England, but there is no indication that he sought out its current leaders. By 1891 three national organizations existed among Englishmen who believed that Christianity requires ethical expression through support of some form of socialism. The two most prominent Christian Socialist organizations, the Guild of Saint Matthew and the Christian Social Union, admitted only Anglicans to membership, while the Christian Socialist Society included Anglicans as well as Nonconformists. As he learned more about the movement he had admired from afar, Rauschenbusch felt a new ambivalence. Its Anglican leaders took their theological cues from F. D. Maurice, centering their thought upon the incarnation and the sacraments and developing these doctrines in ways that did not accord well with Rauschenbusch's own Kingdom-centered theology. Nor did Rauschenbusch appreciate Anglicans' insistence that Baptists and other Nonconformists could not participate in the Anglican eucharist or in their reformist organizations. This theological exclusivity was even more rankling because it was coupled with the attachment of Anglicans to the upper rungs of a strongly class-conscious society. Rauschenbusch appreciated Anglican reformers' desire to mold the entire nation according to Christian principles, but he believed that their grasp of those principles had been weakened by the intrusion of worldliness, symbolized most pointedly by their church's link with the state and its policy of infant baptism.

An afternoon in Westminster Abbey brought the problem painfully into view. At a consecration service for Anglican bishops, Rauschenbush observed richly robed prelates assemble for a solemn procession, then watched with revulsion as they performed their task, "bowing, kneeling, marching, wheeling, and all that to get a man fit to be a successor of the apostles and to draw a salary." So unreformed a church was ill-prepared to reform English society.

Despite the Church of England's shortcomings, English Christianity as a whole received high marks from Rauschenbush. Several months after leaving England he wrote, "For centuries England has had more and purer Christianity than the other European nations. It has since the Reformation been the birth-place of all the progressive religious movements." He had concluded that the mantle of reform leadership rested on Nonconformists rather than on Anglicans, and in succeeding years he looked to English Nonconformist leaders of the Christian Socialist movement as the real guardians of that tradition, and he regarded the Fabian vision and the Birmingham achievement as socialism at its best.[6]

From England, Emma and Walter traveled to their sister's home in Hamburg. Frida Rauschenbusch Fetzer now edited a national paper for Baptist women, and her husband Georg was a mainstay at the Baptist seminary. Walter proudly pronounced their five daughters "good children." He was more impressed than ever with Frida. "She is a superior woman," he wrote in his diary. But he was disappointed to see that the old bitterness between his parents continued. August Rauschenbusch was away much of the time, and Caroline resented the pressure that had been put on her to part from Walter the previous year; she believed her husband "did not want her to be happy" with their son. Several months later, when August visited Emma and Walter in Berlin, the smoldering hostility between father and daughter surfaced. "Emma felt that he was disregarding her and she felt the sores of past years smarting again." Typically, Walter attempted to ease the tensions, but his intervention failed and August left much earlier than had been anticipated.[7]

Walter and Emma rented rooms in Berlin from early June until the end of July. His first business in the German capital was to visit an ear specialist. After a thorough examination the doctor told him that there was little hope of restoring his hearing but that he would try. Walter returned each morning for a week. "Dr. Trautmann . . . treated catarrh and inserted a catheter in the eustachian tubes and passed in air and steams." At the end of the week Walter was dejected. "I felt no benefit and suspected the reverse." A slight ray of hope came in a letter from John Clough, who urged him to consult a noted Vienna specialist who had cured a friend. Walter sent Dr. Adam Politzer a description of his symptoms and the procedures attempted in Berlin. Politzer responded that there was nothing further he could do. The hearing handicap, he judged, was "in all probability incurable." It was a shattering verdict.

Rauschenbusch looked no further for medical treatment, but he did seek relief from another quarter. Germans had pioneered in the development of lipreading, and later in the year he returned to Hamburg for a four-week course. The results were mixed. His new skill allowed him "fragmentary conversation in stores, etc." This was a gain, but he regretted it was so slight. Only with his teacher could he carry on a conversation, and even this was unsatisfactory because his teacher had to shout in order to be heard.

The realization that his hearing was virtually gone and probably would never return brought a time of gloom and soul-searching. Rauschenbusch was not sure he should attempt to continue as a pastor, for his deafness meant he would be unable to engage in the conversations vital to the pastoral vocation. Later he told friends that for a while his faith in God wavered. Letters to Leighton Williams brought his friend's response that he was distressed by Walter's "apprehensions of the future," and Williams offered the consolation that "God is better to us than our fears," as well as the news that Walter's congregation longed to have him back.[8]

Deafness was to remain Walter Rauschenbusch's great burden. For several years near the end of his life, relief came through the use of a mechanical hearing aid, but the help it gave was minimal. People occasionally remarked that the handicap was a "blessing in disguise," for they thought he was spared the distractions of noise. But those closest to him knew he had to cope with an incessant, surflike roar. They sensed rightly that deafness left a mark in other ways as well. The bouts with loneliness and depression he had experienced even before his hearing problem developed now became more severe. There was a recurring temptation to self-pity, and also a sense that his heightened need for help from others required that he avoid risking their displeasure. Rauschenbusch rarely spoke of these things, and people admired him for the courage and apparent ease with which he carried his handicap. He believed God's grace was sufficient to allow him a full life—indeed, he experienced deafness as a steady reminder of dependence upon God and upon the friends who sought to lighten the burden.[9]

During the bleakest period in Germany, Rauschenbusch wondered whether he should begin graduate study and eventually seek a teaching position. Consideration of this possibility was dropped when a more appealing one presented itself. In September he was invited to come to Cleveland as assistant editor of all German Baptist publications in North America at an annual salary of $1,000, with the understanding that he would succeed the current editor. It was an attractive offer. The Cleveland position would make use of his literary and managerial skills, give him a place of national influence among German Baptists, and provide a greater measure of financial security. He especially welcomed the prospect of moving his denomination, "which is on the whole poor and hence often open to Christian thought," toward a more progressive position on ethical and religious issues.

As he pondered his options, however, Rauschenbusch realized how greatly he valued the friends and pastorate in New York. "The fact that Williams and the germ of our association is there," he confided to his diary, "has much force with me." Furthermore, he feared that his duties as an official of a still-conservative denomination might restrict his freedom to do what he now called "God's special work"— helping the churches discover their social mission—and this he must not risk. In the end he turned down the Cleveland offer and reaffirmed his commitment to the people and tasks awaiting him in New York.[10]

German immigrants in New York often brought with them a zealous socialist faith, and Rauschenbusch wanted to study it at the source. He quickly discovered major differences between German socialism and English socialism. Earlier, Bismarck's fear of the Social Democratic party had led to legislation severely restricting its activity. When the antisocialist laws expired in 1890, the party returned to the political fray more committed than ever to a Marxist position, including its open hostility to religion. Rauschenbusch appreciated the steps in the direction of socialism that German city governments had taken, notably Elberfeld's system of public relief for the poor, but he found nothing commendable about the Social Democratic party. He noted that the insurance program for workers instituted by Bismarck in the 1880s had wooed many from the Social Democrats and that party members now were aggressively seeking recruits: "The Party breeds fanatics, enthusiasts, narrow, one-sided, but convinced and persistent, who set about making converts as doggedly as a Salvationist." He hoped that such militancy would eventually be cooled by exposure of the German socialists to the "temperate and practical energy" of English socialist leaders.

Rauschenbusch saw that the hostility of German socialists toward religion was reciprocated by Protestants. "The whole weight of the church," he wrote, "is thrown against the Socialists." Most Protestants knew little about the urban workers whose cause socialists championed, but some believed it was important to concern themselves with the workers and their problems. Rauschenbusch was referred to the best-known leader of this group by Professor Hermann Cremer, his friend from the years at Gütersloh. Since 1878 Adolf Stöcker had sought to save urban workers for Christianity by engaging in political action. As an elected member of the Reichstag, he supported the type of state socialism advocated by German academic economists and implemented by Bismarck's insurance program, but Stöcker also was gaining notoriety by joining those who denounced Jews as a danger to the Reich. In 1890 he took the lead in establishing the Evangelical Social Congress, an organization of pastors, professors, and politicians who met annually to study current social problems. Rauschenbusch called upon Stöcker, but the busy German pastor was not in his office and Rauschenbusch made no further attempt to meet him. Sixteen years later, when he was again in Germany, he did meet with leaders of the Protestant social movement, but in 1891 he judged that German Protestantism's strong attachment to the status quo gave it little to teach him about the church's social mission.[11]

Most of Rauschenbusch's time in Germany was spent writing a book-length manuscript in which he clarified and systematized his learnings as a pastor-reformer. He began the work in June in Berlin, where a cousin arranged for him to use the Royal Library. After two months, when he had completed three chapters of the book he called "Revolutionary Christianity," Walter and Emma accepted an invitation from Professor and Frau Cremer to make the cooler Greifswald their base. Since Walter Rauschenbusch's Gütersloh days, Cremer's eminence as a defender of Lutheran orthodoxy had grown, and he had become a key backer of the cautious social initiatives of Stöcker. Rauschenbusch's response to him was different now: "He did not make nearly the impression on me that he did formerly. I read several of his pamphlets and thought they contained few ideas amid much verbiage, and even those ideas were not clear-cut and plastic." Nor was he as attracted to Ernst Cremer: "He is very conservative and orthodox, and very sure he is right. His interests are so completely theological that he is not a companion of the pleasantest sort." But the Greifswald area, on the Baltic, offered a refreshing environment, and the Rauschenbusches remained there for seven weeks.[12]

Here, as at Berlin, Rauschenbusch consulted dozens of books, most of them by German biblical scholars, historians, and sociologists. By the end of September he had produced a manuscript of 450 pages, which he hoped to complete and revise in New York. Soon after returning, he asked Leighton Williams and Nathaniel Schmidt to read and criticize the manuscript. Although both men praised it, Williams admitted he found the first part dull, and Schmidt drafted a 90-page critique calling for extensive revision, particularly a fuller appropriation of recent biblical scholarship. Rauschenbusch wanted time to rework the manuscript thoroughly, but other duties were too pressing to permit it. Sixteen years passed before he published a substantially altered version of the book.[13]

The fundamental problem addressed in "Revolutionary Christianity" was the church's failure to understand Christianity aright. It has forgotten, Rauschenbusch said, that "Christianity is in its nature revolutionary," for Jesus created an entirely new type of community that was radically different from the world's accustomed ways (p. 70).[14] Other failures result from this key one: The church preaches a message catering to individuals' selfish desire for salvation; it allows itself to be controlled by wealthy members; it neglects groups on the edges of society; and it offers no light to a generation eagerly seeking social reconstruction.

Rauschenbusch contended that the way out of this massive problem is for the church to recover the authentic gospel and be reformed by it. Since its fundamental failure lies in the theological realm, correction must begin there. Recovery and reform, he insisted, can occur only through fresh attention to Jesus and his message. Rauschenbusch agreed with some contemporary biblical scholars that Jesus must be seen in continuity with the prophets of Israel, who heralded the reign of God and called people to live in conformity with the divine will. The coming of God's Kingdom on earth, he said, was the core of Jesus' teaching, around which all its parts revolved. Jesus initiated the Kingdom, embodied its righteousness in his own life, and established the church to exemplify the patterns of righteous life that God intends for all of humanity. Men and women who belong to the church are empowered to do as Jesus did: walk daily in paths of justice and love and seek to extend such righteousness into the world. They thereby make the earth a fit habitation for God and satisfy their own deepest longings for God. But they also meet resistance, for the world does not gladly surrender its evil ways. It killed Jesus and it struggles against his followers.

According to Rauschenbusch, the world uses an insidious strategy to thwart God's design: it infiltrates the church with its own values. Where this effort succeeds, the church has no alternative vision to propose for the world's transformation, and it is reduced to echoing and sanctioning the world's fallen wisdom. He judged that the church has accepted the intrusion of worldly values on many fronts. For example, it relies more on architectural beauty and liturgical pomp to attract members than on the truth of its message, and it imitates the world's elevation of the wealthy to places of power and forgets Jesus' elevation of the poor.

This was a searing indictment of the church, but it was rendered by a man who loved it and believed that change was possible. He said that as the church recovers its true identity it will become an extension of Christ's own ministry, furnishing him "with lips to speak his thoughts, with feet to go his errands, with hands to lift up the sick and check the blow of cruelty" (p. 175). Loving as Christ loved, the church will call the world to discipleship, condemn evil, dress the wounds of humanity, and work to change laws, customs, and institutions that cause people harm.

In the end, Rauschenbusch addressed the outcome Christians should expect from the struggle to make God's cause prevail in the church and in the world. He rejected the cheerful optimism of many in his time who assumed that "every change must be an improvement, every new idea must approximate more nearly to the truth than the one it supplants, every tendency must be just" (p. 280). Such people forget that evolution brings only the possibility of advance, not its inevitability, that history shows that nations both rise and fall, and that experience teaches that people are not naturally good. "None of us individually drifts into purity, justice, and unselfishness, as we all know. And humanity as a whole would likewise, if let alone, by no means roll into the millennium, but by a broad and easy track, into a hell on earth, into rottenness, beastliness and self-destruction" (p. 282). This drift downward is accelerated by a tendency of the human spirit to "give itself to evil and to love it" (p. 282). So bleak an assessment allowed Rauschenbusch readily to second Saint Paul's contention that "our wrestling is not merely with the natural weakness of flesh and blood, but 'against the principalities, against the powers, against the world-rulers of this darkness, against the spiritual hosts of wickedness' " (p. 283). All his life, Rauschenbusch was clear that no right-thinking Christian can ignore the massive power of sin and evil.

But the last word, he insisted, is not one of despair. People are entitled to look to the future with hope, for God is "immanent in the world, forever active and working," making individuals and nations ready for the Kingdom (p. 284). The divine Spirit is present particularly in those persons—both within and beyond conventional religious circles—"who have freely surrendered themselves to the will and service of righteousness" (p. 284). Through their labors, humanity moves toward its God-appointed destiny.

Many years after he wrote this manuscript, Rauschenbusch told a friend there had been few "striking epochs" in his intellectual development, but "perhaps the most important one" was his stay in Europe in 1891. His assessment at the time, recorded in his diary on the voyage back to New York, was that his views had "ripened" during that year in three respects. He freshly appreciated such sociologists as Albert Schäffle, who recognized the important role of religion and ethics in the human drama; in the future he often quoted Schäffle's dictum "History turns on the axis of religion." He also acknowledged that his interests had become "more theological" and that he had a renewed appreciation for traditional Christian teaching about sin and salvation: "I have gained faith in the Christian doctrine of the natural depravity of man, and expect his salvation less from evolution and more from redemption."[15]

A major point of theological growth for Rauschenbusch during this time in Germany was recognition that the Kingdom must receive a place of centrality in the church's thought and life. For years he had affirmed its importance, but never so much as he did now. Only a few months before leaving for Europe, he had made the claim that Christianity, "like an ellipse, has two centers: eternal life as the goal of the individual's development and the Kingdom of God as the goal of the development of all mankind." But study in Germany led Rauschenbusch to conclude that this Ritschlian-sounding formulation inadequately expressed the teaching of Jesus. The Kingdom was more than a major part of his teaching; it was the controlling center. "The entire Gospel," he wrote in his reading notes, "was a *logos tēs basileias*" (word of the Kingdom). About the Kingdom, he said in "Revolutionary Christianity," Jesus' "thoughts circle like a host of planets 'round a central sun" (p. 79). He concluded that the Kingdom must have the same centrality for followers of Jesus.

When Rauschenbusch looked at his own ministry in this light, he discovered a new coherence in its many parts. In 1891, he explained later, the idea of the Kingdom began to embrace all parts of his religious interest. It "responded to all the old and all the new elements of my religious life. The saving of the lost, the teaching of the young, the pastoral care of the poor and frail, the quickening of starved intellects, the study of the Bible, church union, political reform, the reorganization of the industrial system, international peace—it was all covered by the one aim of the Reign of God on earth." He had made a thrilling discovery that would illumine the next important steps of his ministry and remain the centerpiece of his theological horizon.[16]

The third shift that Rauschenbusch believed had taken place in Europe was that his interests had become "decidedly more historical." A fresh appreciation for history was evident in two realms. He had come to a deepened respect for the religious and social patterns evolved over long years by which people organize their lives; hence he turned a disapproving eye toward religious and secular reformers who rejected those patterns without proper regard for their continuing value. The way of true reform, he said, had been exemplified by Jesus, who came not to destroy Jewish tradition but to fulfill it. Rauschenbusch believed that Christianity is "revolutionary," but he never gave that word the destructive and violent content it had for many of his contemporaries.

The other focus of Walter Rauschenbusch's new historical interest was the Anabaptist movement of the sixteenth century. He knew of his father's long-standing attention to the Anabaptists, but until 1891 he had paid them little heed. A trip to Münster, however, introduced him to the German historian Ludwig Keller, who taught a more favorable view of the Anabaptists than was normal among historians. Rauschenbusch concurred with Keller's belief that "the Anabaptists contain more of the future . . . than the Reformers." And in notes made while reading the famed historian Leopold von Ranke, he observed that the chief difference between Luther and the Anabaptists was that "he said the gospel was to free the soul and not the body. They said, both." Rauschenbusch also commented in his notes that "the Reformation went back of the church to Augustine and Paul. We must go back of Paul to Christ." A return to Christ, he knew, had been the intention of the Anabaptists. Their road to reform, together with their understanding of the church as a disciplined, uncompromising band of believers, won Rauschenbusch's favor and made a lasting impression on his thought.[17]

Over the next six years, Rauschenbusch revised parts of "Revolutionary Christianity" and brought them out as separate essays. Had he been able to edit the entire work and publish it in the early 1890s, he would have gained a place of national prominence at that time, for not until later in the decade did a comparable book, treating the theological foundations of the church's social mission, appear. But the months in Europe served him well. He sailed home with fresh clarity about his own vocation and about the great task to which he believed the church must be summoned. "God's special work" awaited him, and he was eager to undertake it.

CHAPTER 6

SERVANT OF THE KINGDOM

The people of the Second German Baptist Church planned a festive welcome for their pastor, but they had to postpone it when word came that his steamer was caught in an Atlantic storm. Finally, on Christmas Day 1891 he arrived safely home, and members of the church and friends from the community converged upon West 43d Street to greet him. The outpouring of affection touched Rauschenbusch deeply. Some knew he had been invited to take the editorial position in Cleveland, and they encouraged him to turn it down. The following week they were relieved when he announced he had decided to remain in New York.

Until 1897, Rauschenbusch continued to be chiefly occupied as pastor of Second Church. In the weeks that followed his return, however, church leaders acknowledged that deafness limited the range of his ministry among them, and they reaffirmed a willingness to transfer some pastoral duties to the man who had substituted for him. Rauschenbusch accepted the proposal gladly, for the presence of a helper ensured that the spiritual needs of the people were met, and it freed him to give part of his time to the wider ministry he believed God had in store for him.

Most of the additional responsibilities that came to him over the next months drew upon his literary skills. He resumed writing the weekly Sunday school lessons for *The Christian Inquirer*, accepted the position of corresponding secretary and treasurer of the Baptist Congress, and agreed to edit *Der Jugend Herold,* a national monthly paper for German Baptist youth. The days became more crowded than ever. Purchase of a typewriter eased the burden somewhat, but it was necessary to organize his time so that every hour counted. He explained to Lina Döring that he ate breakfast and lunch in his tenement apartment, did his writing in the early morning when he was fresh, handled visits to the sick and administrative chores in the forenoon, then took a walk in Central Park and read most afternoons. The evenings were normally occupied with meetings, and he continued to preach twice on Sundays. All this activity, he told his aunt, was controlled by a single purpose: "the building of a Christianity that can transform the everyday life of society."[1]

Attendance at a meeting in May 1892 led to Rauschenbusch's most productive labors on behalf of such a Christianity. In the middle of the month he traveled to Philadelphia with Leighton Williams and Nathaniel Schmidt for the tenth annual session of the Baptist Congress, which was being held for the first time in conjunction with annual meetings of national Baptist agencies. It was an unusually charged week, for Baptists on both sides of the Atlantic were commemorating the one-hundredth anniversary of William Carey's launching of the modern missionary movement by his fateful journey to India. Pictures of Carey and other Baptist heroes hung on the walls of the church where the Congress met, and above them all was a banner with Jesus' admonition to carry the gospel to the whole world. Baptists knew that in recent decades Christianity had spread more widely than ever, and it appeared to be enjoying its most pervasive penetration of American life. For Rauschenbusch the time was ripe for heeding Carey's stirring admonition—"Expect great things from God; attempt great things for God." If Christians could give themselves so effectively to the task of converting all the nations, why not also seek the conversion of America's new urban-industrial order?

In Philadelphia, Rauschenbusch had his first opportunity to proclaim his newfound convictions before a national audience. "The whole aim of Christ," he declared to the Baptist Congress, "is embraced in the words, 'the Kingdom of God.' " He explained, "In that ideal is embraced the sanctification of all life, the regeneration of humanity, and the reformation of all social institutions." Christ's aim defines the church's mission: "Any department of human life which has not been sanctified and brought under the obedience of Jesus Christ is a province to be reclaimed for him by the church." The Christian with eyes to see has only to look out the window of their meeting place to discover a great mission province.[2]

Samuel Zane Batten, the young pastor of a Baptist church in a tenement section of Philadelphia, heard the speech and was stirred to action. Meeting with Rauschenbusch, Schmidt, Williams and two other Baptist Congress members, he proposed that they create an organization of men gripped by a common perception of the Kingdom. They would meet periodically for study and mutual support in their respective efforts to serve Christ and the Kingdom.

Rauschenbusch responded enthusiastically to Batten's proposal. It incorporated something of what he, Williams, and Schmidt had hoped for in their "society of Jesus," but it had the advantage of centering their effort directly upon the Kingdom and of seeking a larger circle of workers. This was perfectly in accord with the convictions about the Kingdom that had come to him in Europe. There was another reason Rauschenbusch responded positively to Batten's idea and pursued it aggressively. Since returning from Europe, he had again become absorbed in the lives of his people, and he knew the daily strain they and their neighbors experienced. "It has been a hard year for many of our people," he told John D. Rockefeller. "Many have been 'laid off' for weeks, and even months." Over the next year the strain worsened as the most severe industrial depression since the Civil War hit the nation. Rauschenbusch later wrote that people were "out of work, out of clothes, out of shoes, and out of hope. They wore down our threshold, and they wore away our hearts." He believed it was more urgent than ever that the church lead America to overcome injustice and poverty, but he also believed this would not happen until Christians recovered Jesus' gospel of the Kingdom.[3]

Because their time in Philadelphia was limited, the group that met around Batten decided to gather again at Rauschenbusch's apartment on 9 July 1892. There, according to Batten's minutes, the six young Baptist ministers agreed they wanted "some association which should serve as a bond of union and a strengthener of convictions." The name Batten proposed for the body was "Brotherhood of the Kingdom." He, Rauschenbusch, and S. B. Meeser agreed to formulate a plan of organization and statement of purpose that would be circulated to the others for comment.

Their next meeting was in Philadelphia on 19 December 1892. The circle had expanded to include several additional people. Under Batten's aggressive leadership, the nine founding members unanimously approved a statement of aims and organization, and they declared the Brotherhood of the Kingdom established. The opening sentences of their charter document stated the group's conviction that this venture was responsive to a divine initiative that called for a two-part reform effort on their part. "The Spirit of God is moving men in our generation toward a better understanding of the idea of the Kingdom of God on earth. Obeying the thought of our Master, and trusting in the power and guidance of the Spirit, we form ourselves into a Brotherhood of the Kingdom, in order to re-establish this idea in the thought of the church, and to assist in its practical realization in the world." It was an ambitious goal, and they had no doubt that God's resources were available to those who pursued it.[4]

Earlier in the century, like-minded American Protestants often had banded together to promote a cause they held dear, such as Abolition or Temperance, but it was rare for them to unite for so comprehensive a goal as the one that gripped these eager Baptists. All over the nation people in such realms as education, business, and labor now were establishing associations to help them reach their goals. Rauschenbusch and his colleagues believed the time had come for servants of the Kingdom to do the same.

The Brotherhood's founders wanted a simple pattern of organization. They agreed that major decisions would be made by a vote of all members and that ordinary business would be handled by an executive committee elected by the members. The only continuing officers would be a corresponding secretary and a treasurer; the chairmanship would rotate among members of the executive committee. The organization was kept simple, Batten explained, to make the Kingdom, not the Brotherhood, uppermost: "We are not associated to perfect an organization but to gain a sight of the ideal and to tell one another our vision."

As plans were considered for 1893, the Brothers decided to publish a book of essays declaring their reformist ideas, much as young Anglican theologians had done four years earlier in *Lux Mundi*. Each author would prepare an essay on a designated aspect of "the social interpretation of the gospel," and they would meet in the summer to read and critique one another's essays. In April, when Batten asked Rauschenbusch to confer with Williams about a site for the summer conference, they had no doubt that the Williamses' summer home on the Hudson was the ideal place for their gathering. It was a spacious Victorian house with ample accommodations and bracing hilltop views in all directions, and the two friends had already discovered how conducive it was to farsighted talk.

Eleven men gathered at Plas Llecheiddior on 9 August 1893. They came ready for a lofty adventure of mind and spirit, and they were not disappointed. Batten's minutes recorded that when Rauschenbusch was asked to lead the group in an opening act of worship, he "briefly reviewed the Providence which had brought us together, and after some tender and helpful words, all present knelt and one by one offered prayer." Over the next four days, as the Brothers read and discussed their papers, they marveled at the spirit of trust and candor that was present. On some matters, such as socialism and women's suffrage, they disagreed, but their differences were contained, wrote Batten, "within the greatest unity of sentiment." Each knew all were committed to making the Kingdom prevail in the church and the world. Each was making a valuable contribution to that task, and each brought distinctive gifts to the group. Nathaniel Schmidt, for instance, was engaged in rigorous scientific study of the Scriptures; George Dana Boardman, in the pursuit of Christian unity and international peace; William Newton Clarke, in the elaboration of a fresh perspective upon the whole range of Christian doctrine; Leighton Williams, in mobilizing support for better municipal government; his brother Mornay Williams (the only layman present), in formulating legislation to protect the rights of workers. Alone, their individual efforts mattered relatively little. Together, they could undertake great things for God.

So rich was the August 1893 conference that the group decided to repeat it the following summer. A small executive committee based in New York City met several times to invite new members and plan for the coming year. In 1894—and for the next two decades—the summer conference at Marlborough-on-the-Hudson remained the Brotherhood's major activity. Some summers, as many as fifty gathered at Plas Llecheiddior to gain clarity about the Kingdom and to support one another in their wide-ranging labors in church and society. The themes varied each year, but always there was consideration both of religious perspectives upon the Kingdom and of the Kingdom's consequences for the social order. Increasing attention was paid to earlier pioneers (many of them Englishmen) who had moved against the tide for the sake of the Kingdom. After 1894 the circle of members widened to include women and non-Baptists, and people from the surrounding area were invited to attend sessions. Contact also was established with sympathetic leaders in England, France, and Germany, and occasionally their writings were read at Brotherhood conferences. At this time there was no other group of American Christians regularly addressing so comprehensive an agenda of religious and social reform.

Until 1897, when he moved to a teaching position in Rochester, Walter Rauschenbusch made the Brotherhood the center of his ministry beyond Second Church. From the beginning he was a member of the executive committee, and between 1895 and 1897 he was the organization's corresponding secretary. In this role he implemented program decisions made by the executive committee, inviting papers from such American friends of the Brotherhood as Henry George,

Richard Ely, Josiah Strong, W. D. P. Bliss, Washington Gladden, and Jacob Riis, as well as from the English Baptists John Clifford and Richard Heath. Few Americans were in touch with as large and potent a circle of reformers.[5]

During the many meetings of the Brotherhood that Rauschenbusch attended, Leighton Williams or another close friend provided instant notes to allow him to follow the conversation. He experienced a spiritual and intellectual atmosphere that evoked the best in him. In 1909 he testified to the power of the experience with words inscribed in the Plas Llecheiddior guest book: "Only where mind touches mind, does the mind do its best work. Where love and confidence draw back the bars and bolt of caution and distrust, thought passes easily from heart to heart, and finds easy lodgment. So we grow. Even a day or two of real fellowship may mean an epoch in our lives." And he added the wish that Marlborough "would do for others in the future what it did for me in the past." It was a sacred spot for him, and some Brothers later referred to it as "Rauschenbusch's Assisi."

His chief contribution to the Brotherhood in the 1890s was a thoughtful exploration of the significance of the Kingdom for the church. Later his interest shifted more toward the bearing of the Kingdom upon the world, but initially he believed it critical that he and his colleagues understand and articulate the message they wanted to reestablish in the mind of the church. "I am still at it trying to get clearness for myself and others on the Kingdom," he wrote to a seminary classmate in 1894. He added that the idea of the Kingdom had not "come in for any real investigation till the latter half of this century. And an amount of collective work is necessary for a generation to get hold of and elaborate such an idea." But there was no doubt in his mind that patient toil would be rewarded: "The fullness of time has come for this aspect of Christianity."[6]

Substantial clarification was necessary because for centuries the church had misunderstood Jesus' teaching about the Kingdom, and as a result, contemporary Christians' perception of their message and mission was gravely skewed. Rauschenbusch summarized the magnitude of the problem in the first of several pamphlets he wrote for the Brotherhood. It was as though he were nailing theses to the door of Christendom:

> Because the Kingdom of God has been dropped as the primary and comprehensive aim of Christianity, and personal salvation has been substituted for it, therefore men seek to save their own souls and are selfishly indifferent to the evangelization of the world.

Because the individualistic conception of personal salvation has pushed out of sight the collective idea of a Kingdom of God on earth, Christian men seek for the salvation of individuals and are comparatively indifferent to the spread of the spirit of Christ in the political, industrial, social, scientific and artistic life of humanity, and have left these as the undisturbed possession of the spirit of the world.

Because the Kingdom of God has been understood as a state to be inherited in a future life rather than as something to be realized here and now, therefore Christians have been contented with a low plane of life here and have postponed holiness to the future.

Because the Kingdom of God has been confined within the church, therefore the church has been regarded as an end instead of a means, and men have thought they were building up the Kingdom when they were only cementing a strong church organization.

To begin to understand the Kingdom properly, he continued, is to recognize that it reaches both to individuals and the wider society, to this life and the afterlife, to the present and the future, to the church and all other forces for righteousness. The Kingdom "embraces all pure aspirations god-ward, and all true hopes for the perfection of life"; it is "a perfect humanity on earth, living according to the will of God." No one knows when or how it will arrive in its fullness, but key parables of Jesus suggest that its growth toward consummation will be gradual. What can be known is that men and women must prepare for it now by seeking to make God's will done here as it is in heaven.[7]

Rauschenbusch contended that when the church places Jesus' teaching about the Kingdom at the center of its faith, it will constitute a historic change comparable to the Reformation of the sixteenth century. Then it was Paul's teaching about justification that was recovered; now it is Jesus' teaching about the Kingdom that must be recovered. Only a shift of such magnitude will bring the church into the role God intends for it. This modern-day reformation, he insisted, must reach eventually to every realm of the church's life:

We desire to see the Kingdom of God once more the great object of Christian preaching; the inspiration of Christian hymnology; the foundation of systematic theology; the enduring motive of evangelistic and missionary work; the religious inspiration of social work and the social outcome of religious inspiration; the object to which a Christian man surrenders his life, and in that surrender saves it to eternal life; the common object in which all religious bodies find their unity; the great synthesis in which the regeneration of the spirit, the enlightenment of the intellect, the development of the body, the reform of political life, the sanctification of industrial life, and all that concerns the redemption of humanity shall be embraced.[8]

It was a compelling vision that Rauschenbusch articulated for the Brotherhood, and he and his colleagues were thrilled by the conviction that God had placed them in the vanguard of a mighty new movement.

But calling for so complete a reform of the church was bound to provoke opposition from Christians who were convinced that the older views were from God and thus could not be surrendered. Rauschenbusch had met resistance to his ideas earlier, but formation of the Brotherhood and publication of its views brought more intense attack than before. The first public opposition surfaced in November 1893 in the pages of the *National Baptist,* a denominational paper published in Philadelphia. Dr. James Willmarth, a prominent pastor there, argued that the attempt of Batten and his cohorts to push the church into social reconstruction was without scriptural warrant, for neither Paul nor Jesus had concerned himself with such temporal activity. Moreover, Willmarth contended that Scripture teaches the coming of the Kingdom only in the future, after a series of apocalyptic events and the return of Christ. He concluded that the Brotherhood's erring position "tends to heresy," destroys the "spirituality of the church," is "the essence of Romanism," and plays into the hands of socialism, which "is of the Devil, . . . no matter if it is called Christian Socialism."

A sensitive nerve had been struck, and in several subsequent issues of the *National Baptist* Rauschenbusch and Willmarth exchanged letters. In their debate, as well as in other debates that were to occur, Rauschenbusch attempted to engage in controversy irenically, for he regarded his opponents as Christian brothers to be respected for their desire to serve Christ. Normally he sought first to identify the theological ground they shared, then to identify what he regarded as the fuller dimensions of Christian truth not yet acknowledged on the other side.[9]

His quarrel with Willmarth and other early critics focused mainly upon the question of the positions Christians should take on the millennium and on socialism. Willmarth voiced the growing "premillennialist" (or "millenarian") conviction of many Protestants that Christ's future reign will be preceded by a succession of catastrophic events about which Christians can do nothing. Rauschenbusch acknowledged that the people who hold this view properly remind all Christians to look forward expectantly to a time when God's intentions for humanity will triumph over all that resists them. But he added that their vivid pictures of apocalyptic events and protagonists—rapture, the Antichrist, the conversion of Israel, Satan, final judgment, the new Jerusalem—err gravely. The premillennialists rely upon "a narrow and unhistorical system of interpreting Scripture," selecting certain passages from the Bible and treating them as the key to understanding Christ and Christianity.

In taking this stand, Willmarth and the others ignore Christ's teaching that the Kingdom already has begun to be present and that it grows gradually toward fulfillment in an indeterminate future. "There will be no absolute cessation of evil," Rauschenbusch continued.

> The wheat and the tares will grow side by side till the end; but there will be an increasing and victorious power of truth and good, overcoming evil and steadily answering the prayer, "Thy Kingdom come! Thy will be done on earth!" This progress will be due, not to the inherent powers of humanity, but to the spiritual and redemptive forces implanted in humanity by Christ.
>
> Finally the end will come. Christ will judge the quick and the dead. There will be a new heaven and a new earth. God will dwell among his people, and we, seeing him as he is, shall be like him.

Rather than working now to spread "truth and good," the premillennialists surrender the world to the devil and wait soberly for Christ's return. This, concluded Rauschenbusch, is "a practical abdication from the task of conquering the world in all its relations for Christ."[10]

The second major issue of controversy with Willmarth and other critics was the stance of Christians toward socialism. Willmarth charged that because it diverts attention from humanity's spiritual needs it stands condemned as a child of the devil. Rauschenbusch's response to Willmarth on this score was subdued, partly because it remained a nettlesome issue for the Brothers. Many considered themselves Christian Socialists, but the term was not used in public statements about the Brotherhood, probably because they did not agree about socialism and feared that use of the term "Christian Socialist" to describe their organization might lead outsiders to conclude that the Brotherhood was a socialist organization.

In August 1895 members of the Brotherhood discussed a paper by Rauschenbusch that they agreed he should publish as a statement of their views. It took a "yes and no" position toward socialism. Rauschenbusch urged Christians to welcome the movement for social reform sweeping across the West because it follows Christ's lead in affirming the inherent worth of the lowly and in seeking humane patterns of community. It is, he contended, "a river flowing from the throne of God sent by the Ruler of history for the purification of the nations." He added, however, that in the socialist portion of this movement there is a regrettable alloy mixed with the good. Socialists do not properly respect the liberty of the individual, the stability of the family, and the integrity of nations, nor do they recognize the danger of using force to achieve their goals. Moreover, most socialists in continental Europe are so wed to a materialistic philosophy that they pursue economic reconstruction without proper attention to changes that must be made in individuals and in the larger social fabric to ensure just and humane conditions for all.

Rauschenbusch argued that, despite these defects, Christians dare not reject socialism. Some must stay close enough to it both to learn from its passion for social justice and to help correct its errors. "For working purposes I am myself a Socialist," he admitted, though neither at this time nor later did he affiliate with a socialist political organization. Increasingly he would be asked to clarify his position on socialism and to explain why he could affirm the movement but not join the party.[11]

If Rauschenbusch and the Brotherhood would not endorse socialism as the great bearer of God's Kingdom in American life, friends wondered, what were they prepared to do to assist in the coming of the Kingdom? Some members, including Rauschenbusch, urged that the Brotherhood take collective action on several important social fronts, but the majority preferred that the organization limit itself to supporting the individual initiatives of members. Most of them gave leadership to an array of reform organizations emerging among the middle class in the 1890s. This was appropriate, Rauschenbusch explained, because most Brothers are "members of the classes that have money, culture, and power"; they enjoy "inside influence with those classes"; and they use their influence to encourage peers' acceptance of the cogency of reform proposals rising from radical groups and to initiate gradual steps toward justice for workers.

Rauschenbusch's own early contributions to social reform occurred chiefly in proposals to city leaders that they undertake innovations like the ones he had observed in Birmingham. On several occasions he spoke on municipal reform at forums in New York City, along with such leaders as Theodore Roosevelt, Samuel Gompers, Carl Schurz, and Felix Adler. By November 1894 he had gained enough stature in the field to be invited to Detroit with Batten to address prominent citizens who were meeting to establish a civic federation for their city.[12]

Only once in the early years of the Brotherhood did the group take direct action on a social issue, and Rauschenbusch played a key role in this venture. In 1896 he persuaded the Brotherhood to urge the New York Park Board to install sandpiles in city parks for small children, and he was assigned the responsibility of designing and implementing an advocacy campaign. He wrote a statement that was circulated widely in the name of the Brotherhood, urging New York to follow the lead of Berlin and other European cities that had provided sandpiles in which youngsters could play and enjoy the outdoors. He explained that they were needed especially for children living in the city's tenement districts, where there were no play areas save the streets and sidewalks. This innovation, Rauschenbusch argued, could be made easily and inexpensively, and it would promote the health and happiness of thousands of children, "the worthiest and most important class of our citizens."

Requests for support were sent to a dozen newspapers and many prominent New Yorkers, and later in the year the Park Board agreed to experiment by placing a one-hundred-square-foot sandpile in East River Park on East 86th Street. Park Board members had received hundreds of letters, and the *New York Herald* acknowledged that the board's decision was the result of "agitation by the Brotherhood of the Kingdom." The first steps had been taken toward a policy that was eventually widely implemented in New York and beyond. No record remains of Rauschenbusch's response to the board's action, but he doubtless took pleasure in it, for Jesus had accorded children— and the qualities they embody—a privileged place in the Kingdom. Here was a small way of nurturing what was best in human experience.[13]

Rauschenbusch's interest in playground opportunities for children had been stimulated by his observations in Europe several years earlier, but by the time of New York's first sandpile he knew the need for it more intimately, for he had been married three years and was the father of two children.

Rauschenbusch first met Pauline Ernestine Rother in September 1889, when he attended a German Baptist convention in Milwaukee. She taught German in a local school and participated actively in the First German Baptist Church. Pauline had been born into a rural family in Prussian Silesia in 1864, and after the wartime death of her father she had emigrated to Wisconsin with her mother and younger brother. She was a bright, brown-haired, blue-eyed woman, whose beauty was often accented by a flower worn in her hair. When Pauline first met Walter, she was engaged to another man; in later years she told her children the worst nightmare she ever had was that she had married him rather than Walter.

Walter saw Pauline again in 1890, and for the next two years they maintained contact through correspondence. During Rauschenbusch's third visit to Milwaukee in September 1892, there came the realization that friendship had blossomed into love, and they decided to marry. To his seminary classmates Rauschenbusch wrote that "the proud and independent bachelorhood of the bachelorest one of us all" was soon to end. To Pauline he confided that he felt he had successfully resisted "the usual effects of loneliness and deafness . . . but it has been a steady lifting of a weight and in time I would begin to bend under it." Pauline, he knew, could make him strong: "With your help we can between us do a good and enduring life's work." They were married in Pauline's church on 12 April 1893, and following a honeymoon in Racine the newlyweds returned to New York and made their first home in the top-floor apartment of the church on West 43rd Street.[14]

It proved to be a happy match for both. Pauline adored Walter: "What a heaven this earth would be," she exclaimed, "if everyone had a husband like mine." She believed she had a special calling from God to be a "help-meet" to him in his tasks as pastor, and she quickly endeared herself to the congregation. "Pauline helps in all directions," Rauschenbusch wrote Aunt Lina, "and enjoys the hearty affection of the people." She often called on members with him, favored them with baked delicacies, and conveyed messages between congregation and pastor when he was away. In numerous settings she acted as his "hearing ear" by penning shorthand summaries of statements he could not hear but, thanks to her speedy note taking, he could respond to.

Pauline believed unreservedly in Walter's calling as a reformer. When he met opposition, she comforted him, and when he won victories, she rejoiced with him and urged him to continue. "I delight in the influence for good that you carry wherever you go," she wrote. "God bless you and widen that influence more and more."

Both found joy in their sexual union and believed that it was touched by divinity. The "reproductive faculty," Rauschenbusch told his congregation, "comes closer to the divine power of creation" than anything else in human ken. Wrote Pauline to Walter:

> I am so thankful that to both of us it is such a sacred, holy thing to become one flesh. It is something incomparably sweet to me. It fills me with a keen realization of God's infinite wisdom and love as scarcely anything else does and my heart is often full of the deepest gratitude

that I am permitted to drink from this cup. While you are lying at my breast deep in the rapture with which it fills you, my heart is sometimes ready to burst with thankfulness.[15]

Walter knew that in Pauline he had found a jewel, and he marveled at the love she lavished upon him: "I always feel that your rich and constant love is the greatest thing any being can give to another, and that I have nothing to weigh as heavily." Never did he have so loyal a friend, so intimate a confidant, and so resourceful a helper.

He looked to her increasingly as the one with whom he could share the journey of his soul. Before marriage he had discovered that she knew better than he the "restful side of religious life." By contrast, religion for him was "conflict, work," and he looked to Pauline to help him discover biblical religion's green pastures and still waters. As husband and wife they at first prayed together daily, but after two years Rauschenbusch confessed to concern for the devotional life of each of them, as well as his continued need for her spiritual ministrations. "I need more meditation and prayer," he confided to Pauline.

I do not feel that I have receded exactly, but I have not advanced in real fellowship with Christ and I feel a gap.

I have often wondered how it is with you, dear one, whether the life within was warmer and devouter in Milwaukee than in New York. Perhaps the hurried life here has been a a danger to you that I have not helped you to overcome. Perhaps too the religious thoughts as I hold them have weakened your faith and you have not found new props to replace the old.

I am glad we are both Christians, dear wife, and it is always sweet and helpful to me when you speak of the Savior to me. You mustn't think that I don't need it because I express perhaps the same thoughts to others. . . .

It's almost only when you and Leighton talk to me that I can peel my humanity out of its official relations. You know, I told you long ago that you must be my pastor.

The chief tension between the pair was occasioned by a chronic shortage of money. Walter admitted, "Our finances are a constant drag on my peace of mind." His salary had doubled since coming to New York, but not his sense of security: "I have never earned so much nor been so short." He feared they had surrounded themselves with too much comfort, and he urged Pauline to help them economize. That way she could rescue him from the insidious temptation of responding to writing and speaking invitations on the basis of the income they produced rather than their usefulness to the Kingdom.[16]

The coming of two children added to the couple's anxieties about finances, but it also brought new joys. "The soul of a child," Rauschenbusch told the people of Second Church, "is the most valuable and solemn trust" God gives a man and a woman. Together they have the opportunity to make their home "a small Kingdom of God in miniature," but it is the mother more than the father who plays the central role. "She is engaged in a service to God and humanity, in a work second to none on earth, a work royal in its dignity, sacrificial in its ministry and eternal in its effects."[17]

The Rauschenbusches' first child, Winifred, was born in March 1894. She was unusually large at birth, and the delivery caused difficulty for Pauline. They named their daughter after Rauschenbusch's brother who had died many years earlier in Canada. In a memory book started for Winifred (but not repeated for other children), the proud parents carefully recorded milestones in her development. The first word spoken after "Mama" and "Papa," noted Walter, was "book," and he added wryly, "Blood will tell."

Their second child, a boy, was born in May 1896. He was named Hilmar Ernst after two Rauschenbusch ancestors, who, Walter explained, had been "pious ministers and stout hearts." The necessity of caring for two children would have greatly limited Pauline's role as her husband's helpmeet had the young couple not been able to rely upon Caroline Schaefer. "Tante Schaefer" was a widowed member of Second Church who doted upon Rauschenbusch and in 1894 volunteered her services to the family as nurse, maid, and cook. For the rest of Rauschenbusch's life she lived with the family and was treated affectionately as one of its members.

The arrival of children made Pauline uneasy about their life in New York. She worried about the family's cramped quarters and the limited opportunities for outdoor play. As early as 1894 she told Walter she wished they could live in Rochester; her "favorite daydream," she said, was that they eventually would live in the old Rauschenbusch home on Arnold Park.[18]

Pauline's dissatisfaction was heightened by her friendship with Laura and John D. Rockefeller. Through Walter she met Charles and Bessie Rockefeller Strong, and by 1895 she had visited Bessie's parents in their luxurious home on West 54th Street. Pauline and Laura Rockefeller quickly found common ground in their shared Baptist piety, and over the next two decades the women exchanged scores of letters and occasionally visited in each other's homes. Pauline often showered the Rockefellers with gifts of flowers or cookies, and the

Rockefellers, moved by the Rauschenbusches' near-poverty and grit, sent them checks from time to time. The first, in 1897, was a gift of fifty dollars from Laura to Pauline, which the older woman asked the younger to use any way she wanted.

Many years later, when Winifred told her own children about their grandmother's charm, she said John D. Rockefeller was one of the men who was "very much attracted" to Pauline. There is no trace of how Walter Rauschenbusch felt about the Rockefellers at this time or about the tie between the two families. In his Sunday school lessons he had observed that Jesus enjoyed contact with people of all classes, and as always Rauschenbusch sought to do as his Master had done. He probably viewed the Rauschenbusch-Rockefeller relationship as an opportunity for him to gain influence with the man who wielded extraordinary power in American life. Perhaps it was also a reminder of his family's long-standing kinship with the upper strata of society. Laura Rockefeller's hope expressed to Pauline in 1900 that Walter, like her own husband, might spend two or three afternoons a week golfing, doubtless brought a smile to the Rauschenbusches. How far their world was from that of the Rockefellers! But as later years were to demonstrate, there was something about wealth and comfort that attracted Pauline and Walter Rauschenbusch.[19]

More and more Rauschenbusch viewed his ministry at Second German Baptist Church as an integral part of his work for the Kingdom. Every congregation, he told his people, is called to be a "small Kingdom of God in miniature" that shows the surrounding community how God intends the human family to live. Worship on Sunday morning and evening, week after week, continued to be the focal point of his leadership. Except when he had to be away from New York, he rarely missed the opportunity to preach. His foremost desire always, he told the congregation near the end of his New York ministry, was to "preach Christ . . . simply, clearly and boldly." As had been true before the ten months abroad, the dominant note of his sermons after 1891 was the personal religious journey. But now the theme of the Kingdom was pervasive. As individuals meet Christ, they are freed from sin and made channels of God's action to make the ways of the Kingdom prevail in the family, the church, the city, and the nation. Never, however, must the gaze of Christians be so fixed upon their larger tasks that they neglect the task closer to hand. Believers cannot effectively fight evil in the world, Rauschenbusch warned, "if you have not mastered it in your own heart." After the end of their journey, servants of the Kingdom go to "the greatest prize of individual existence," a joyous life beyond the grave.[20]

More than before, the congregation heard Rauschenbusch talk about needed changes in the world around them. He admonished them especially to accept their responsibility as Christian citizens, working through the ballot box to bring public life under the "control of Christian ideas and Christian men." Prior to elections each autumn, he discussed key issues to be decided at the polls. He explained that he would not take partisan positions for political parties because that would be a misuse of the pulpit; besides, he found none of the major parties consistently arresting enough to win his loyalty. But on some issues that immediately impinged upon his congregation, such as the question of a rapid transit system for New York, he did not hesitate to suggest how his parishioners should vote. His feeling about the importance of immigrants' participation in the political process was so great that several years later he published a small book in German about the American system of government.[21]

Under their pastor's prodding, members of the congregation came to realize that they must minister more actively to one another and to the community, and their new church building became the center of an expanding variety of activities throughout the week. Rauschenbusch especially wanted to provide opportunities for youth to develop wholesome patterns of play and work. None responded more spiritedly than Company L, Third Regiment, of the Baptist Boy's Brigade. Its young members practiced their marches and music weekly, competed against units from other churches, and went with Rauschenbusch on excursions to the countryside and harbor. They pledged to abstain from liquor, tobacco, and profanity and to attend Sunday school faithfully. Older youth enjoyed the church's mock legislative sessions, where such issues as tariffs and prohibition were debated and voted upon. Working mothers appreciated the church's establishment of a day nursery where they could leave their small children.

Rauschenbusch admired the proliferation of services to people of the neighborhood that had occurred at Leighton Williams's church, and in 1894 he persuaded his congregation to collaborate with Amity Baptist in sponsoring a "deaconess association" for women trained to care for the sick and needy. Members of Second Church agreed to the joint effort, but some were lukewarm and a few were actively opposed. Rauschenbusch believed that "institutional churches" such as Amity ran the danger of moving so far toward providing social services that they compromised their spiritual mission, but to his people he confessed regret that they did not undertake more in this realm.

The congregation continued to grow, and by the time of Rauschenbusch's departure in 1897, its membership was nearly double what it had been when he arrived in 1886. He had baptized 207 people, and he rejoiced that a new spirit pervaded the church and that it had gained both the goodwill of the neighborhood and the respect of other churches. But he admitted that at times his duties as pastor had brought him pain, especially when he guided the process of removing members who violated their vows by such offenses as drunkenness, dishonesty, and erratic attendance.[22]

The congregation's respect and affection for Rauschenbusch was evident when in June 1896 they celebrated the tenth anniversary of his coming to the church. Leighton Williams and other ministerial colleagues praised Rauschenbusch, but no one moved him as much as the butcher Julius Dietz, who spoke on behalf of the church. The ragged manuscript of Dietz's remarks remained one of Rauschenbusch's prized mementos from the New York years. Said Dietz of Brother Rauschenbusch:

> We have found in him more that is Christ-like than in any human being we have ever met. And because of this we have . . . been brought closer to Christ than any of us were previous to his coming into our midst.

> We have in him a perfectly fearless preacher, one caring nothing about criticism of any kind, but who always stands up, and in a manly, fearless way teaches and adheres strictly to Christ's teaching. . . .

> My heart says, Praise God from whom all blessings flow, who has placed our brother among us.

Second Church had held Rauschenbusch far longer than it had any other pastor, and by the time of the tenth anniversary celebration, members suspected that his days with them were numbered. He was one of the most prominent younger pastors in the German Baptist Union and a key member of the committee that oversaw the German Department of Rochester Seminary. His talent and energy had been further demonstrated in 1895 when he published a small study book for German Baptist youth about the life of Christ.[23]

The invitation that took Rauschenbusch away from Second Church came from the seminary in Rochester. He had twice before rejected offers from President Strong, and in 1892 he had turned down a feeler about graduate study and a teaching position in sociology at the University of Chicago. But in May 1897, when Professor H. M. Schaeffer of the German Department died and Rauschenbusch was asked to consider the position, he was strongly attracted. Deafness had continued to be a hindrance to his pastoring, and he believed it would affect teaching less. He knew Pauline would be happier in Rochester than she had been in New York. His assessment of the seminary had grown more positive in the last three years, especially because of President Strong's apparent shift in a liberal direction. More than ever Rauschenbusch believed that the mission of German Baptists was in the "forefront of radical Christianity," doing "outpost duty" for the entire Christian movement. By training the denomination's future ministers, he could do more to shape its destiny than he could as pastor of a single church. And as Schaeffer's successor as professor of New Testament, he would work in the discipline that had long been one of his favorites.[24]

After Rauschenbusch's nomination to the position, President Strong urged him to allow his name to go to the school's trustees, but he also warned that there were two problems. Because the board of trustees had just concluded its annual meeting, the nomination could be acted upon at present only by the executive committee; hence he must serve provisionally for a year until the following spring, when the entire board could consider him for a permanent appointment. More serious, though, was President Strong's admission that there was a question about Rauschenbusch's acceptability to certain unnamed wealthy trustees: "We have one or two brethren on our Executive Committee who have a great horror of socialism, and who suggested that we go slowly." Strong asked that in order to allay their apprehensions Rauschenbusch write him "a note, expressing in two or three sentences your present view of the Socialistic movement." He added that he understood Rauschenbusch's position to be advocacy of "no revolutionary action, but only legal changes as would result from mutual sympathy of rich and poor." This presumably would not ruffle feathers.

Rauschenbusch responded by sending Strong an article published the preceding year in which he weighed the strengths and shortcomings of socialism. The hesitant trustees were satisfied, and on 14 June 1897, Strong informed him that he had been elected unanimously by the executive committee. Several days later Strong added that he hoped "we shall yet get money in large amounts" from the men who had wavered, and he showed Rauschenbusch their cautionary letters.[25]

The appointment was secured, but Rauschenbusch had been stung. During the past year he had watched with shock as his friend Nathaniel Schmidt was fired from a teaching position at Colgate Theological Seminary because of his views on biblical authority, and he knew that similar proceedings were under way, or threatened, at other seminaries. No such incident had occurred at Rochester, but Rauschenbusch saw he must be on his guard because his views were suspect in high places. At the time he kept to himself whatever distress he felt. Sixteen years later, however, an autobiographical comment revealed that he viewed reservations about his appointment in 1897 as part of a larger struggle and that the episode still smarted.

> This is one of the saddest things that I can say, but I cannot get it out of my mind. The Church held down the social interest in me. It contradicted it; it opposed it, it held it down as far as it could; and when it was a question about giving me position or preferment, the fact that I was interested in the workingman was actually against—not for me. They did not say: "Now here is a young man who loves the workingman, and has some thoughts about him—let us put him into a theological professorship." No! "The fact is, this young man thinks like the workingman. . . . therefore, he ought not to be a theological professor." That is the way they looked at me.

But at least for the moment doubters had been satisfied, and Rauschenbusch returned to the city of his birth for whatever battles lay ahead.[26]

❋❋❋ CHAPTER 7 ❋❋❋

GERMAN BAPTIST

When Professor Walter Rauschenbusch arrived in Rochester in July 1897, all seemed remarkably well for the school and for Christendom. Two months earlier, Rochester Seminary had graduated the largest class ever, and by September a record number of new students was enrolled for the fall semester. President Strong believed the recent raising of admission standards in the English Department had brought Rochester the best class of entering students in any of the Baptist seminaries. He perennially worried about the need for additional operating funds, but he could take comfort in the school's $600,000 endowment—the largest among the Baptist seminaries—and in his knowledge that John D. Rockefeller still took a keen interest in the school.

Leaders of Rochester Theological Seminary were also happy about the larger picture. Their institution was contributing significantly to the Baptist tide sweeping the nation. In the last fifty years, while the population increased threefold, Baptist ranks grew nearly five times— there were now 4 million Baptists of all stripes in the United States. But it was not numbers alone that mattered. The witness of Baptists to such principles as freedom of conscience and the supremacy of Scripture had made so deep a mark upon American Christianity that some plausibly claimed the nineteenth century as "pre-eminently a Baptist century." Rochester men also were doing their part in American Christianity's global expansion. Each year an appreciable number volunteered for foreign missions, and the unprecedented openness of the entire world to Western ways made the time seem more ripe than ever for these messengers of the gospel.[1]

103

Leaders of the seminary's German Department shared the optimism of colleagues in the English Department. The enterprise begun by August Rauschenbusch constituted one of the premier attempts by Protestants in America to reach German immigrants, and it now enjoyed a measure of stability never known before. The five-story building erected in 1890 to house German students was fully paid for; the enrollment of thirty-three students in the German Department's theological program was the largest ever; and the campaign to raise a $100,000 endowment was more than half subscribed. Across the United States and Canada, German Baptists looked with confidence to Rochester for a continuing supply of ministerial leaders.

The German Baptists had grown rapidly during the past half-century, and by 1897 there were 22,000 members and 240 congregations. A network of committees, publications, and institutions had evolved to link the congregations and to facilitate their missionary outreach. The use of German in worship set them apart from other Baptists, and a distinctive spiritual ethos was increasingly evident. It was not yet customary to speak of the German Baptists as a denomination, but that time would soon come.[2]

During the 1890s most German Baptist leaders expected their growth to continue into the twentieth century. Even when immigration from Germany markedly declined at the end of the decade, they believed there was still an evangelistic opportunity among the unchurched German-speaking population already present. They were especially hopeful about German-speaking immigrants from Russia who had been under Mennonite and Baptist influence there and had recently settled in the western regions of Canada and the United States.

German Baptist leaders counted as a favorable sign, too, English-speaking Americans' greater acceptance of German immigrants. The fear present only a decade earlier that all immigrants were corrupting American institutions had given way to an appreciation of the contributions of northern Europeans to American life and a nervousness about the large number of immigrants arriving from southern and eastern Europe. The view of one Baptist official was typical; he lauded German immigrants as "industrious, intelligent, cleanly, economical, social and law-abiding," then went on to say that "a German converted by God's grace makes the best kind of Christian." Samuel Zane Batten voiced the corresponding conviction of many with his lament that arrivals of the "allied races from Protestant and enlightened Europe" had fallen, while those of the "alien races from Catholic and illiterate Europe" had risen.[3]

Since the early years of his New York pastorate, German Baptists had learned to look to Rauschenbusch for articulate defense of their interests within the American Baptist community. In 1888, against the threat of restrictions upon all immigration, he had asserted the traditional theme of American inclusiveness to a Baptist Congress audience: "I believe in throwing open this country to all who will come, for I believe God made it for all." A few years later, however, in two widely distributed appeals for funds for the German Department, his call for an infusion of German blood reflected the growing race-consciousness of Americans. The first statement played shamelessly upon the fears of contemporaries: "Is the American stock so fertile that it will people this continent alone? . . . Are the whites of this continent so sure of their possession against the blacks of the South and the seething yellow flocks beyond the Pacific that they need no reenforcement of men of their own blood while yet it is time?" The other made the point only a little less blatantly: "The Germans . . . are of the same stock as the English, readily assimilated, and a splendid source of strength for America, physically, intellectually, and morally." Here was a moral blind spot that Rauschenbusch appears not to have recognized. His rhetoric was good—America is intended for all. But under the pressure of having to make an effective case for acceptance of the German immigrants, he concluded that it is intended for some more than for others.[4]

By the late 1890s two major problems faced German Baptists, and they looked to Walter Rauschenbusch to help them find their way through both. The first problem arose from the lingering conviction of some American Baptists that the best means for evangelizing and assimilating German immigrants was to bring them as quickly as possible into English-speaking congregations. In this view, the goals of evangelization and Americanization were poorly served by maintaining a host of German-language congregations and institutions, for they delayed the absorption of immigrants into the Baptist mainstream. The recent decline of immigration from Germany seemed to make all the more imperative an orderly phasing out of the parallel (and expensive) Baptist enterprise built upon the German language.

German Baptist leaders disagreed with the Americanizers and sought to persuade them that a strategy of evangelization and cultivation based upon the English language alone risked losing the immigrants altogether. Far better to proceed slowly by bringing the newcomers into a religious community where the gospel is preached and faith is nourished in the language they know best. This approach requires not only preserving German-speaking Baptist congregations and institutions, but also making them strong and attractive. Advocates for the German Baptist cause went on to admit that eventually, when the German immigration has subsided and the German language is no longer an appropriate medium of spiritual life in the United States, there will be no need for a distinct German Baptist fellowship; then individuals and congregations will gladly melt into the American Baptist community. Explained Rauschenbusch: "We have loyally accepted the task of building a structure which is destined to last forever in its effects, but to perish in its outward form, and to carry the names and the memory of the toilers to oblivion with it." But the theory of German Baptist provisionality proved far easier to state than to implement.[5]

The second problem facing German Baptist leaders was maintaining the loyalty of younger members. Almost universally, in their eager embrace of American life, immigrants' children saw no room for the Old World ways of their parents. The problem struck close to home for Rauschenbusch, for by 1900 it became evident that fewer young German Baptists were enrolling in the German Department. Moreover, some observers estimated that already ten thousand Baptists had left German-speaking churches to join English-speaking churches. This shift pleased the Americanizers, but for Rauschenbusch and his cohorts it posed a grave challenge. They believed there still were many Germans in America who needed conversion and nurture, and presumably many others would come in the future when immigration from Germany resumed. This was not the time to dissolve the German Baptist community. The key step toward preserving it was holding the second generation.

These two problems set the stage for Rauschenbusch's five-year career as a professor in the German Department. He had no doubt that most German Baptist congregations embraced distinctive qualities of spiritual devotion and missionary ardor that raised them above English-using counterparts and justified his all-out effort to ensure their preservation. Eventually, though, he had to decide whether concentrating his energies upon this task allowed him also properly to honor his commitment to seek reform of the church and the nation.[6]

The precipitous decline of German immigration forced numerous German-language organizations in the United States into the same struggle for survival. Success was elusive, and one by one institutions as different and alike as German-language congregations and German-language newspapers disappeared. A key strategy of the survivors was to foster such pride in Germany and its culture that young German-Americans gladly blended affection for the Old Country with loyalty to the new homeland. German Baptists believed Rauschenbusch was ideally equipped for leading them into this uncharted territory. He was steeped in the ways of Germany and America alike, and as the son of the great August Rauschenbusch he was viewed by many as the model second-generation German Baptist.

Young Rauschenbusch knew his responsibility and rose to it willingly during his years on the German Department faculty. One tack was to testify openly to his love for Germany and its ways. In a major address in Rochester, he praised German religion's "sense of mystery in the face of the inscrutable universe" and its "pondering of the riddle of the human soul and its destiny." Germans, he contended, traditionally have taught qualities of honesty, trustworthiness, dutifulness, and tenderheartedness that put to shame the coarse materialism of American life. And this new nation, he added, has been immeasurably strengthened by immigrants' contributions of the best fruit of German art, science, social idealism, and theology.

He also borrowed theories then emerging on both sides of the Atlantic to argue that Germans, the English, and Americans belong to a single Teutonic racial stock. In their hands today, he averred, are much of the world's wealth and power, as well as the responsibility of shaping its future. The unfortunate tension among the three nations must give way to a new sense of shared destiny. "Let the Teutons of the old home, the Teutons of the island and the Teutons of the farther continent look each other in the face and stand shoulder to shoulder in whatever mission for the world God has in store for us."[7]

The plea for a three-way Teutonic alliance fell on deaf ears, for by the late 1890s the imperial ambitions of the three nations had brought them into conflict. Moreover, as the interests of the United States and England increasingly converged, they found themselves standing together against Germany. Rauschenbusch regretted the rift and attempted to prevent its widening. When it became apparent in 1898 that Germans were angered by what appeared to them to be unwarranted American interference in Spanish colonial affairs, he wrote a letter published in the *Frankfurter Zeitung* maintaining that American action in Cuba was triggered principally by moral revulsion at Spain's abominable treatment of the Cuban people, not as a ploy for the sake of commercial or political expansion.

When Rauschenbusch realized Americans needed help in understanding Germany's seemingly unconscionable hunger for colonial expansion, he sought to persuade his countrymen that the new German imperialism was essentially no different from the old English imperialism: "Is it strange or ridiculous that the Continental Teutons, now that they have at last found their organic unity, should seek to do what the insular Teutons have been doing for ages?" Americans should not be surprised, he continued, if resurgent Germany and other ambitious continental powers seek to expand their colonial reach in territories long dominated by England.[8]

Walter Rauschenbusch's fresh interest in international politics was shared by growing numbers of Americans, for his return to the German Department coincided with the aggressive entry of the United States into global affairs, which had been building quietly for decades and was ignited dramatically by the Spanish-American War. Rauschenbusch took no public stand about whether the United States should go to war with Spain, but once the war was over he spoke out vigorously on its significance for the United States. In November 1898 the bright new professor in the German Department preached at the annual Thanksgiving gathering of Rochester Baptists. It was the most jingoistic of all his public addresses, but his audience probably was struck by the reflective, cautionary tone not often present at this time of intense nationalistic fervor.

Rochester Baptists heard their native son claim that God's hand had been present in the war, working through events to bring the United States victory and to teach Americans important lessons. Among them was the recognition by a people only three decades from bitter fratricidal strife that they now shared a single national destiny and could harness immense resources for national ends. More important, the defeat of Catholic Spain and the victory of Protestant America demonstrated the "decay" of a nation whose culture sprang from a religion of authority and submission, and it revealed the vitality of a nation whose life had been shaped by a pure religion of "freedom, justice and love." Americans must acknowledge that God had laid upon their nation an imperial destiny they did not seek but must accept in obedience to the divine will.

Rauschenbusch went on to warn that God's new summons to the nation provides no warrant for assuming divine approval of all that presently constitutes America. It will not do, he insisted, to foist upon the occupants of America's overseas domain the problems associated with its shabby political and business ethics. "We are bound to mend our own faults, if we propose to be missionaries of good government and exemplars of humanity in foreign parts." Nor can American Protestants rest content with their accomplishments. They must work to ensure that the religious faith underlying American civilization remains vigorous, in order to be able to address recurring internal threats to liberty and justice. America the chosen must be America the vigilant.[9]

Rauschenbusch told his Thanksgiving Day audience he hated war and hoped the clash with Spain would make nations quicker to pursue roads leading to the peaceful settlement of conflicts. Less than three months later he vigorously advocated travel along the road opened up by Russian Czar Nicholas II's proposal that Western nations confer about means to limit armaments and arbitrate disputes. Rauschenbusch judged that the bellicose national mood and cynicism about the czar's motives might keep the McKinley administration from agreeing to U.S. participation in the talks, and that therefore there must be efforts to generate an outpouring of public support for the czar's proposal. On 31 January 1899, after laying the groundwork through private conversations, Rauschenbusch and fourteen other Rochester clergy issued an appeal to all the city's ministers to address the topic three weeks hence. Parallel efforts were made to raise the issue in schools, labor unions, and the Chamber of Commerce. He also wrote friends in other cities to urge similar initiatives. The Rochester planners agreed that the public launching of their campaign should come on 12 February in the form of a Rauschenbusch sermon.

This was Walter Rauschenbusch's first public pronouncement to gain a wide hearing beyond Rochester. Local papers reprinted the sermon; he preached it again in Pittsburgh; and W. T. Stead, an English journalist active in the peace movement, published it in his periodical *War Against War.*

The aim of the sermon was to arouse Rochesterians to agitate in favor of purposeful U.S. participation in the conference scheduled to open soon at The Hague. After describing the ominous armaments race under way across the Atlantic, and its nearly inevitable outcome if unchecked in a "great European war," Rauschenbusch noted that Americans unfortunately still think the Atlantic Ocean gives them immunity to European wars. Some even enjoy the prospect of profits from sales to the belligerent nations and capture of their global trade. But surely, he argued, there is no long-term gain if Europe is wasted by war, nor are there grounds for supposing the United States can any longer remain untouched by events in Europe. Had not Spain's foreign policy sent the United States to war the previous year, and was not Italy's domestic policy bringing multitudes of impoverished immigrants to American cities? Americans must accept the fact that the world has changed irreversibly: "The sooner we learn that this earth is a very small planet and getting smaller every year, and that our welfare is bound up with all the other passengers, the better it is for us. Paul says we are one body and members one of another, and if one member suffers, all the rest suffer with it." This, insisted Rauschenbusch, is not just religious talk. It is "a great sociological law and all modern science and all modern progress thunders its amen to that."

The Hague Conference, he concluded, might not achieve the grand goal of eliminating war, but it will be amply justified if it succeeds in limiting the area, the frequency, or the cruelty of war. The urgent need now is for the peoples of the world to want the conference to succeed, for in the last analysis, participants will be moved to attempt little or much at the conference depending upon what they think their citizens want.

It was as an advocate of international peace that Rochester first responded to Rauschenbusch the reformer. Numerous churches and civic bodies took their cue from him, and Rochester became the first American city to push strongly for U.S. participation in the conference. Rauschenbusch was pleased when President McKinley appointed a delegation and when participants succeeded in establishing an international tribunal for settling disputes. In 1907, after several minor incidents had been referred to it, Rauschenbusch wrote optimistically that the Hague Tribunal would be remembered as "the faint beginning of a new era in international relations." It was a historic step for the nations, but unfortunately they had made no serious effort to address the problem of arms limitations, and within a few years it became painfully evident how little this initiative had accomplished. In 1914 Rauschenbusch again faced the issues of armaments and war, but then with a heavy heart that the nations had ventured so little fifteen years earlier.[10]

Professor Walter Rauschenbusch's students and colleagues in the German Department of Rochester Theological Seminary knew him more as a teacher than as an internationalist. Few of the students had attended college, and many had not completed high school. But the German Baptist constituency held high expectations for them. Through a grueling six-year program they must become skilled in German and English and knowledgeable in the classical and theological disciplines. Nearly half of Rauschenbusch's fifteen hours of weekly class time was devoted to eight courses offered over a two-year cycle in the preparatory section: English literature, American literature, physiology, physics, civil government, political economy, astronomy, and zoology. His duties in the theological section of the German Department were more satisfying but no less demanding. A course on the life of Christ was the one fixture offered annually. Other courses dealt with individual books of the New Testament and such themes as the history of the New Testament canon.

In a report to the school's governing board, Rauschenbusch explained that his approach to teaching Scripture was to help students understand major themes of the German Bible rather than to focus upon small segments of the Greek text. His published reviews of scholarly treatises show that he read and respected new critical literature in the field, but neither heart nor mind was heavily invested in this realm. "I am thankful," he admitted, "that we have competent critical investigators, but also that we are not all compelled to do their work." The reason, he explained, is that one's comprehension of the Bible is not chiefly dependent upon proficiency as a critic. "The deep things of the Spirit in the Bible are revealed to the humble and childlike of heart." Better for him to help people grasp those "deep things" than to become mired in the host of technical issues that increasingly attracted biblical scholars.

During the five years he taught in the German Department, Rauschenbusch published occasional Sunday school lessons and other short hortatory articles on biblical themes. His only book-size contribution to New Testament literature was an English translation of German scholar Gustav Zart's brief, popularly written essay, *The Charm of Jesus*.[11]

Rauschenbusch's concentration upon Jesus reflected the blend of Pietist-Evangelical piety in which he had been raised, but it was also the dominant note of the German Baptist ethos, and his earnest commitment to Jesus was a badge of membership in this community of faith. Attention to Jesus was more than a matter of personal piety, however; it also sprang from his theological conviction that the fullness of God's revelation had occurred in Jesus Christ. Uniquely revealed in Jesus, wrote Rauschenbusch, is the loving will of the One to whom every person must be obedient. Those who encounter God in Christ know their responsibility to lead others to the same experience: "We take our brother by the hand and bring him to meet Jesus, and there he learns to know God. . . . True Christianity puts a man face to face with Christ and bids him see what he can find there." No one who has met Christ can fail to be an evangelist.

The Gospels present the most complete picture of Jesus' personality, words, and deeds, and Christians must use all the tools available to understand this picture. In the last analysis, however, people's encounter with God through Christ is not tied to the Bible, for Jesus Christ lives now and seeks them. He comes mystically to individuals in earnest search of him, opening their eyes to the truth of the biblical record, winning their allegiance, and uniting them with God. Christ "draws us; he masters us; he transforms us. In him we see God; in him we possess God, in him God possesses us."

Rauschenbusch believed that because the different parts of the

Bible (even the different parts of the New Testament) do not present Jesus equally well, not all parts are equally authoritative for Christians. "Jesus Christ," he said, "is the standard of judgment about the Bible, as about all things." Rauschenbusch acknowledged that this approach to the Bible challenged the conviction widespread among Protestants that the Bible is an inspired, infallible book equally authoritative in all its parts. But he believed his view reflected better the position that guided the church through much of the past. Furthermore, it corresponded better to the way believers actually use the Bible. "Each Christian," he argued, "has his own inner Bible, a narrower set of books and passages that speak to his spirit with the unmistakable sweetness and power of the Master, and from which he draws comfort and strength and holiness." The real issue for Christians is determining the content of this inner core.[12]

What is striking about Rauschenbusch's application of this principle during the years as a New Testament teacher is the widening that occurred of his "inner Bible." The picture of Jesus and his teaching presented in the Gospels continued to be central, but a greater appreciation for other biblical voices that either prefigured or echoed Jesus came to be a part of his thinking. He concluded that there was far more in the Mosaic law, in the Psalms and Proverbs, and most notably in the prophetic books than Professor Howard Osgood had dreamed. These Old Testament writings must be taken seriously, Rauschenbusch insisted in 1899, for they "contain a real revelation of the will of God" from which Christians can learn about God's wrath toward those who oppress the weak, as well as about God's intention that religious faith be expressed in deeds of mercy and justice.

He went on to claim that in portions of the New Testament reflecting the mind of the early Jewish-Christian churches, one meets the high ethical traditions of Israel in which Jesus was steeped. They are seen notably in the Letter of James and the Revelation to John. The former, wrote Rauschenbusch, has "the ring of the old prophets in its denunciation of the property distinctions that were creeping into the Church. With him, as with the prophets, the rich are the oppressors, and the poor are the heirs of the Kingdom." But unfortunately, he concluded, Christians in churches that are today under the sway of the rich rarely hear James' denunciation of oppression either read or preached upon. For Luther, the Letter of James had been a mere "epistle of straw," but for Rauschenbusch it brought a ray of searing light.[13]

Students in the German Department immediately took Walter Rauschenbusch into their hearts. One later recalled that he had been strict in his requirement that assignments be done punctually, but also that he had cared deeply about students' growth as persons and ministers. The son of another German student recalled his father's gratitude for Rauschenbusch's continued support after graduation. This marvelous teacher, wrote M. L. Leuschner, counseled his father "how to be a good minister of Jesus Christ, how to meet the problems of that day in the spirit of Christ, and encouraged him in the service of the Lord." More striking is the testimony of former students about Rauschenbusch as a man of prayer. "To have heard him pray," remembered a graduate of the German Department, "was to have felt a benediction. He was like a child at his father's knee, speaking with simplicity, confidence and hope concerning his request to God. How beautiful, how direct, how heartfelt were his prayers." It was a testimony echoed by generation after generation of Rochester students.[14]

Prayer and the commitments from which it springs particularly concerned Rauschenbusch during his years as a professor in the German Department. Here was the rich soil in which he believed the distinct identity of German Baptists was rooted. But these matters needed attention also because of threats rising from two sources. He admitted in 1900 that preoccupation with "social salvation" too often distracts contemporary Christians from proper attention to the cultivation of personal spirituality. Something of this sort, he confessed, had happened in his own life: "While I had been busy clearing the forest on the hill, the bottom-lands where my father raised abundant harvests had been lying fallow." But he believed that even more destructive of prayer and personal religion is the doubt generated by modern science. In the light of new knowledge about physical causality, the vastness of the universe, and the seeming waste and cruelty of nature, many thoughtful people have concluded that traditional views of a beneficent God to whom prayer can be expectantly addressed are no longer tenable.

A closer look, he said, reveals that personal religion need not be extinguished by either social concern or modern science. Any perceptive champion of social reform knows that the moral convictions essential to the quest for justice are powerfully generated by religion, for the religious person wants nothing more than to will and to love what the God of Jesus and the prophets wills and loves. Hence it is crucial for the cause of social justice that faith in this God be respected and cultivated.

As for the challenge of science to personal religion, Rauschenbusch argued (in an uncharacteristic philosophical vein) that human beings are part of a "great cosmic life," on the one hand bound to the necessities of the natural order but on the other hand free to will, to think, and to know themselves as standing over against the world. They reach out instinctively for God, whether through traditional religion or through such surrogates as philosophy and the movement for social justice. Satisfaction of this groping brings a person's deepest joys. The search for God, insisted Rauschenbusch, is itself responsive to God; it comes in answer to a "faint and far call, sweeter than the rhythm of the spheres, the voice of the Father of spirits calling to his child." When people respond to this voice, they are lifted from bondage to nature up to the threshold of a new realm of uniquely human existence: "The husks of necessity, which we share with the beasts, drop from our hands, and we long for the bread of freedom and peace in the eternal habitations of our Father. And with that conscious turning to God, we leave slavery and enter sonship." Human freedom thus has its ultimate source and sanction in divine grace: God calls people to freedom, gives it to those who respond, and despises every assault upon it.[15]

The response to God's call comes grudgingly, however, for people are more ready to satisfy their selfish drives than their higher instincts. "Whether we have fallen and have been corrupted by ages of sin, as the Bible says, or whether we are slowly mounting from the purely animal life to the spiritual, as the doctrine of evolution asserts, in either case it remains true that the spiritual life is as yet feeble in humanity. If it is to grow, it must not be left to the rude conflict with the hostile forces of the flesh and the world, but must be consciously fostered." Growth of the spiritual life requires deliberate, sustained cultivation. Rauschenbusch's advice to German Department students about such growth drew upon the wisdom of generations of spiritual counselors: Practice the presence of God through frequent prayer; seek the company of saints past and present; test one's purposes and wishes against the highest that is known of God's will; eschew corrupting influences; and persevere when the road to holiness seems tortuous and long.[16]

The warm and reflective piety of Walter Rauschenbusch reminded German Baptists of August Rauschenbusch and made them grateful for a son so worthy of the father. Increasingly, they venerated the man who had educated their pastors and placed his stamp upon their churches in dozens of ways. During the last years of his life, the elder

Rauschenbusch taught at the Hamburg seminary and wrote several short works for Baptists in Germany. In December 1899 word came that he had died peacefully and had been buried near the Hamburg school. Financial assistance from the Rockefellers had made it possible for Walter to spend the previous summer working in Germany with Emma and his father to complete the autobiography started by August earlier. It was a happy time for Walter Rauschenbusch; in the twilight of life, his father had mellowed and developed warm ties with his wife and daughter. "He was so loveable," wrote Emma to Pauline, "his former stern and severe way was all gone."[17]

Over the next year, researching and writing his father's life story became Walter Rauschenbusch's chief after-class pursuit, for the elderly man had asked his son to take up the task if he died before he could complete it. Parts of the ten chapters that August Rauschenbusch had drafted needed revision, and an additional ten had to be written. The result was a volume of 274 pages—part autobiography and part biography—that friendly reviewers hailed as both an engaging story of "the father of the German Baptists" and a revealing chapter of Baptist history.

Walter Rauschenbusch explained in the book's introduction that his father did not want the kind of biography that bordered on hagiography, and that consequently readers would find lights and shadows, a portrait of one who knew he was "no perfect saint." As it turned out, the volume was read widely among German Baptists, for it provided the most substantial look at their origins and growth yet written. At a time of uncertainty about the future, German Baptists could discern in August Rauschenbusch's fervent commitment to mission and education clues about who they were.

But Walter Rauschenbusch had not told all. He admitted his father's "singularity" and "sternness," and he acknowledged that at times August Rauschenbusch had spoken harshly to students. This behavior, Walter explained, resulted from a combination of nervousness, insomnia, and recurring illnesses. Moreover, it usually was followed by contrition and apologies to those he had treated offensively. Walter Rauschenbusch said nothing, however, about the troubled home life of his parents, and he scarcely mentioned his mother. This was not the occasion for lifting the veil he had spread over the family's private life many years earlier. He knew that neither their wish for privacy nor the need of the German Baptists for a hero would be served by such candor.[18]

German Baptists not only read Walter Rauschenbusch frequently in their publications, they met him more and more as well. His skill as a spokesman for ministerial education was needed to help raise the German Department's $100,000 endowment, and he was sent on numerous trips during vacations, some as far away as the Dakotas, to solicit support. The combination of teaching and traveling was wearying, but for the German Department his labors were indispensable, and when the last dollars were collected in 1913 it was clear that Walter Rauschenbusch had played an important role in securing the endowment.

The qualities that won his students also brought Rauschenbusch the respect of the wider circle of German Baptists. In September 1901, when delegates to the triennial General Conference voted upon a new editor for their national weekly paper, *Der Sendbote*, they elected him on the first ballot. The show of confidence was flattering, but he knew he could not accept the position. Conference minutes indicate that "in an emotional address Brother Rauschenbusch definitely declined to accept the election." He was a member of the committee that had decided not to nominate the incumbent editor for an additional term, and in the tempest surrounding that decision he did not want to appear to have been angling for the position.[19]

More significant, Rauschenbusch knew he could neither accept a new position among the German Baptists nor remain much longer as a teacher in the German Department. All his adult life he had given himself to the work to which his father had pointed him long ago, but he knew now that his ministry among German Baptists was deflecting him from his more fundamental calling to do "God's special work." As a pastor on New York's West Side, he had been able to address the tasks of reform along with his work to build up the German Baptist fellowship. But now the heavy instructional and promotional responsibilities he carried so crowded his schedule that there was virtually no time for the reform-oriented research and writing he wanted to do. Furthermore, the number of German Department students had declined year after year, and those presently enrolled seemed less well prepared than earlier classes. In these circumstances, lectures no longer were a satisfactory pedagogic tool, and the necessity for constant verbal exchange with individual students was a draining, frustrating experience for the hearing-impaired professor.

He knew also that though his personal stock within the German Baptist community appeared to be high, he was making little progress in his effort to awaken it to a lively sense of social mission. The increased prominence of German-Russian immigrants, coming as they did from a background of devout sectarian separation from the world,

Walther (later Walter), Frida,
Caroline, and Emma
Rauschenbusch, 1869. (Courtesy of
American Baptist Historical Society)

August Rauschenbusch, 1869.
(Courtesy of American Baptist
Historical Society)

Walter Rauschenbusch as
graduate of the Rochester Free
Academy, 1879. (Courtesy of
American Baptist Historical
Society)

Main building of Gütersloh
Gymnasium. (Courtesy of
Evangelisch-Stiftisches
Gymnasium zu Gütersloh)

Pauline Rother Rauschenbusch, circa 1893. (Courtesy of American Baptist Historical Society)

Members of the Brotherhood of the Kingdom, August 1894. Rauschenbusch is near the center; Leighton Williams is the second to his right. (Courtesy of American Baptist Historical Society)

The five Rauschenbusch children, 1907. (Courtesy of American Baptist Historical Society)

Rochester Theological Seminary professors. Front row, left to right: Thomas Harwood Pattison, William Arnold Stevens, Augustus Hopkins Strong, J. W. A. Stewart. Top row, left to right: Walter Rauschenbusch, Walter R. Betteridge, John P. Silvernail. (Courtesy of American Baptist Historical Society)

Rauschenbusch home at 4 Portsmouth Terrace, Rochester, New York. (Courtesy of American Baptist Historical Society)

Rauschenbusch summer home in Ontario. (Courtesy of American Baptist Historical Society)

Walter Rauschenbusch, 1909. (Courtesy of American Baptist
Historical Society)

Rauschenbusch with People's Sunday Evening colleagues Paul Moore Strayer (center) and James Bishop Thomas (right). (Courtesy of American Baptist Historical Society)

Walter Rauschenbusch with Edmund Lyon. (Courtesy of Carolyn Lyon)

Walter Rauschenbusch, circa 1916. (Courtesy of American Baptist Historical Society)

augured an even greater reluctance to attempt social reconstruction. To some of his former students Rauschenbusch admitted in 1904 that he had felt isolated within the German Baptist community "because of my convictions." The painful truth was that the reforming career he had begun among German Baptists could no longer be constructively continued among them.[20]

In the summer of 1902 the Rauschenbusches considered the possibility of his leaving the German Department. "While you can get along without them," Pauline admitted, "I don't see how they can get along without you. . . . It would take the heart out of many of the best men if they felt you were not with them." Walter conceded her point and decided he would not initiate a change; if he should move on, God would make it clear. Soon a door opened and he saw it as a sign. On 6 September 1902, following the death several days earlier of Benjamin True, professor of church history in the seminary's English Department, President Strong conferred with Rauschenbusch about the possibility of his succeeding True. An aide-memoire written by Rauschenbusch reveals that Strong pressed him hard to accept the position. His heavy load in the German Department, Strong argued, did not bring out his "best gifts"; as a professor in the English Department he would have a considerably lighter teaching load, would be freer for research and writing, and would be able to develop his courses as he wished. Strong perhaps clinched his case with the assurance that he considered church history "not merely the doings of an organization, but the history of the Kingdom of God on earth." That, Rauschenbusch noted, was the way he viewed the matter too.

The two men did not duck the tough issue of what a move would mean for Rauschenbusch's relationship to the German Baptist community.

> When I spoke of the effects of leaving the Germans, he asked if I could not still be of great service to them by advice etc. I said, Yes, if they would let me and would not regard me as a renegade. He said he would wish this to draw the Depts. nearer together and would be sorry to have the Germans feel as if they had been robbed. I said, if there was any feeling, it would not be against the English Department but against me. But that I thought it could be overcome, and that I had thought I might retain my membership in a German Church and attend their Conferences etc. He liked that.[21]

Two weeks later the announcement was made that Rochester Theological Seminary had called forty-year-old Walter Rauschenbusch to become Pettengill Professor of Church History in the English Department. At the same time, Walter wrote a letter published in *Der*

Sendbote explaining that his move bespoke no lessened sense of the need for a German Baptist mission in North America and that he did not intend this step to end his ties with the fellowship in which he had been reared and which he would always cherish. "In the most important decisions of my life," he concluded, "God always gave me an inner clarity and certainty, and whatever happened later on, He never made me think I had taken the wrong step. Now I have the same clarity and certainty that this is the next step God wills for me." Walter knew this was not the step August Rauschenbusch would have wanted for him, but he also knew he was captive to a higher obligation and must go where it led.

Most of the flood of letters that came in the next weeks strongly supported the decision. Many echoed William Newton Clarke's wish that Rauschenbusch now would be able to do his "duty with such fidelity as to disturb the calm somewhere." German Baptist friends, though pleased he had the opportunity for wider service, confessed their disappointment. "What will become of our German Department?" asked one of his former students. "I for one deeply deplore the loss we have sustained," said another.

Walter Rauschenbusch continued as professor of church history at the Rochester school for the rest of his life. During those sixteen years he retained membership in the German congregation in which he had grown up, and from time to time he accepted invitations to write for *Der Sendbote*, to advise German Baptist leaders, and to speak at their conferences. But never again were his ties with German Baptists as close or as consuming as they had been. Some in the emerging denomination attempted to steer it in the direction he had wanted for it, but without notable success. After 1902 Rauschenbusch was free to give himself wholeheartedly to the tasks that had been slighted since his return to Rochester.[22]

CHAPTER 8

ROCHESTERIAN

During his five years in the German department, Rauschenbusch was involved enough in local civic and religious affairs to begin to attract a following and win a reputation. "All Rochester knows," wrote a journalist in 1902, "that when Walter Rauschenbusch rises to speak, they have a treat in store." That same year his contributions as citizen and educator were recognized when the University of Rochester awarded him a Doctor of Divinity degree—the same honor bestowed upon his father forty years earlier.

This was only the start of Rochester's discovery of its talented native son. For the rest of his life, but especially over the next six years, Walter Rauschenbusch repeatedly involved himself in the public life of the city. By the time he became a nationally prominent figure he had been long known to Rochesterians as a leader of local reform efforts. The experience he gained among them was evident in the books that eventually brought him fame. Those writings bore the stamp of one who not only had seen lofty visions of a better America and a renewed church, but also had actually journeyed along the winding roads leading toward their realization.

Action to improve Rochester came easily for Rauschenbusch. "I love this city," he told fellow Rochesterians in 1903. "I was born here and all my boyish memories are twined about this city. God willing I hope to bring up my children here." It was, he added, "one of the fairest cities of our country," made so by a rare combination of elements: natural beauty, vigorous churches, prosperous educational institutions, expanding wealth, a growing population, and a proud community spirit.[1]

But as the twentieth century began, much of this seemed to be threatened, and Rauschenbusch was alarmed. Workers and their families crowded into wretched housing; children found few opportunities for wholesome recreation; factories polluted the air and the Genesee River; powerful business and political interests put their own prosperity ahead of the people's welfare. But Rauschenbusch rejoiced that a remarkable corps of public-spirited men and women saw the threats and attempted to address them. They had first been mobilized in the mid-1890s under the leadership of businessman Joseph Alling and his bipartisan Good Government clubs. Alling and the others were respected members of the community; most were either pastors or lay leaders of local churches (the Alling-taught Bible class of one thousand men was said to be the largest in the nation). For them religious commitment and reforming zeal went hand in hand. When in 1910 journalist Ray Stannard Baker lauded Rochester's reform movement as one of the most progressive in the nation, he remarked that his study of the city's efforts led him to conclude that "many of them had their roots in some form of religious enthusiasm." This group welcomed Walter Rauschenbusch into its ranks and came to appreciate his leadership. Far more than New Yorkers, Rochesterians were ready to listen to a man who spoke about reform in a biblical idiom.[2]

During the early years of his participation in local civic affairs, Rauschenbusch often reflected upon the grounds and objectives of this activity, and there was ample opportunity to refine his thought in talks and articles. The starting point for him was always Jesus and the Kingdom: Those who follow Jesus Christ continue his work of spreading Kingdom ways of justice, freedom, and love. Rauschenbusch believed that people who take up this task must come chiefly from the ranks of the laity, for they are daily in touch with realms of life that are not yet conformed to the Kingdom. They must be prepared for patient labor on a variety of fronts, for there is no single remedy for social ills, no panacea that will abruptly end accumulated wrongs. Jesus' parables of the Kingdom stressed the slow processes of its growth; hence, those who toil now in its behalf must "settle down to the task of gradually transforming society."

Laborers for the Kingdom also must learn to deal "scientifically" and "preventively" with social ills by identifying and addressing their causes. This does not mean ceasing to provide charitable relief for present victims of injustice, but it does require sustained attention to the creation and maintenance of a social order in which the rights of everyone to a full life are upheld. Followers of Jesus desire this for neighbors far and near, for they know the sacred worth of every person. Moreover, they crave humane social conditions that attest to the goodness of the Creator and the wisdom of the gospel, and that thereby prepare people for commitment to the One who seeks their allegiance.

Finally, Rauschenbusch recognized that those eager for the spread of Kingdom ways will not always agree about how to conceptualize or realize them. None can claim that their particular economic or political program is identical with the divine will. At times, Christians will find themselves working shoulder to shoulder with non-Christians who share their commitment to a better world; this should not surprise them, for biblical perspectives are plowed deeply into Western civilization and human souls. For all, the way ahead can be illuminated only by careful attention to the relevant facts and full debate about the options. Crucial to this process is full participation by all parties, with no one allowed arbitrarily to dominate it and no one arbitrarily excluded from it. More than most of his contemporaries, Rauschenbusch recognized the right of women and blacks to a share in the process, but he played no leadership role either locally or nationally in assuring their participation.[3]

Rauschenbusch's initial engagement with local issues of reform occurred in 1902. For years the city's gas needs had been supplied by a single firm, the Rochester Gas and Electric Company, and strong resentment had risen over its rates. Early in 1902 the prospect of relief came with the request for a franchise by a new company proposing lower rates. Public opinion favored the Common Council granting the franchise, but Rauschenbusch proposed a more intricate strategy. In a speech to the Economics Club, he stressed the importance of lowering the price of gas, principally to make it accessible to poorer families now dependent upon the cheaper but less desirable kerosene. "Irreparable injury," he said, "is done to the eyesight of children and adults by cheap and poor kerosene lamps." Moreover, gas lessens the risk of fire, lowers insurance rates, and provides a quality of light that makes homes more pleasant.

He conceded that competition from a second firm might well drive gas prices lower, but he cautioned that admitting the firm into Rochester would create difficulties. Experience with competing utilities in other cities had shown that they bring such inconveniences as streets torn up to lay new mains. More important, competing firms find the costs of doing business so great that they eventually take steps to combine, with the result that consumers again face exorbitant rates. Rauschenbusch proposed that the city refuse a second franchise—on condition that the monopolistic Rochester Gas and Electric agree to a 20 percent reduction of its rates. This move, he claimed, would be in the utility's best interest as well, for lower rates would bring an expanded circle of customers.

He went on to argue that if Rochester Gas and Electric did not agree to a rate decrease, the city should award a franchise to the new firm, but on three conditions: that the quality and rates of its gas be fixed, that the franchise continue for only a limited period, and that it acknowledge the city's right eventually to purchase its equipment. Rauschenbusch said municipal ownership would be best of all, but he conceded that public opinion was not yet ready for that step.

As it turned out, two weeks after he floated his proposal Rochester Gas and Electric announced it was prepared to move in this very direction. Provided the city agreed to award no new franchise, it promised to lower its rate. Rauschenbusch greeted the announcement warmly and urged its acceptance by city officials. Mere consideration of allowing a competing utility into the city, he wrote, had provided just the leverage needed to force the reduction; it was "one of the most effective clubs ever swung in Rochester." When word came a month later that the two firms had merged, some feared Rochester Gas and Electric would renege on its pledge to reduce rates, but it assured the city no such change was contemplated. Walter Rauschenbusch had tasted victory in his first public skirmish with big business.[4]

Correcting the abuse of public responsibility was also a key theme of his involvement in James Johnston's 1903 campaign for election as mayor of Rochester. For a decade Johnston had been active in city government, first as alderman than as comptroller. As the functions and costs of city government grew, Johnston fought vigorously against padded budgets and kickbacks. A Republican, he had been precariously aligned with George Aldridge and his powerful Republican political machine. But in 1903 "Boss" Aldridge became so miffed at Johnston's criticisms of cost overruns and inefficiencies that he left Johnston off the ticket. Outraged, Johnston and his supporters moved quickly to establish a third party to run Johnston for mayor.

Rauschenbusch admired Johnston's aggressive independence, and when Johnston asked him to make a nominating speech at the Citizens' Party rally, he accepted. This he did despite an eleventh-hour appeal from President Strong to avoid a public endorsement of Johnston. Strong explained that he feared Johnston would not pursue reform of the school system and that votes cast for him would draw support from the reform-minded businessman picked as the Republican candidate.

Rauschenbusch's speech on 15 October 1903 was his only public statement on behalf of a political candidate. Johnston's record, he said, had demonstrated his interest was more in improving Rochester than in furthering his own career; he had clearly shown his desire to address "the needs of the plain people." Moreover, as a third-party candidate, Johnston embodied two important principles: that candidates' positions on local issues rather than loyalty to a national political party should determine how a person votes in a municipal election, and that Rochester's future should be decided in the open by its citizens, not manipulated behind the scenes by a political czar.

Rauschenbusch was unusually pointed in insisting that Rochester, like other American cities, had suffered too long at the hands of an unchecked autocrat. "There is an unseen power, a man whom we have not elected, whom we can not depose nor hold responsible, and who yet exercises more power in our affairs than anyone else. And he is the really disturbing element in city administration . . . he is not after principles but after profit." A vote for Johnston would be a blow struck for Rochester and against "Boss Aldridge and the whole party system."

Johnston waged a vigorous campaign, but he was not elected. The Republican, James Cutler, won by a narrow margin over the Democratic candidate, 13,013 to 12,103, and Johnston captured 6,523 votes. Citizens' Party leaders believed this was a promising beginning and talked of redoubled efforts in the 1905 campaign, but nothing came of their third-party hopes. For Rauschenbusch there was consolation in the fact that Johnston's candidacy had pressured Aldridge to select an unusually able person as the Republican candidate. Over the next several years he discovered Mayor Cutler was a formidable ally to the reform movement.[5]

Three months after the election, Rauschenbusch again took a public role in local affairs. The Rochester branch of the Young Men's Christian Association embarked upon an ambitious investigation of social conditions in the community, and Rauschenbusch accepted an invitation to chair the volunteer committee conducting the study. Most of its twenty members were clergymen, and though they proceeded without the benefit of professional staff trained in the new sociology, their gaze ranged widely over the life of Rochester. After some twenty meetings, on 29 May 1904 Rauschenbusch presented their report to a large and appreciative gathering. In it he urged Rochesterians to recognize that despite the high quality of life in their city "the forces of evil are strong," and he proceeded to identify twelve realms in which enlightened citizens must work to improve the city. In most of these areas Rauschenbusch and his muckraking colleagues believed their strategy should be only to make the city aware of the dreary evidence: "Frank self-criticism is the first step toward better things," he said, for it will help people see the directions in which they must move.

Most of the recommendations gave little specific indication of what must be done. For example, after detailing the recent arrival of large numbers of immigrants from southern and eastern Europe, the committee was content with the limp admonition, "Look after the new immigrants, the Italians, Slavs and Jews." Several recommendations were more pointed. The increase of "sexual evils among boys and girls," said the committee, should be countered by supplementing parents' instruction of their children through hygiene classes in the public schools.[6]

The committee uncovered numerous facts and recorded its opinions about reform, but the report was bland, and Walter Rauschenbusch knew that more was necessary to precipitate change. In three of the realms the committee considered, he took it upon himself later to identify precisely the remedial steps required and to mobilize public opinion. A major target was the Rochester Railway Company, operator of the controversial Monroe Avenue streetcar line. Rauschenbusch believed that here was a glaring instance of a major menace to American life. Again and again public service corporations were found to be more interested in milking cities than serving citizens. In a growing community like Rochester, cheap and efficient public transportation between downtown workplaces and suburban residential areas was essential if workers and their families were not to be forced into urban ghettos.

Nor was the streetcar company sufficiently attentive to the needs of middle-class people like himself. "We have a number of grievances," he told a mass meeting of Monroe Avenue commuters in September 1904. Fares have gone up, but without an improvement of service. Open cars ("pneumonia incubators") are used in cold weather; cars frequently fail to complete their scheduled routes; and they run dangerously close to sidewalks. The Rochester Railway Company, he contended, is not interested in change. "The company gives just so much service as to be able to get the best dividends for themselves. That is all." Consumers must insist upon better service and support the efforts of Mayor Cutler and other city officials to require improvements. He concluded shrewdly, "Let us ask for more than we expect to get, and they may think it advisable to give us something to buy us off." Over the next several years conditions improved, partly because Rauschenbusch remained a persistent thorn in the flesh of the streetcar company.[7]

A gentler effort was made to secure recreation facilities for the people of Rochester. In a front-page Sunday newspaper article in July 1904, Rauschenbusch pleaded for the city to build "swimming baths" on the Genesee that would be open to the public during the summer. This innovation, he reported, had proved popular in England and Germany; its introduction into Rochester would be a boon to all, especially to youngsters. "Certainly the habits of cleanliness, of physical self-reliance, of hard breathing, of glowing skin-action, created by swimming, must do a great deal for the children." Mayor Cutler was persuaded, funds were appropriated, and Rochesterians enjoyed a new public pool the following summer.[8]

The YMCA committee had urged enlightened citizens to launch "a moral and scientific crusade against the drink evil," and some Rochester reformers took up this cause. Walter Rauschenbusch believed in it and often spoke out against the insidious influence of alcohol. In February 1905 he was one of four local sponsors of a conference initiated by the Anti-Saloon League to consider state legislation against abuses of the Raines Law by saloons posing as hotels and claiming the privilege granted only to hotels in 1896 to sell liquor on Sundays. From time to time, too, he spoke out in favor of local option laws. A recurring theme in these statements was the effect of alcohol upon workers and their families. He charged that saloons, and the entire liquor industry, seek profit without regard for the human consequences of their trade. Although alcohol dulls the senses of everyone who consumes it, this is especially dangerous to workers, for men who drink and then work with machines are prone to terrible accidents. Alcohol also impairs the brain's ability to think clearly, thus impeding workers' struggle for better conditions and higher wages. "If working people are to get ahead they must think."[9]

This scion of a long line of German university graduates came instinctively to the conviction that all people must learn to make maximal use of their rational faculties. The nurturing of the ability to think and to communicate one's thoughts is essential to the progress of a free, self-governing society. This, he believed, was the great mission of public schools, but observing his own children's experience in Rochester schools, Rauschenbusch concluded it was not being properly pursued. Earlier he had supported removing the local school system from control by the politically driven Board of Aldermen and placing it under a small group of concerned citizens constituting a Board of Education. But he and other parents of elementary school children grew uneasy about changes made by the new board to implement its perception that traditional patterns of education neither adequately encouraged youngsters to express their individuality nor properly developed the practical skills necessary for life in industrial America.

At an open meeting of parents on 10 September 1908, Rauschenbusch was named to a committee charged with investigating complaints and preparing a report for a follow-up meeting. This group asked him to chair a subcommittee to conduct an immediate investigation and draft the report. It was an assignment with all the appeal of a hornet's nest, but Rauschenbusch consented. "I know how you shrink from strife," Pauline wrote him, and she added, "It was brave of you to go into it." Over the next three weeks he squeezed the new duties into an already crowded schedule, reading dozens of confidential letters solicited from parents and teachers about the new system, conducting interviews with school officials, administering spot tests among students in spelling and arithmetic, then compiling a thirty-five-page report. It was first discussed privately with board members to give them an opportunity to prepare their response, then on 13 November, highlights were presented to a packed auditorium of parents and teachers at the new East High School.[10]

The "Rauschenbusch Committee" commended the Board of Education for attempting to move the schools in a new direction. The fruits of the shift were evident, said Chairman Rauschenbusch: "Our children like to go to school. They do become interested in many things of which children of the same age used to know little. They do seem to have greater freedom and readiness in expressing themselves on anything that comes along. These results are a distinct advance in education, and we would not surrender any of them."

The gains, however, were purchased at a high price. Rauschenbusch contended that the hours given such activities as dramatization and exhibit making allows too little time for attention to "the three Rs." Moreover, eagerness to win students' lively interest in their work has brought a diminished concern for discipline. And with teachers required to teach subjects and use methods for which they have neither training nor relish, many of them are demoralized. But the problem goes even deeper, charged Rauschenbusch. The schools' failure to teach boys and girls how to engage in intense study leaves them unprepared for their role as builders and preservers of civilization. "The fundamental distinction between the civilized man and the savage is that the civilized brain can concentrate attention and keep it up, while the wandering interest of the savage picks things up with grunts of delight and swiftly wearies of them." More time must be spent on the processes necessary for producing the civilized brain.

He went on to propose seventeen specific remedies, most of which were accepted by the Board of Education. Included were admonitions to spend more time on the basics, tighten discipline, allow teachers more latitude in their classrooms, seek higher salaries for them, and hire specially trained instructors to teach such subjects as music. The board also agreed to cooperate with a continuing body appointed by the Rauschenbusch committee to implement certain of the recommendations and address other grievances that might arise in the future.

In the end, Rauschenbusch felt satisfied about the agreement, though from time to time over the next several years he privately regretted that some of the same deficiencies continued in the schools. In December 1908 he told Pauline that leaders of East High School (whose teachers had criticized the poor preparation of children coming to them) were pleased at the results. "Every teacher in the high school," said Principal Albert Willcox, "is under a life-long obligation to you." And a faculty associate at the seminary wrote Pauline, praising her husband's "strong, shrewd, playful, efficient way" of conducting the investigation and adding, "There are many grateful souls who feel deep kindness for what he has done." The outcome of the school controversy gave him lasting satisfaction.[11]

This episode reinforced what he had learned from involvement in earlier local reform ventures. He saw that aroused citizens could reach significant agreements about changes needed in the community and that through united action they could move people in authority toward the desired reforms. It was clear, too, that Rochesterians shared enough of Rauschenbusch's blending of religious faith and democratic idealism that he could appeal effectively to their best hopes for the community. Within the next few years, as he moved to a national platform, he discovered that many people across the United States were ready for the same message.

Rauschenbusch's record in public affairs, together with his oratorical talent, made him a sought-after speaker among local organizations, and he accepted numerous invitations. The breadth of his topics and his audiences is striking. The YMCA, for example, heard him speak on the question "What About the Woman?" (said to be "an unsurpassed lecture on personal purity"). The Labor Lyceum heard him on "Impressions of Germany"; the Men's Civic Club on "Non-Partisan Political Ideals"; the City Club on "Is There Sense in Socialism?"; the Delta Upsilon fraternity on "The Pleasures of Life"; and the University Club on "The Forces at Work in the Social Movement." A prominent Rochesterian who had watched his friend's role develop, declared in 1915 that the strong local interest in "Rauschenbusch of Rochester" proves a prophet can have honor in his own hometown.[12]

The Reverend Walter Rauschenbusch was equally comfortable in the pulpit, and especially in the early years of his teaching he often spoke in local churches. The wish "to still make myself useful to the plain people," whose friendship he had treasured in New York City, led him in 1904 to write the pastors of small Baptist churches in the area offering his services gratis as a speaker.

> If you prefer it, I will preach an evangelistic sermon or a sermon aiming at a higher life among Christian people, at some Sunday service. Or I will deliver a lecture or address on a week evening on one of the following topics: 1. Why I am a Baptist. 2. An Education; what it is worth and how to get it. . . . 3. New Light on the Temperance Question. 4. The Social Problem. 5. Rochester as it might be. 6. The Pleasures of Youth.

He explained that the offer was an experiment on his part and that although he hoped he could accept all invitations, other commitments would place constraints upon him. It was a generous gesture, but his hunch about the limitations of his availability proved accurate, and the offer was not repeated later.[13]

Part of the reason for not involving himself more actively with local churches was that most of them ignored what he increasingly regarded as the great task of Christians everywhere—to close the gap between Christianity and the growing masses of workingpeople. The chief reason for their alienation, he declared in 1904 in a widely distributed essay entitled "The New Evangelism," is that the church's message is still shaped by the mind of an earlier era, and its destiny is controlled by the same affluent people who govern the political and economic realms. The common people simply do not find this church honoring their values or addressing their needs.

Christians, continued Rauschenbusch, must now so develop "the latent moral and spiritual resources of the Gospel" that its full power is unleashed for all citizens of the modern world. This requires a process of reformulating the Christian message that listens to what the church is being told, both by the Spirit of Jesus and by the spirit of the age. No better means exists for hearing the latter than by turning an attentive ear to workingpeople. The church must go to them, claimed Rauschenbusch, not only to preach its message but also to learn from them what God is now attempting to teach the church about the message.[14]

Rauschenbusch's major continuing engagement with the workingpeople of Rochester began in 1908, when he joined an innovative ministry in the downtown area. Paul Moore Strayer, pastor of the affluent Third Presbyterian Church on East Avenue and a member of the Central Labor Council, shared his friend's anxiety about the estrangement of workers and proposed an imaginative method of reaching them. Under Strayer's leadership, a team of ministers would plan and host Sunday night programs in a large downtown theater, to which workers were invited. There would be familiar elements of worship, such as prayers and hymns, but there would also be enough unusual features, such as speeches on contemporary subjects and audience talk-back, to mark this as a departure from conventional Christianity. "We propose to attempt to take the church to the habitual non-churchgoer," said Strayer; he is "an honest and reasonable man, and we aim to put the Gospel in such form and present it with such sympathy and reasonableness that he will receive it." It would be the kind of new departure the time seemed to require.

Strayer invited Walter Rauschenbusch and Henry H. Stebbins, a retired Presbyterian clergyman, to work with him as ministers of this unique congregation. Backed by a committee of prominent businessmen and labor leaders, and endorsed by the Protestant clergy of downtown Rochester, the three men launched the People's Sunday Evening on 1 November 1908. After a five-month trial period, the ministers and their supporters concluded that the venture had succeeded beyond all expectations. Attendance had exceeded 30,000; the program was financially solvent; employment had been found for some idle workers; the ministers had developed pastoral ties among people with no church affiliation; and a new appreciation of Christianity had emerged. Rauschenbusch acknowledged that the experience had brought something to the three ministers as well. He explained that at first they had thought they would need to offer entertainment to attract the workers. But they soon found that their "audiences were most profoundly interested in strong, vital, earnest discussions that got at the marrow of the solid questions of life. . . . On the whole, our respect for the intellectual grasp and the moral earnestness of the people has grown." It was a promising venture that must continue.[15]

The People's Sunday Evening remained a part of Rochester life for five months each year until 1916. Throughout this period Rauschenbusch continued with Strayer in the ministerial leadership (Stebbins was succeeded by an Episcopal clergyman, James Bishop Thomas). For Rauschenbusch it was a valued association. The energetic Strayer handled most administrative matters and did much of the speaking. Rauschenbusch spoke often and relished the opportunity for exchange with workingpeople. In 1915 he wrote a friend that the People's Sunday Evening had become the second-largest Sunday evening congregation in Rochester, that it was composed almost entirely of thoughtful workingpeople unreached by the churches, and that encouraging signs had come of a "change of temper . . . among some of the radicals." But new city ordinances now permitted theaters to show Sunday movies, and attendance at People's Sunday Evenings dwindled. The following year, with war clouds looming, it was decided to end the programs.[16]

Rauschenbusch's other long-term leadership role in Rochester religious affairs came in his association with the local chapter of the Brotherhood of the Kingdom. In 1902 he urged Leighton Williams and other leaders of the Brotherhood to acknowledge that if their organization were to have continued usefulness, it must form local units to inspire and support an expanding circle of new members, much as the Marlborough meetings had done for the original members. Clergy and laity, professional men and workingmen, must be sought for membership in local chapters across the United States.

When the Rochester chapter was established in December 1903, Williams greeted this new step for the Brotherhood as "the boldest and most important for a long time." Rauschenbusch remained the guiding spirit of the Rochester group and brought into its membership some twenty leaders in business and the professions who shared his commitment to religious and social reform. Other Rochester reformers (such as Joseph Alling and Clarence Barbour), though not members, often participated. The group's usual pattern was to meet for supper several times a year and to invite friends to attend as guests. "We do not intend to compete with other organizations," Rauschenbusch explained to a prospective member, "but to stimulate all. We resist the temptation of numbers and public display, and believe in spiritual quietness and social courage."[17]

During Rauschenbusch's years as professor of church history at Rochester Theological Seminary, he remained in touch with the Brotherhood's Marlborough-based activities, but they no longer captured his interest as they had earlier, nor did they command as much of his energy as the local chapter did. At the time the Rochester chapter was formed, Leighton Williams confided to him that he thought the zest of the Brotherhood's earlier years had been lost. Part of the problem, wrote Rauschenbusch in 1907, was that many of the avant-garde causes for which the Brotherhood had fought in its earlier days—Christian unity, critical study of the Bible, a Kingdom-centered theology, a just economic and political order—had moved into the mainstream of American Protestant consciousness. "Everything is now coming our way," and Brotherhood members could be proud they had promoted the shift. But there no longer was clarity about a distinctive mission for the Brotherhood.

Besides encouraging Brotherhood leaders to form local chapters,

Rauschenbusch also contended that they should invest the organization's slim resources in hiring a staff person to implement decisions made at Brotherhood meetings. On neither point was he successful. In 1912, obviously disappointed, Rauschenbusch confessed he believed the organization had been held back by its excessive dependence upon "my dear friend, Leighton Williams," who with other key leaders had dissuaded the Brotherhood from taking bold stands on social issues; consequently "we have marked time on the vague statements of an earlier day while all the world has swept forward. So we have lost the young men." It was a sad admission.

Rauschenbusch concluded that the only useful future for the Brotherhood would be to have it join forces with comparable organizations. Earlier in the year Harry F. Ward, executive of the Methodist Federation for Social Service, had proposed to him that they work to create "a league for all the social propagandists for mutual protection against the reaction that is likely to come." Rauschenbusch urged Brotherhood leaders to negotiate with Ward and others at the forthcoming Chicago meeting of the Federal Council of Churches. Whether the Brotherhood ended its existence this way or some other, members could be proud of its record. His words were a kind of epitaph:

> Whatever happens, the Brotherhood has not lived in vain. It is justified by its children. It has had a tremendous influence on the early group, and it has been of inestimable value to the entire national movement to have a number of mature minds at its command early. A handful of seed-corn in April is worth more than a bushel of corn in November.

Brotherhood leaders did not pursue the Ward-Rauschenbusch proposal, and the organization gradually petered out, never recapturing the luster of its first five years.[18]

When word went out in the city that "Rauschenbusch of Rochester" was scheduled to speak, there were sure to be large audiences. By the early years of the new century, people in much of the nation were reaching out for ways to cope with the enormous changes in American life, and they were ready to listen to voices that offered hope for a new order—especially to voices that linked reform with basic Christian and American ideals. Walter Rauschenbusch provided such a message, but there was more to his popularity than that. Audiences were struck by the man himself. It was partly that he was a physically commanding person: tall (just under six feet), slim, erect, neatly dressed in the formal style expected then of professors, with a large forehead, heavy eyebrows, straight nose, a full head of dark-brown hair, a trim auburn beard, and a firm mouth often wearing the trace of a smile. Most people noticed his deep-set, dark eyes; a painter who knew him well said they possessed "that quality which seemed to see through superficiality and to penetrate to the utmost that on which his attention was focused. To a remarkable degree also they expressed solicitude and friendliness and kindness." Some spoke of his "Lincolnesque" appearance.

He impressed audiences, too, with the way he made his case. There were always illuminating metaphors, an economy of words, a fairness toward those he opposed, and a disarming sense of humor ("one reason why people tolerate me as they do," he confided to a close friend, is that "I respect my audiences, and I laugh at myself as well as at them"). His voice was enough on the high, thin side that one had to listen carefully to catch all he said. Again and again the ease with which he handled his handicap proved to be an endearing quality.

Rauschenbusch sparkled in the question-and-answer sessions that usually followed his talks. Notes made by a family member or friend stated the query he could not hear; then he responded quickly and incisively. He gave the impression, wrote Paul Strayer, "that these were just the questions on which he had been thinking for weeks." But when he was uncertain about his answer to a query, he did not hesitate to admit it; he despised pretense and wanted to give it no foothold in his own life.[19]

Friends marveled at his ability to accept so many responsibilities and to carry them so well. The key, one of his student secretaries aptly observed, was "rigid self-discipline by which he restored frayed nerves, conserved vital energy, and utilized to the full each hour." His working day usually began before other members of the family were up; even on summer vacations he put in an entire morning of reading and writing, often beginning before sunrise. His methodical mind was also evident in the careful organizing of the day's activities and in his extensive files. He knew that his capacity for effective work depended upon allowing himself times for the right types of play; forms of recreation that brought a complete change of activity and scenery were deliberately selected. Favorites were those that brought him into touch with nature—especially gardening, hiking, canoeing, swimming, and fishing. In his later years he also became an avid woodcarver.

His friends knew how greatly Rauschenbusch valued the ties that bound them together and how consistently he worked to nurture those ties. He had a "genius for friendship," said Strayer. People who wanted his counsel found him eager to help, and through prodigious correspondence he kept in touch with many whose lives had touched his, offering a quiet word of encouragement at times of stress and a light word of affirmation at times of joy.

Those who knew him best marveled at the range of his friendships. "His ability to love people, all people, and to make them love him," said his daughter Winifred, was her father's great legacy. Many years earlier he had testified that the key to this all-encompassing love was the firsthand knowledge he and Pauline had of people at all levels of society, from the tenements of West 43rd Street to the mansions of Fifth Avenue. "We try to love and appreciate the humanity and beauty in all of them." These were qualities he believed had been placed in them by their Creator; hence they could not be erased either by themselves or by others.[20]

Since the move from New York City, Rauschenbusch's close friendships had been established increasingly with men in the professions and business who shared his commitment to reform. A few, like John Strong (son of President Strong), were teachers at the seminary, but most were prosperous business executives. Closest to Rauschenbusch within this circle were Joe Alling and Edmund Lyon, who with their wives often shared happy times with Walter and Pauline. Not only did such friends share his commitment to reform; they also admired his good works and offered their support. For some the support typically was a word of commendation they knew this modest man appreciated. "During the time that you are more or less alone with your thinking and dreaming," wrote Paul Strayer, "remember also that you are helping us who are working in the shallows, doing better the things we have to do because you are moving in the deeps." For several businessmen the support came more tangibly through gifts of money to expand the impact of Rauschenbusch's work. Only one of them was a Rochesterian; in 1910 Edmund Lyon established a joint bank account into which he placed funds for Rauschenbusch to use to subsidize such projects as French translations of his books.[21]

The Lyon support of $1,200 was small compared to the monetary gifts that continued to come from the Rockefellers. Between 1900 and 1918, John and Laura Rockefeller gave Rauschenbusch and his family approximately $8,000. The periodic gifts of cash covered a variety of expenses: $1,500 was given to pay off the mortgage on their first Rochester home; $1,500 went toward the purchase of a new home; $1,000 helped support Walter Rauschenbusch's widowed sisters; $625 financed his niece's college education; and checks for $100 or $200 came most Christmases.

The Rockefeller funds were given with no strings attached. Usually there was only the word that the money should be used to ease the burdens of the Rauschenbusches' busy life. "We enjoy our rest better," Laura Rockefeller once explained, "by sharing it with others." The elderly Rockefellers appear greatly to have enjoyed and admired these young friends of their daughter and son-in-law. The Rauschenbusches were overnight guests at least three times in Rockefeller homes in Cleveland, Manhattan, and Pocantico Hills. "We rejoice in all that you are doing for the Master," wrote the Baptist capitalist to the Baptist reformer in 1904. Six years later Rockefeller commended Rauschenbusch for his "long, continued, and most intelligent efforts for the general uplift." His example, Rockefeller believed, had helped many "to struggle to do their best."

Neither the Rockefellers nor the Rauschenbusches made public mention of the support given the one family by the other (Rauschenbusch did not even tell his sisters the name of their benefactor). For the Rockefellers these gifts were a tiny ripple on a giant wave of philanthropy. Still, one can wonder about them. What prompted the gifts? Was there some hope of creating a dependency that would prompt Rauschenbusch to soften his criticism of the economic system that brought Rockefeller his wealth? The Rockefeller-Rauschenbusch correspondence (consisting of about three hundred letters, most of them between Pauline and either Laura Rockefeller or her sister, Lucy Spelman) provides no support for such a conjecture. It seems more plausible to conclude that the pious Rockefellers admired the pious Rauschenbusches and wanted to lighten their load.

For their part, Pauline and Walter appear to have had no qualms about accepting the Rockefeller gifts, and they did so with genuine gratitude. Walter perhaps remembered the support his father had received from well-to-do relatives in Germany. He never joined the chorus of reformers who criticized Rockefeller's business practices, but this was typical of him, for he believed strongly that blame for America's economic woes lay more with the capitalist system than with the individuals who profited from it. The Rauschenbusches believed that a door was open for whatever impact Walter's message could make upon the Rockefellers, and they regularly sent them inscribed copies of his books and of some articles. In response came polite expressions of appreciation, including the message that Laura Rockefeller was keeping one of Rauschenbusch's sermonic essays in her New Testament. But there is no record of a more substantial Rockefeller response having been triggered by the Rauschenbusches.[22]

Although the affectionate support of friends meant much to Rauschenbusch, the greater sustenance came from his family. In the years following their arrival in Rochester, three additional children were born to Pauline and Walter: Paul in 1898, Carl in 1900, and Elizabeth in 1904. The expanding family soon outgrew the Rauschenbusch's first house, a rented frame building on Avondale Street, and in 1900 they bought their own home, a new, five-bedroom, one-bath dwelling on nearby Shepard Street. Initially, when weather permitted, Rauschenbusch covered the distance between his house and the seminary on a bicycle given him as a farewell gift by the youth of Second German Baptist Church. Two incidents, however, made him a regular commuter on the Monroe Street line—the first a collision with a streetcar whose approach he had not heard, the second a two-dollar fine for riding on the sidewalk.

As the Rauschenbusch children grew older and Walter became a more prominent figure in Rochester and the nation, he and Pauline began to look for a larger, more comfortable house closer to the seminary. The opportunity to move came in 1911 when the widow of Rauschenbusch's teacher C. Harwood Pattison decided to sell the family home at 4 Portsmouth Terrace. This was an older place requiring extensive renovation, but the Rauschenbusches were attracted by its charm and spaciousness and by the fact it was only a short walk to the school. The house was two doors from East Avenue, around the corner from George Eastman's showplace mansion, and three blocks from the Edmund and Carolyn Lyon home. The Rockefellers' munificence again was accepted, and the Rauschenbusches moved a final time in March 1912.

Rochester seminarians often came to 4 Portsmouth Terrace for an evening of food and relaxation, and the Rauschenbusch children waited table much as their father and his sisters had done at the August Rauschenbusch home many years earlier. The students saw immediately that this was a happy home. The children were industrious and bright and clearly devoted to their parents. All five knew that their father prized the family's tradition of academic achievement, and they sought to please him by hard work in school. They knew, too, that their father wanted them to attend the finest colleges and that an important reason for his accepting so many speaking and writing invitations was to earn the funds that would make this possible. Indeed, so important to Rauschenbusch was the raising of this money by his own labors that he declined Edmund Lyon's offer to help with the children's education. Between 1912 and 1918 he had the satisfaction of seeing four of the children attend top colleges— Winifred at Oberlin, the three boys at Amherst—and three of them win election to Phi Beta Kappa (Elizabeth later earned that honor at Cornell).

The children also knew that religion was important to their parents, and they regularly attended Sunday school and morning worship at the First German Baptist Church. Bible reading and prayers at the dinner table were a fixed part of family life. Many years later Lisa Rauschenbusch remembered that at a time when she had been particularly gloomy her father gently told her, "You would feel better if you would come to Jesus." Rarely, however, did he engage the children directly in discussion about religion. Nor did he press his sons to carry on the family's tradition of ministerial service. He did not want to make the mistake his own father had made by too aggressively attempting to shape the children's religion.

The family's happiest times came during summer vacations in Canada. A camping trip with Rochester friends in 1905 had introduced Rauschenbusch to the Canadian woods, and in 1908 he purchased a three-and-a-half acre tract on Lake Sturgeon, near Bobcaygeon, Ontario, one hundred miles south of Algonquin Park. That summer he built a rustic cottage and began preparing the soil for a garden at this new "Rauschenbuschhof." Until 1915 the family spent two months there every summer, though Walter often was away lecturing for several weeks. This spot, remembered one of the daughters, was the Rauschenbusches' "paradise." All shared Walter's love of the outdoors, and week after week they swam, canoed, hiked, gardened, and fished. So special did the area become that the summer following Rauschenbusch's death the five children returned a final time and spread his ashes upon a lake in Algonquin Park.[23]

There also were strains in the Rauschenbusch home. Walter held high standards for his children and was disappointed when they were not met. "It always grieves me," he wrote them in 1910, "that you are so slow to take hold of your new chances. . . . When I think how eager many poor people are to learn, and what sacrifices they make to go to night school, etc., it makes me feel bad. . . . You know that I love you all, and want to see you grow into fine men and women, and it hurts me when you hurt yourselves." There was a distance, too, created partly by his frequent absences and partly by his deafness. The children learned to communicate by speaking directly into his ear or by using the manual alphabet, but they knew—and he knew— that his inability to participate in their banter and casual conversation prevented the closeness they all desired. Nevertheless, there was an abiding affection and admiration for their father.

The children adored their mother and Tante Schaefer, but not the third woman in the family circle. Following the death of her husband in 1910, Emma Rauschenbusch Clough moved to an apartment near the seminary and was often in her brother's home. During the years in India she had developed a keen interest in theosophy and believed that she was the reincarnation of her long-deceased brother. It became evident that Emma believed Pauline was unfit for Walter, and tensions developed between the two women. The children plainly disliked Aunt Emma. In later years Lisa remembered "we detested her" for the way she treated their mother.

Through all the years in Rochester, Pauline continued to pour herself out for her husband, much as she had done during the early years of their marriage. "No one realizes how many things you are to me," she wrote him in 1911. But with his prominence reaching new heights and fresh expectations pressing upon her, there were more frequent periods of depression and a recurring fear of failing him. At times there also was regret that though she could know his deepest convictions through his writings he did not always comprehend hers. She longed for him to know her equally well.

Pauline's love for Walter was never in question, nor was his for her. Despite the strains, he had no doubt about the continuing affection of his family and closest Rochester friends. His testimony in 1910 bore the ring of truth: "I have an amazed sense of a great and growing world of love about me. So many people love me, and they love me so vastly more than I ever deserved at their hands, that I can only accept it as a mystery and a beautiful gift of God." This gift of love made him eager to love in return, and it steadied him in the difficult times that were to come.[24]

✦✦✦ CHAPTER 9 ✦✦✦

HISTORY PROFESSOR

During its first fifty years, Rochester Theological Seminary had earned widespread trust and support by the respect it paid doctrinal landmarks dear to most American Protestants. As the new century began, however, some wondered how long the school would maintain its conservative stance, for powerful theological winds were moving many in directions explored earlier by liberals such as Bushnell, and it was not yet clear how sweeping the changes would be. Augustus Hopkins Strong had no doubts about where he stood and where he wanted his school to stand. "Let others teach as they will," he declared to Rochester trustees in 1906, "we propose to walk in the old paths and hand down to our successors the old gospel." It was a welcome word for most of his Baptist constituents.

A decade earlier Strong felt kindlier about the ferment present in religious thought, but now he had profound reservations. Thanks to the pernicious influence of "Ritschl and his Kantian relativism," too many Christian intellectuals were rejecting Christ's deity and atonement, even to the point of denying the validity of praying to Christ. Strong feared that this drift from orthodoxy was leading American Protestantism to the brink of a "second Unitarian defection" more divisive than the first a century earlier. In common with a growing number of alarmed Protestants, he believed the time had come to insist upon acceptance of doctrinal fundamentals and to fight the assault upon them. Strong hoped the enlarged edition of his three-volume *Systematic Theology* (published 1907–9) would help, but even more he hoped the seminary he had led for more than three decades would strike telling blows for the true faith.[1]

President Strong knew wealthy Baptist businessmen who shared his vision of the school's task, and he effectively cultivated a commitment from them to make Rochester one of the finest seminaries in the United States. The mainstay, Rockefeller, continued his long-standing beneficence (giving the school altogether about $500,000); in 1905 a bequest of $560,000 came from the estate of John J. Jones, a New Jersey industrialist; and two years later Strong's brother, Henry, president of Eastman Kodak, gave $140,000 for a new building named after their father. The school's assets now were valued at more than $2 million.

The handsome Alvah Strong Hall was a fitting addition for an institution set in Rochester's most attractive and prestigious neighborhood. President Strong took special pride in the new four-story building. There was enough space for every two students to occupy a three-room suite. In addition, Strong Hall boasted a richly furnished parlor, comfortable faculty offices, spacious lecture halls, even a bowling alley and gymnasium. People from the community now came often for special lectures and musical performances. The students' elegant surroundings were considered an integral part of their education. Strong and other prominent Baptist ministers in Rochester mixed regularly with the upper strata of the community, and he believed it was important for young aspirants to the ministry to learn to "mingle with ease in cultivated society," so that they would be able to perform their ministerial tasks among "refined and educated people."

The new money also made possible several additional faculty positions, expanded library facilities, and increased scholarship aid for students. President Strong's financial worries seemed to be over, and he believed that the school now attracted not only the largest number of students ever, but also the brightest. Best of all, he said, this had happened without a dilution of the faith; indeed, it was a sign of God's pleasure at the seminary's continued faithfulness.

The school stood as a bright example of Rochester's prosperity and the Baptists' success.[2]

President Strong valued Walter Rauschenbusch's role in the seminary's ascent. He was a favorite of Rockefeller, and earlier had helped attract John Jones' interest in the school. Strong felt uneasy about some of his history professor's views, but he could tolerate them because Rauschenbusch's fundamental soundness was attested to by his sterling character and his frequent addressing of prayers to Christ. Strong also welcomed Rauschenbusch's talent as a bridge builder—between rich and poor, Americans and Europeans, German-speaking Baptists and English-speaking Baptists, conservatives and liberals.

Rauschenbusch had a knack for recognizing values on each side of divides and for helping those divided see them too.

Rauschenbusch's faculty associates knew his place in Strong's esteem, and they chose him for a delicate mission in 1909. Over the last several years they had wondered when the school's prosperity would be reflected in their salaries. Finally they decided to address the issue openly, and at their behest Rauschenbusch presented the faculty's case to Strong. For thirty years, he said, professors' annual salaries had remained fixed at $3,000, despite sharp rises in the cost of living. It now was nearly impossible to maintain their place "in the class of the population with which the professors are naturally thrown into social contact." Comparable seminaries had raised salaries; if Rochester did not follow suit, present faculty members would be forced to increase outside remunerative engagements that unfortunately would deflect them from single-minded performance of their seminary duties. Moreover, failure to raise salaries could mean that professors would accept positions elsewhere and that able replacements might be turned away by Rochester's low compensation.[3]

Strong's response was sympathetic but unbudging. He explained that benefactors had designated most of the new monies for other purposes and that the remaining funds were not adequate to allow the desired increases. He also told the faculty that Rochester salaries were the envy of professors at other Baptist seminaries, that they exceeded salaries at the University of Rochester, and that the seminary practiced the unusually generous policy of granting year-long sabbaticals with pay. Eventually, he concluded, the school should increase each professor's compensation enough to match what the city's best-paid Baptist preachers received, but this step lay in the future.

Rauschenbusch and his colleagues felt so strongly about the issue that several took it to individual trustees. When Strong reported the professors' concern at the trustees' annual meeting in May 1910, that body endorsed Strong's judgment, but Rauschenbusch did not let the matter drop. He knew that faculty at several other schools (including the University of Chicago) had expressed interest in hiring him and that he could not adequately provide for his large family on his present salary. Intimations of this to several close faculty and trustee friends brought from one of them a strong affirmation of his usefulness to the seminary, and from another the insistence that he, more than others, had first claim upon any increases that might be granted. But no raises came, and Rauschenbusch decided that because he did not want to teach elsewhere he must continue to expand his writing and outside lecturing commitments to ensure an adequate flow of income.[4]

President Strong was engaged with the faculty and trustees in another, more far-reaching drama. During the period he was overseeing the school's financial stabilization, questions began to occur about how much longer the Baptist patriarch would continue at the helm, as well as about what would happen to the school after Strong's retirement. The second question was especially disturbing to those who shared the president's conservative outlook, for they knew that some Rochester professors and trustees had been influenced by the new theological currents. Might not these Baptist liberals seek a president who would move the school in a fresh direction?

A clue about the faculty's mind on this issue came in 1906 at the time of Strong's seventieth birthday. A public tribute by Walter Rauschenbusch included the jocular observation that "any Baptist from Texas to the North Pole feels free to write to Dr. Strong as the court of final appeal to settle how a Baptist church should be run and what a Baptist ought to believe if he wants to be marked 99 98/100 per cent pure." Then came the more serious acknowledgment that "he has managed to write bigger books and solider books than all the rest of the faculty combined." At this point in the address, conservatives doubtless hoped Rauschenbusch would applaud Strong's defense of the faith once and for all delivered to the saints. Instead came a commendation of his capacity to think fresh thoughts. "It is rare indeed that a man of such precision of conviction will keep his mind open to the tuition of the Holy Spirit in such a degree. It takes grace to do that." If Rauschenbusch thought it took grace to defend the old faith, that was not said.[5]

Finally, the long-anticipated announcement came. In May 1911 Strong told the school's trustees that after one more year—by which time he would have completed forty years as president and professor of theology—he would retire. Strong made it clear that, although he would stay out of the search for a successor, he hoped the school would not change course: "What work I have done should not be undone in the years that follow." By this time Strong believed he knew how the school should move ahead, for five years earlier he had brought his son John to the faculty with the thinly veiled hope that young Strong would succeed him. Some now speculated openly that the trustees would select John Strong, but during the next several months it became evident that they would not do so and that a substantial bloc wanted new presidential leadership capable of moving the school to creative engagement with modern theological currents. The search process proved more difficult than had been expected, and Dean J. W. A. Stewart, who became acting president, stayed in the position for three years. Some of Rauschenbusch's colleagues talked about having Rauschenbusch assume the presidency, but the board of trustees was set upon bringing in someone from outside the faculty. Not until January 1915 did the board announce its selection of Dr. Clarence A. Barbour, an active member of the board who for many years had been pastor of one of Rochester's largest Baptist churches.[6]

After 1912 the liberal complexion of Rochester Theological Seminary became steadily more pronounced. For Augustus Hopkins Strong it was a discouraging sight; he complained to his son that "criticism and doubt has taken the place of faith and of prayer to a considerable extent," and in succeeding years his dissatisfaction grew. But for Rauschenbusch it was a time of ripe possibilities. A key step was the replacement of retiring faculty, and he had an active hand in helping bring most new appointees to the school. When George Cross, a Canadian scholar whose doctoral dissertation at the University of Chicago had focused on Schleiermacher, asked about the school's policies, Rauschenbusch assured Cross that the administration had never interfered in his work, and he successfully encouraged Cross to accept the invitation to come as Strong's successor in theology. When a new appointment was being considered for the German Department, Rauschenbusch wrote President Barbour that his longtime friend Frederick W. C. Meyer fruitfully combined warm devotion with a grasp of historical-critical methods learned from Chicago's President Harper; he had just what it would take "to wake those German boys up." And to his former student Justin Wroe Nixon he encouraged interest in an opening in Old Testament: "We want to breed prophets here, and . . . we need you for just that thing."[7]

In these years of transition for the school, Rauschenbusch increasingly occupied a place of respect and influence within the faculty. It derived partly from the renown he was winning outside. Seminary publications regularly carried news of his accomplishments and honors, and it was evident that none of the Rochester teachers had an influence as far-reaching as his. One of the school's leaders said publicly in 1915, "Dr. Rauschenbusch not only teaches church history but in a true sense is a maker of church history by his epoch-making addresses." The following year, when he was projecting a sabbatical leave, President Barbour encouraged Rauschenbusch not to publicize his absence lest potential students be deterred from enrolling at Rochester. Barbour knew that Rauschenbusch was a major drawing card for the seminary.

Rauschenbusch's place within the school was won equally by his skill and effectiveness as a teacher. During the two decades he taught there, repeated commendations came for his pedagogical talent. One observer reported in a local newspaper in 1903 that Rauschenbusch had the ability to make "history live before his students with all the interest of contemporary events." President Strong reported the following year, "Professor Rauschenbusch is scoring a brilliant success in History." An outside examining committee observed in 1906 that because of Walter Rauschenbusch seminarians "all alike seem to have given themselves *con amore* to the study of Church History." Comparable words continued to flow.[8]

Student evaluations of their teacher reflected appreciation of the same qualities of humor, clarity, and humility that outside audiences admired. But students were struck, too, by additional qualities that helped make enrollments in his elective courses usually the largest in the school. Among themselves students often spoke of him affectionately as "Rauschie." Some especially appreciated the simple, earnest prayers with which he began classes. Repeatedly, events and issues from earlier centuries were illumined by reference to present events and issues—which in turn gave new insight into the current scene. Students also appreciated the printed summaries of his lectures and wall charts of dates and events he prepared to help them grasp the vast field of church history. He was available to talk with them about their work through systematically scheduled individual and group consultations. They knew they could see him about other matters too. Many years later one Rochester graduate remembered that students "could go into his office at any time and he would pay the closest attention to what they were concerned about." A student wrote Rauschenbusch that he would "never forget the many times you have helped me when illness has hindered my work." Another recalled the day when his teacher's message had been suddenly clarified for him when, upon being late for class, Rauschenbusch explained he was delayed because he had tried "to right a saleslady's mistake without endangering her position." "Students all loved him," said a former student secretary. "He was really the most Christlike man that I ever knew."[9]

Faculty colleagues appreciated Rauschenbusch's skills as a teacher and his determination to pull his weight in the school despite many outside engagements. His course load normally was the same as others—seven or eight hours of class a week. He accepted no speaking invitations that would take him away during the middle of the week, for arrangements had been made for his classes to be conducted on Tuesdays, Wednesdays, and Thursdays. He was also active in the administrative matters that befall faculty members in small schools; most notably, he was one of three professors responsible for planning the school's shift in 1913 to a curriculum substantially embracing the elective system and introducing such novel subjects as psychology of religion and religious education.

Other professors also admired his determination to master the field of church history. He had been disappointed that when he began teaching the subject in 1902 he was forced to plunge into a full load of courses with scant preparation; a sabbatical leave, he believed, was due him so that he could repair the deficiencies in his knowledge. When the school granted him a leave during the 1907–8 academic year, no one was surprised that Rauschenbusch chose to spend the time in Germany. For the first three months the entire family was in Kiel, then for the remainder of the year they moved to Marburg (where Pauline and the children remained a second year so that the Rauschenbusch youngsters could become fluent in the language).[10]

Rauschenbusch delighted in introducing his German family and his American family to each other. There also were nostalgic trips to such places as Gütersloh, and for husband and wife there was a visit to Rome, where they were impressed by the earnestness with which Pope Pius X presided over a beatification ceremony in St. Peter's Basilica. For Rauschenbusch the chief academic objective was study of two areas in which he wanted to do more teaching and writing—the history of baptism and medieval Christianity. At Marburg most of his time was spent reading in the university library, but he also enjoyed contacts with members of the theological faculty. To friends in the United States he reported his fascination with the recognition by German scholars freshly exploring "the history of religions" that numerous traces of alien oriental religions made their way into early Christianity. He also declared his sympathy for German pastors who sought to preserve the faith of parishioners shaken by the results of university professors' aggressively scientific study of religion.

Most significant among his new Marburg acquaintances was Martin Rade, professor of theology and editor of *Die Christliche Welt*, a principal organ of the Christian social movement in Germany. The tie with Rade led to an invitation to publish an extensive article on the social awakening in the United States and to deliver a critique of German drinking habits at the 1908 annual session of the Evangelical Social Congress. There Rauschenbusch met the distinguished president of the Congress, Adolf von Harnack, whose seminal historical study of the hellenization of Christianity he had incorporated into his analysis of early Christian history. Through Rade and Harnack, Rauschenbusch became directly acquainted with the theological party that made Albrecht Ritschl its chief mentor, and though he never completely shed his dissatisfaction with the German theologian, some of his subsequent writings reflected a higher degree of Ritschlian influence than earlier writings. Through Rade and Harnack, Rauschenbusch also saw more of the German Christian social movement than he had observed before, and though he made no major issue of it, he expressed disappointment that so little had been done to generate church support for German socialists' championing of workers' rights.[11]

Rochester faculty associates respected Rauschenbusch not only for his work as a historian but also for his role in teaching Christians to discover the social dimensions of their faith. Often the school's commitment to the church's social mission was expressed in ways that heartened him. A key early note was struck in 1903 with the appointment of J. W. A. Stewart, the school's first dean, to teach Christian ethics; in subsequent years Stewart and Rauschenbusch were close friends, and Stewart's courses reflected many themes articulated in Rauschenbusch's writings. From year to year, too, outside speakers brought to the school by Presidents Strong and Barbour included leaders of the social movement. The clearest signal of the faculty's and administration's commitment to social Christianity was the new curriculum introduced in 1913. It included one elective course offered in each of the four academic divisions (biblical, historical, theological, and practical) on some aspect of the church's social mission.[12]

Anguish arose over his relations with some colleagues during the last several years at Rochester Theological Seminary, but for most of the two decades Rauschenbusch served there, he considered it an ideal base for his professional career. He had been linked to the school since birth, and he did not hide his love for it. "I miss it all more than I can tell," he wrote from Marburg in 1907, "this press of ardent and noble life in the dear old Seminary." As the years passed, evidence mounted that students who took his courses not only loved him but embraced the causes he held dear. This brought perhaps the deepest satisfaction of all. "I rejoice," he wrote about his students in 1909, "that we can all multiply ourselves in those whom we raise and who take up our work when we have to drop it." Hundreds of Rochester graduates were proud to carry forward their professor's work and to see their school later honor him by establishing an annual lectureship in his name.

There was another reason he felt comfortable at the school and never sought another position. Rochester Theological Seminary's conservative tradition and its hesitant move toward liberalism reflected well the mind of American Protestantism in these years, and Rauschenbusch both respected that mind and wanted to help reshape it. Some liberals, he believed, were moving too far from Christian foundations, and he was pleased to be part of a tradition that kept the foundations squarely in view. Also, he believed his effort to awaken the church to its social mission was enhanced by association with a school that, as a microcosm of American Protestantism, provided him a laboratory for research into the mystery of continuity and change. If he could develop ideas and arguments that passed Rochester's testing procedures, they might well succeed in the national arena.[13]

When Rauschenbusch completed his first year as a history teacher, one colleague complimented him for making the "dry bones of Church History live." The new historian realized that although history courses had always been included in the school's curriculum, most students did not look forward to them. In Germany the discipline of church history had shared in the nineteenth-century rejuvenation of all historical investigation, but in the United States there was little of that excitement. Rauschenbusch believed the problem was posed partly by the culture: This young nation contained few visible reminders of a historical tradition. "We have very little historical feeling," he observed, "because we are not on historical soil," nor does the American penchant for practicality and immediate results place a high premium upon historical study. But the problem has a religious root as well, he added. American Protestants are conditioned to value the Bible and preaching but not history; they look at it "the way people looked at the Bible before the Reformation, . . . as something needless to learn." Thus, a major issue for Rochester's professor of church history was to make students recognize the value of their history courses. This, he saw, was part of the larger task of helping American Protestants learn to appreciate the Christian past as a resource for their present religious life.[14]

His approach built upon commitments he knew were present already in most of his students. He explained that those who truly desire to be citizens of the modern era will become thoroughly acquainted with the scientific-historical methods that are a distinctive badge of current scholarship. Those who want to understand Scripture will learn to view biblical figures and events in relation to the total social and religious environment of the ancient world. Those who want to distinguish between what is enduring and what is ephemeral in Christian teachings will develop an awareness of how doctrines have evolved across the centuries. Those who want to avoid being trapped in sectarian narrowness will learn to prize the spiritual treasures developed in other churches. And those who want to be wise architects of social change will seek to discover the recurring patterns by which communities shape the lives of their members.

Rauschenbusch urged students to accept the historiographical methods that he had learned at Gütersloh and that now were practiced widely in American university circles. The study they undertake must be critical; they must not accept claims about the past without rigorous testing, especially by reference to the sources. And their study must be scientific; it must seek cause-and-effect connections between earlier and later events. But he also believed that scientific-critical methods alone were inadequate for the church historian. Some scholars had become so enamored of the new historiography that they made little attempt to bring religious commitments into their practice of the discipline. Rauschenbusch thought this was a mistake. Better, he believed, to combine one's reasoning processes as a historian with one's faith commitments as a Christian. In fact, it was the way Rauschenbusch's fundamental religious perspectives guided his interpretation of the data of Christian history that gave zest to his courses and made his work, according to one recent observer, unique among American church historians of his generation.[15]

The key to his distinctive approach was the set of christological convictions that came from his Pietist-Evangelical upbringing and were applied to the past in the style of Neander. The lecture notes first prepared for students in 1905 began by declaring, "With the life of Jesus Christ a new type of life and a new creative force have entered humanity." Christianity is not principally about ideas, institutions, or feelings; it is about this life that entered the ebb and flow of human history with the intent of changing all subsequent history. It is clear, Rauschenbusch continued, that "in moving through history this power has transformed individuals, created organized fellowship, and affected all life." The task of historians is to tell the story of this palpable, manifold impact. Within their purview historians include what has happened to the "organized fellowship"—the church—but they also look beyond it to the total impact of Christianity, assessing the ways and the degree to which Christianity has accomplished its purpose "to regenerate all human relations and transform natural humanity into Christian humanity." By tradition these scholars are called church historians (and that was the title Rauschenbusch proudly bore), but in actuality they know that the "history of Christianity . . . is larger than Church History."

Rauschenbusch's delineation of the role of church historians continued with the claim that they must focus upon two features of Christianity's interaction with the world. First, they must trace the actual effects of Christianity upon the great variety of individuals, nations, and civilizations it has sought to transform. The religion has had such a great impact upon three successive civilizations—the Greco-Roman, the Teutonic, and the modern—that they define the major epochs into which the field should be divided for purposes of analysis. The church historian also must tell the story of how the "transforming force" that issued from Jesus Christ has been affected by its alliances, for the cultural worlds Christianity has sought to remake have repeatedly introduced "processes of change and adulteration" into the religion itself. But because the power working within Christianity is divine, said Rauschenbusch, its contamination has never been absolute; instead it has repeatedly generated fresh movements for reform—indeed, Christianity's "divine vitality is proved by its perpetual tendency and power of self-purification." A key task of historians, then, is to trace and interpret Christianity's dramatic swings between adulteration and purification.

But how does the historian distinguish between an adulterated Christianity and a purified one? According to what standard is this judgment made? Here again Rauschenbusch appealed to his fundamental religious commitment. "The spirit of Jesus," he said, "is the ultimate canon by which every historical personality, institution, or movement must be judged, and our personal absorption of his mind and spirit is the ultimate qualification for a really useful study of the history of the Church." Rauschenbusch's attempt to clarify this hermeneutical principle put him on relatively unfamiliar and unexplored ground. Certain things, however, were clear for him. First, he believed that the New Testament is an essentially credible record of the impact Jesus made upon the first community of men and women who sought to follow him. The New Testament's accounts of Jesus' life, as well as of his followers' corporate and individual lives, provide a lasting, normative picture of the new life he embodied and continues to impart to those who follow him. Next, Rauschenbusch believed that because the church embraces the Bible as its sacred book, "it carries a norm through history by which its present condition can always be tested." In fact, he added, "every reformatory movement has thrust the New Testament in the face of a degenerate Church" and allowed it to rediscover its true self there.[16]

Rauschenbusch's strong interest in early Christianity was more than a matter of a historian's preoccupation with origins. He wanted truly to be a *Baptist* historian, and he believed the principal mark of his tradition was its advocacy of the original religion of Jesus and its opposition to every departure from that core. Looking at the biblical records from this vantage, he concluded, "the Christianity of Jesus was democratic and fraternal in its organization, simple and spiritual in its worship, undogmatic and ethical in its ideas." Looking at developments of subsequent centuries, he saw Christianity becoming "clerical and hierarchical in organization, sacramental and super-stitious in its worship, speculative and dogmatic in its ideas." Given this Baptist key to the past, the entire subsequent sweep of Christian history fell into focus as a struggle between forces that distanced Christians from Jesus and those that returned them to him. It also encouraged Rauschenbusch to view his own time as a new era of re-form: "Christianity is growing less clerical, less ceremonial, less dog-matic; more democratic, more spiritual, more ethical." This "eman-cipation," he said, gives Baptists an enormous responsibility and opportunity. They must become the vanguard of modern Christianity's purification by recovering and championing the fundamentals that lie deep in their heritage.[17]

For Rauschenbusch the Baptist, this mission led in two directions. One was toward his own spiritual kinspeople: He must help Baptists recover the essentials of faith and reject their own compromises of it. A four-part article entitled "Why I Am a Baptist" was his major published contribution to this effort. There he argued that even though all Christian churches have the same basic aim, "to bring the human soul into saving contact with God through Christ and to secure for it the knowledge and power of a holy life," none places so few hindrances in the way of that task as the Baptist church. At their best, Baptists know it is not creed, ritual, or priesthood that is central but one's own direct and transforming experience of God. However, Rauschen-busch acknowledged that many Baptists had compromised their foundational principles—some by allowing shallow emotionalism to substitute for life-changing experience of God, some by letting the Bible impose law and bind thought rather than impart a spirit and awaken thought, and others by making worship more a matter of repeating ritual than of renewing love for God and neighbor. Whatever the fault, Baptists can correct it by returning to the New Testament and using it as their vehicle for "hewing our way back to original Christianity." It was clear to Rauschenbusch that as they did so, they would rediscover Jesus' social mission and claim it as their own.

Rauschenbusch's understanding of his mission as a Baptist led him also to active concern for Christians of other denominations. To-ward some this required a critical word, for he believed they retained compromises made centuries ago with non-Christian patterns of thought, worship, and organization; regrettably these churches' com-promises hinder their members' access to God. Most guilty was the Roman Catholic church. He asked, Has Rome not "interposed a lot of man-made ceremonies between the soul and God, so that thousands who punctiliously go through all this ritual never experience God in fact, and are kept from doing so by the very things in which they are taught that they meet him?" But Lutherans err, too, with their excessive reliance upon confessional statements—and Episcopalians, with their reliance upon priests. Baptists must fearlessly identify such compromises and "speak the truth in love" to the churches perpetuating them in order to provoke them toward reform.[18]

Other churches, fortunately, have recovered more of primitive Christianity, and Rauschenbusch believed that Baptists must take a different stance toward them. He maintained that six major Protestant denominations played major roles in shaping the American ethos, in the course of which they were also shaped by American life. Through that shared history these bodies increasingly have come to resemble each other in polity, worship, and thought. The groups constituting this "true American Church"—Baptists, Presbyterians, Reformed, Disciples, Methodists, and Congregationalists—now have an opportunity to heal the splits of the past and lead the way to Christian unity.

He explained that most Christian denominations arose from great theological and social differences that have lost their earlier power. Today denominational divisions are "kept alive artificially" and at a high cost. Theological differentia are so magnified that they divert attention from the basics of Christianity shared across denominational lines; and denominations that struggle to perpetuate separate, competing institutions and ministries forfeit the opportunity to work together for a more effective mission in the world.

The prophetic Baptist ecumenist said that a time may come when the six denominations will have converged sufficiently to allow them to effect "formal union." He concluded that for now their task is the critical preparatory one of recognizing the bonds already present and of finding fresh ways to share their faith and witness.[19]

Rauschenbusch taught church history for sixteen years and was a prolific author, but he wrote no book and few articles about history. He explained in 1913 that most of the six books he hoped to write were on historical issues and that had he been able to undertake them earlier they would have enhanced his scholarly prominence. The one he most wanted to write, he told a friend in 1917, would allow him "to do for Church History what has been done for the Bible by a great number of writers in recent years—to give it a social interpretation, to see it from the Kingdom point of view, to view the Church not as an end in itself, but to judge it by what it has done for mankind." None of his historical books was completed because always the first claim upon Rauschenbusch's writing remained the present demands of Jesus and the Kingdom. Nevertheless, as a conscientious teacher of history, he spent long hours carefully preparing lectures and, for some of his courses, making detailed outline notes available for students. The surviving unpublished documents provide a glimpse of his treatment of the four realms of Christian history that interested him most.[20]

The realm engaging him chiefly was the evolution of Christianity in the first several centuries after Christ. Like many Protestant historians, Rauschenbusch found here both Christianity's golden age and its most crippling fall. Drawing heavily upon the writings of Harnack, he contended that from primitive Christianity's alliance with Greco-Roman culture came the Catholic church. There was, he said, a "profound difference" between its Christianity and that of the first century. But more than most Baptist scholars, Rauschenbusch acknowledged that there also were "elements of good" in the transition. Greatly to its credit the church accepted its mission to the Greco-Roman world and the need to adapt itself to that culture. "It had to speak the language of its age to lead its age." And the Catholic church did achieve major successes in its transformationist mission. Polytheism, nature worship, and dualism were overcome; and ethical monotheism became "the religion of civilized humanity," which, he noted, ranks as "a first-class achievement in the history of religions."

He also acknowledged that internal developments within the Catholic church, although obscuring many marks of apostolic Christianity, had served vital functions:

> Orthodoxy cramped, but it also protected against rank emotionalism and erratic speculation. The Catholic Church departed from primitive Christianity, but it saved Christianity from going still farther into Gnosticism. Local organization meant efficiency; Catholic unity was a noble expression of the larger Christian fellowship. . . . In spite of rigidity and ossification, there was still a strong pulsation of the Christian spirit and an abundance of beautiful Christian characters.

Most significant, the Catholic church established normative Scriptures that preserved the vision of its true character for all subsequent centuries. So, despite the departure from its origins, the church "enshrined the record of those origins, and thereby kept itself reformable." No church with this scriptural endowment is beyond its reform-producing potential. There was hope, Rauschenbusch believed, that even the churches that had strayed most might yet travel the road to reform.[21]

The second major focus of Rauschenbusch's historical interest was the sixteenth-century Reformation. In lectures on this subject he looked first to preparatory movements that had broken out earlier in such prophetic figures as Francis of Assisi and John Wyclif. They recognized that Christianity was compromised, but the time was not yet ripe for its self-purification. The fact that religious reform began in the sixteenth century, and not earlier, illustrated one of Rauschenbusch's key convictions as a historian: Religion is so connected with the total fabric of society that no major religious shift can occur without an accompanying upheaval throughout the social structure. By the early sixteenth century, thanks to profound political, economic, and intellectual changes sweeping through Europe, the stage was set for a great religious reformer.

Martin Luther's work, however consequential for subsequent Christian history, did not constitute the most important development of the Reformation era, because he and the other major Protestant reformers remained attached to much of traditional religion. In Rauschenbusch's eyes the truly heroic figures of the Reformation were the Anabaptists, because more than other Protestants they recognized the church's failures and courageously sought a restoration of primitive Christianity. For these "radical Protestants," Christianity centered in believers' direct experience of God, their disciplined ethical life, and their striving to be a church filled with the Holy Spirit, uncontaminated by alliances with the state and committed to a religious transformation of social life.

Rauschenbusch regretted that most Catholic and Protestant historians had treated Anabaptist zealots at Münster as representative of the whole movement, and he welcomed the correction of that caricature by some contemporary historians. As a result of their revisionist labors, one could see these embattled and misunderstood Christians in their original splendor. "The Anabaptists took Jesus Christ as their leader and the Holy Spirit as their inward light, and that combination raised them with a single uplift far beyond their time and gave their movement a prophetic power and grandeur." Rauschenbusch believed that although the Anabaptists made no notable impact upon their own time, they stood as a beacon pointing twentieth-century Christians to God's intention for the whole church.[22]

The third major realm of his historical interest was American church history. He believed that too few Protestant historians had yet recognized the importance of the United States as "an unexampled proving-ground of organized religion" and as the place where older religious bodies had modernized themselves. Here they were impeded far less than in Europe by the hand of the state and the weight of tradition. Rauschenbusch's lectures in his American church history course traced the evolution of various denominations in this benign climate. He observed that Baptists had fared especially well, both through their numerical growth and through their impact upon the nation's religious life. Largely because of Baptist influence, the "right of private judgment in religious matters has become an axiom of American thought. Most of our denominations have accepted the Christian principle of democracy for their church organization. . . . Sacramentalism is almost gone; conscious spiritual experience is everywhere recognized as the great aim of religion. Thus the essential principles of Baptist life and thought are triumphant." He believed it was this triumph that had brought major denominations to the threshold of far-reaching new steps toward Protestant unity.[23]

Rauschenbusch called the fourth realm of his special historical interest "the history of social redemption." Although he did not inaugurate a course with this title until 1915, its major themes had been present since the early years of his teaching and were sketched in two major books. He explained that the intent of the course was to determine how the great social hope of early Christianity declined, and how it reappeared in modern times. His major thesis was that the failure of Christians to pursue "the social redemption of the race on earth" constitutes an aberration from the original genius of Christianity and that a return to Christian origins must include a recovery of this great aim.

More than a dozen historical causes for this failure were identified. Some could be accounted for by pressures from the early church's hostile environment. The mighty Roman empire, for example, appeared too vast and too corrupt to be changed by a small band of Christians. Some came in the form of the impact of alien forces upon the mind of the early church. The dualistic, otherworldly complexion of ancient philosophical and religious movements, for example, was allowed to shift attention from Jesus' purpose to make God's will "done on earth as it is in heaven." Other causes were associated with the Catholic church's overreaction to perceived threats. For instance, intense preoccupation with defending and building the church deflected Christians' energy from the task of aiding the Kingdom's growth in the wider society. And tragically, as later Christians made the church of the first three centuries the norm for their own life and thought, they found there confirmation rather than rebuke of their failure to attempt social transformation.[24]

Rauschenbusch was convinced that just as it had taken centuries for the aberration to develop, so a correction had been evolving for over four centuries. The decisive early steps had been taken in the sixteenth century, and numerous others had followed in the last one hundred years. God's providential presence had been active in such diverse but complementary forces as socialism's commitment to alleviate the suffering of the masses, the social sciences' recognition of the plasticity of human life, biblical scholars' rediscovery of the historical Jesus and the Kingdom, and Christians' awakening to the ethical character of their religion. Through it all, Christianity was becoming more Christian—thus better fitted for its social mission than ever before.[25]

To later generations, Walter Rauschenbusch's optimism about the churches' turnabout appeared excessive, but it can not be gainsaid that he was living in the midst of profound changes within Christianity, one of which was a prodigious burst of social engagement. He repeatedly said there was no guarantee the churches would rise to the historic opportunity to give their social mission its due. One thing was certain, however: he was ready to commit all his talent and energy to the task of helping make this happen.

CHAPTER 10

"APOSTLE OF A MIGHTY GOSPEL"

Requests for Walter Rauschenbusch's services as a speaker continued to come from fellow Rochesterians for the rest of his life, but after his return from Germany in 1908 he was able to accept fewer and fewer of them. Likewise, though students and faculty colleagues found him available for classes and conferences during the middle of the week, at other times he was not as available as before. Fame had come, bringing with it repeated demands upon his time from Americans eager to learn his views about the nation's ills and the steps necessary for health. Increasingly, he was either on the road, taking his message all over the United States, or in his study, writing the essays and books that were to extend his impact to other circles, other generations, and other nations.

The event that catapulted Rauschenbusch into national prominence was the publication in April 1907 of his *Christianity and the Social Crisis*. The book had undergone a gestation period of sixteen years. Following criticisms by Schmidt and Williams of "Revolutionary Christianity" in the early 1890s, he had continued to believe such a book was needed, but two attempts at revision failed to produce a manuscript that satisfied him. Then, for two months during the summer of 1905, while he and his family vacationed at nearby Lake Canandaigua, he started over. Some sections of the fresh draft incorporated earlier papers and lecture notes, but most were new, the result of his recent reading of German, British, and American authors

157

and of his own maturing reflection. The following summer, spent with his family in Ontario (near the spot on which he built a cottage in 1908), he returned to the manuscript and finally brought it to the point that he was ready to submit it to a publisher.

Rauschenbusch later described the anxiety that dogged the entire process of writing. He believed his message made this a "dangerous book," one likely to generate "a good deal of anger and resentment" and perhaps even to jeopardize his job. But as at other turning points in his life, he took courage from the conviction that his labor was "for the Lord Christ and the People" and that God would strengthen him for so important a task. He said, too, that renewal had come particularly while writing about the social aims of Jesus: "I often was overwhelmed with feelings of loyalty and love for him. He seemed so great to me."[1]

When the Rauschenbusches returned to Rochester in August 1906, Walter sent a sample chapter to the Macmillan Company. In October word came from George Brett, president of the large publishing house, that he wanted to see the entire manuscript. The following month Brett wrote that it had been accepted and could be published with few alterations. Now decisions had to be made about such matters as a title for the book and compensation for the author. Rauschenbusch sent a list of eleven titles that had occurred to him (including "The Forgotten Purpose of Christianity," "The Social Ideal of Christianity, Its Defeat and Revival," and "Revolutionary Christianity"); the one agreed upon was his first choice—"Christianity and the Social Crisis."

After considering the two payment options presented by Brett— either a 10 percent royalty on all books sold, or half the profit after all publication and marketing costs were met—Rauschenbusch chose the latter, for it promised a greater return if the book did well, and despite his worries about its effect, he believed prospects were good for a large sale. In March 1907 Macmillan sent the embarrassing news that printing had been delayed because the shipment of paper for the book had been lost in transit. Finally, in April 1907, just before the Rauschenbusches sailed for sabbatical leave in Germany, *Christianity and the Social Crisis* appeared.[2]

It was a book of extraordinary power. The appeal resulted partly from the stylistic grace Rauschenbusch already had demonstrated hundreds of times: the compactness and clarity of his prose, the telling use of metaphor and wit, the vigorous pace of his argument. Even more, it came from the personal charisma that had endeared him to many and that were evident in chapter after chapter. "Seldom have I read a book," wrote Dean Stewart, "which was so truly the precious lifeblood of its author, as this book is. The splendid intellect, the warm heart, the keen conscience, the wide knowledge, the deep conviction, the religious faith and hope, the daring and chivalrous spirit, the lofty idealism, so well known to the friends of the author, are all here." Readers sensed they were encountering both a message and a man— a message that had been lived before it had been written. Rauschenbusch explained in the opening pages that he had produced the book to discharge a debt to workingpeople in New York he pastored for eleven years.

> I shared their life as well as I then knew and used up the early strength of my life in their service. In recent years my work has been turned into other channels, but I have never ceased to feel that I owe help to the plain people who were my friends. If this book in some far-off way helps to ease the pressure that bears them down and increases the forces that bear them up, I shall meet the Master of my life with better confidence (p. xv).

It was a winsome word and a skillful setting of the stage.[3]

The chief force of *Christianity and the Social Crisis* lay in the cogency of Rauschenbusch's plea for Christians to undertake the task of creating a new social order. He built his case upon three arguments. For the first (which consumed half the book) he marshaled substantial biblical and historical data to push Christians to rethink their understanding of the Christian life. It was not enough, he believed, to attempt to persuade them to build a sense of social responsibility upon deficient theological foundations. Instead, those foundations must be reconceived, so that involvement in social mission could be seen to flow directly from them. As always for Rauschenbusch, the key to this reform was helping Christians realize that to follow Jesus means recovering his social purpose and making it their own.

He explained that Jesus' purpose continued the inspired mission of the early prophets of Israel, who strove to raise the collective life of their people into the paths of justice and mercy willed by God. Jesus' way of fulfilling that mission was to embody a wholly new style of being human. He lived a life of unconditional love for God and all God's children, proclaimed the coming of a Kingdom in which the same quality of love eventually triumphs over all obstacles, and called every person to embrace Kingdom ways and struggle like him for their realization in the world.

But if this was the character of original Christianity, how did later Christianity fall so far short of it? Rauschenbusch the historian answered in considerable detail, explaining that Jesus' mission was compromised by alien influences upon his followers and that for centuries the church had been in retreat from its proper mission, serving Christ with a flawed vision and a halting march. But he also stressed that through the mysterious movement of God in human affairs, recent developments in both church and world had brought a promising change. Christians at last were beginning to recognize that to serve Christ they must attempt to construct a social order in which the ways of the Kingdom prevail.

The second part of Rauschenbusch's case argued that substantial rewards for the world and for the church could issue from a recovery of the church's social mission. In the United States and the whole of Western civilization, he said, such recovery might mean deliverance from a threatening collapse like that which befell Rome centuries ago. The key problem, he explained, is that Western industrialized society has become dominated by an economic system that victimizes everyone it touches. Workers receive less than they deserve for their labor and suffer the loss of health and dignity, while owners take more than they deserve and suffer the loss of those qualities that make life most human. Between the rich and poor, moreover, capitalism has created a chasm that continues to widen, even to the point of portending class war.

Rauschenbusch argued that Western civilization's best chance of staving off collapse lies in the emergence of a moral vision that causes people to perceive the immensity of the crisis and to make a determined effort to build a just and humane society. A church awakened to its social mission, he contended, is the only source of such an energizing vision. "It is either a revival of social religion or the deluge" (p. 286).

He went on to argue that such a revival also will serve the church's interest, for the social crisis has damaged Christianity, most grievously by alienating the poor from churches they perceive as captive to the rich and by blunting the Christian message to make it palatable to the affluent. As Christians sense afresh their responsibility for society, they will recognize the need to free the church from this cultural bondage and recenter it upon Jesus and the Kingdom. They will work to "rechristianize the church" (p. 337) so that the gospel message can be unleashed in all its transforming power.

The third part of Rauschenbusch's case sought to persuade aroused Christians that effective corrective action was within reach, especially for the expanding class of professional and business people who constituted a large segment of the Protestant churches' membership. The Pietist-Evangelical heritage lodged deep in Rauschenbusch's soul made him insist that most important of all the corrective steps is a spiritual regeneration that awakens individuals to their complicity in the sins of society and to a commitment to social reform. For the regenerated preacher this will lead to a proclaiming of Jesus' gospel of the Kingdom in the knowledge that "if he really follows the mind of Christ, he will be likely to take the side of the poor in most issues" (p. 361). For the regenerated layperson, it will mean steadily seeking to extend Kingdom ways in daily work, there modeling more just and humane patterns of thinking and behaving.

Laity and clergy alike, he continued, must recognize that direction of the movement toward a new society presently lies chiefly in the hands of the working class, and that for them socialism holds the messianic promise once enjoyed by religion. Rauschenbusch saw the likelihood of a grim struggle ahead between the haves and have-nots, and he argued that, as that struggle unfolds, aroused Christians must use their ties with both sides to help shape the outcome. "All that we as Christians can do is to ease the struggle and hasten the victory of the right by giving faith and hope to those who are down, and quickening the sense of justice with those who are in power, so that they will not harden their hearts and hold Israel in bondage, but will 'let the people go' " (p. 411). This mediating role—characterized by work in both camps to seek change in each and build bridges between them—was actually the style of Rauschenbusch's own ministry, and he acknowledged that those who venture it must be prepared for misunderstanding and anger to be heaped upon them from both sides. But they undertake the task like sowers, confident that God and history will bring their labors to fruition.

Here was a conception of Christianity and its earthly task quite different from what most Christians held, and Rauschenbusch was understandably nervous about how the book would be received. During his first several weeks in Germany on sabbatical, he waited anxiously for news. The first word was a letter of praise from Rochester: Dean Stewart wrote that he thought so highly of the book he was advising everyone to buy it. A Rochester friend reported that people at the seminary "all act and speak as if a big baby boy was born to the faculty." Augustus Hopkins Strong said he believed the book would be "as epoch-making as Henry George's *Progress and Poverty*. . . . Church people are going to read it, as they never read Henry George, and it is going to do much to show Christians their duty." The book's one serious flaw, he added, was that Rauschenbusch consistently took "the side of the underdog, regardless of the fact that the underdog sometimes deserves a pounding."[4]

Strong was right in his prediction about the popularity of *Christianity and the Social Crisis*. In 1911 Rauschenbusch was told that during the last three years more copies of his book had been sold than any other religious volume. Macmillan repeatedly did fresh printings, producing thirteen by February 1912. In all, some 50,000 copies were sold, and about $5,000 came to the author in royalties. Scores of reviewers on both sides of the Atlantic praised the book. Hundreds of letters expressing appreciation came to Rauschenbusch, and many sought counsel from the author about how to implement his message. In 1909 Ray Stannard Baker concluded on the basis of conversations with religious leaders throughout the nation that *Christianity and the Social Crisis* had done more than any other book to instruct the new generation of social Christians. Rauschenbusch was particularly pleased it had taken hold among such a broad spectrum of groups; in 1912 he wrote a brief autobiographical sketch for a publicist, noting that his book "has been used as a textbook in conservative institutions, prescribed by the Methodists for their young ministers, and is also advertised and sold by the Socialists." Years later Harry Emerson Fosdick spoke for multitudes of Protestant ministers, saying the book "struck home so poignantly on the intelligence and conscience . . . that it ushered in a new era in Christian thought and action."[5]

Not all responses were laudatory, however. Some Episcopal reviewers were miffed by his insistence that sacramentalism was a vestige of heathen religion impeding the rise of a Christian social consciousness. Several writers for New York newspapers (which Rauschenbusch believed consistently voiced the views of big business) rejected both his critique of capitalism and his call for a Christian social mission. Two sociologists at the University of Chicago praised the book but went on to make important criticisms. Dean Albion Small thought Rauschenbusch had inadequately defined the particular variety of socialism he endorsed, and Charles Henderson argued that he had not sufficiently acknowledged either the good fruit of capitalism or the effectiveness of current governmental efforts to correct its abuses.[6]

Rauschenbusch had hoped his message would make a positive impact in Baptist circles, and the criticisms that stung most came from there. An ominous word reached him in Germany that the Cincinnati-based chairman of the seminary's trustees objected vigorously to the book and that other protests had been received by the school. But both President Strong and Dean Stewart stood up for Rauschenbusch, and no action was taken against him. Other rumbles continued to be heard from Cincinnati, however. The *Journal and Messenger*, a conservative Baptist paper published there, carried a review calling Rauschenbusch "a Socialist of the German school" and charging that he had imposed socialist doctrine upon the New Testament. A German

Baptist friend claimed in another paper that Rauschenbusch had ignored biblical teaching about Christ's sacrificial death and his second coming to usher in a new age. A strong premillennialist case was argued against him by I. M. Haldeman, a prominent New York Baptist minister, in a forty-two-page pamphlet published in 1911. True believers, he said, will heed the biblical word to turn away from such teachers of false doctrine.[7]

The criticisms upset Rauschenbusch, but he was undeterred and took steps to expand the book's impact. In his original negotiations with Macmillan he had kept control of all matters regarding translations, and he soon was attempting to arrange for editions in several European languages. The effort did not bear the intended fruit, but his correspondence and conversations led Rauschenbusch to warm ties with such European stalwarts of social Christianity as Elie Gounelle, Wilfred Monod, Leonhard Ragaz, and Hermann Kutter. When a missionary professor at the Doshisha University in Japan asked if copies could be given to English-reading Japanese ministers, Rauschenbusch arranged with James E. Franklin, a wealthy banker in St. Louis, for a hundred copies to be sent. Franklin was also the benefactor making possible gifts to a larger set of key readers. Through his generosity, two thousand seminarians received the book in 1911. The gift had been made, explained Rauschenbusch in a cover letter, with the hope that it would help each of the young ministers become "an apostle of a mighty Gospel that is to revolutionize both men and institutions, and to turn the anarchy and sinfulness of our present life into a kingdom of peace and love." It was a treasured gift from a man rapidly becoming known as just such an apostle; it was also a shrewd planting of seed in fallow ground.[8]

The ground was fallow because Americans were passing through the period of self-criticism and hopeful reform called the Progressive Era. Rauschenbusch later acknowledged that *Christianity and the Social Crisis* had appeared at the "psychological moment" that allowed it to become "an expression of what thousands were feeling." His experience in New York City and Rochester had taught him both what Americans were feeling and also how to speak their language of indignation and hope. Although considerable theological and historical learning underlay his message, it was delivered with such verve that Rauschenbusch enjoyed a hearing with the American middle class that was rarely matched among the scholars of his generation. He meant his message to be a religious one from beginning to end, and he was particularly grateful, he said later, when people told him "that it gave them a new experience of religion and a new feeling about Christ." It was a message addressed to the soul of the nation, in the great tradition of the Prophets of Israel and the Puritans of New England—and a succession of other prophetic figures who periodically arose in American life. It told all who would listen that a decisive moment in their national life was at hand, called them to repentance and reform, assured them that God's power was available to assist the awakened ones, and warned that the consequences of success and failure alike were monumental.[9]

The message made no promise of easy victory. Rauschenbusch knew that sensitive attention to the record of the past forbade that: "History laughs at the optimistic illusion that 'nothing can stand in the way of human progress' " (p. 279), and he added that a thousand years hence "some Gibbon of Mongol race" may chronicle the decline and fall of Western civilization (p. 285). And though less was said about it here than in his other books, he knew too the continuing power of sin and evil. Nevertheless, the dominant tone of Rauschenbusch's message plainly was optimistic. And why not? In these years missionaries were demonstrating Christianity's power to influence religions and cultures around the world. Christians in Rochester and across the nation were addressing long-deferred tasks of social reform. Optimism was in the air, and Rauschenbusch knew that if the church was to speak effectively to the age it must speak the language of the age. To be sure, there was a risk of acculturation, but there also was a risk of irrelevance, and he judged the latter more dangerous.

The message was indeed optimistic, and he sought to make it an authentic Christian optimism. No claim was made that righteous men and women either can construct the Kingdom by themselves or command the divine blessing upon their social striving. God, insisted Rauschenbusch, is "the real creator of the Kingdom" (p. 63), and he added that in human affairs there can be only "an approximation to a perfect social order. The Kingdom of God is always but coming" (p. 421). But God wills human effort to spread Kingdom ways, and God uses that effort to overcome resistance and accomplish the divine intention. On this point, Rauschenbusch was making an important theological statement and raising an important theological issue. He was in line with earlier generations of Christians (some called "Semi-Pelagians," others "Arminians") who taught that divine grace and human agency cooperate for the transformation of individual lives. That position now was pushed a step further to include social institutions within the scope of God's transformationist intention and to affirm divine-human cooperation as the means of accomplishing it.

Walter Rauschenbusch believed that the message of Jesus Christ indeed is a "mighty Gospel," for it proclaims God's gracious intention to transform individuals and institutions alike and to use the faithful labors of men and women to move toward whatever final outcome God has in store for the human drama.

A chief strength of Rauschenbusch's "first book" (often called this by those who did not realize he had written earlier books in German) was the comprehensiveness of his call for religious and social reform. Increasingly, however, he saw that individual parts of the argument needed greater development. Consequently, his lecturing and writing over the next decade undertook such elaboration, some of it by attempting to refocus the devotional life of Christians, some by clarifying their social task, and some by building theological foundations for the work of reform.

He had contended in *Christianity and the Social Crisis* that "a new type of Christian" must be raised up—men and women whose love for God is expressed in love for God's children and social engagement on their behalf. He now saw that a key arena in which he must address this issue was prayer, for most written prayers bequeathed from earlier centuries reflected a piety that fostered only minimally the yoking of love for God with love for neighbor. His own private prayers, as well as those he offered in public worship, had long united the two, and in 1909 the opportunity came to take a major step toward teaching the church this vision of prayer.

The push in this direction came from an unexpected source. Editors of *The American Magazine*, who had opened the pages of their popular monthly to such reformist figures as Ray Stannard Baker, Jane Addams, Ida Tarbell, and William Allen White, were impressed by Rauschenbusch's book and invited him to write something for the magazine. John S. Phillips, the publisher, favored a life of Jesus, but when Rauschenbusch declined, it was agreed he would write a series of prayers. The first two appeared in December 1909, along with an appreciative profile by Baker. Throughout 1910 a new prayer was strikingly set on the frontispiece of each issue.

In the summer of 1910, officials at Pilgrim Press, a Congregational publishing house, asked if the prayers could be collected and published in book form. Rauschenbusch responded positively, quickly composed additional prayers, wrote an introductory essay entitled "The Social Meaning of the Lord's Prayer," and rushed the material to Pilgrim Press in time for the little book to appear several weeks before Christmas. The publisher made *For God and the People: Prayers of the Social Awakening* an unusually handsome volume. Its pages were edged in gold, and each prayer was framed with an intricate border in fifteenth-century style. Later Rauschenbusch acknowledged it was his "favorite book." Composing the prayers had been an enjoyable chore, for they expressed the movement of his soul over the last two decades and allowed him to utilize the poetic style at which he was a master. Most important, they gave him access to the deep reaches of the human spirit where he knew the decisive battles for reform were won and lost.[10]

There were fifty-eight prayers altogether (including two by Mornay Williams, a friend from the Brotherhood of the Kingdom). They were preceded by a compact exposition of the Lord's Prayer in which Rauschenbusch claimed Jesus' words as the model for all Christian prayer. That prayer, he said, is "the purest expression of the mind of Jesus" (p. 15) and demonstrates his dedication to "the ultimate perfection of the common life of humanity on this earth and . . . the divine revolution which is to bring that about" (p. 18). None of Rauschenbusch's essays captured the heart of his message more lucidly and incisively.

As with Jesus' own prayer, the themes of Rauschenbusch's collected prayers varied. In some, there was reverent affirmation of the holy God and grateful acknowledgment of dependence upon the divine mercies:

> For the Fatherhood of God
> O Thou great Father of us all, we rejoice that at last we know thee. All our soul within us is glad because we need no longer cringe before thee as slaves of holy fear, seeking to appease thine anger by sacrifice and self-inflicted pain, but may come like little children, trustful and happy, to the God of love. . . .

> For This World
> O God we thank thee for this universe, our great home; for its vastness and its riches, and for the manifoldness of the life which teems upon it and of which we are part. . . . Grant us, we pray thee, a heart wide open to all this joy and beauty, and save our souls from being so steeped in care or so darkened by passion that we pass heedless and unseeing when even the thornbush by the wayside is aflame with the glory of God. . . .

In most of the prayers, concern was focused upon a specific group, either one that modern society mistreats or one upon which it is especially dependent:

> For Children Who Work
> O Thou great Father of the weak, lay thy hand tenderly on all the little children on earth and bless them. . . . But bless with a sevenfold

blessing the young lives whose slender shoulders are already bowed beneath the yoke of toil, and whose glad growth is being stunted forever. . . .

For Employers
    We invoke thy grace and wisdom, O Lord, upon all men of good will who employ and control the labor of men. . . . When they are tempted to follow the ruthless ways of others, and to sacrifice human health and life for profit, do thou strengthen their will in the hour of need, and bring to naught the counsels of the heartless. . . .

Finally, some prayers expressed hope for the transformations of heart, church, and nation that must yet occur:

For a Share in the Work of Redemption
    We pray thee, O Lord, for the graces of a pure and holy life that we may no longer add to the dark weight of the world's sin that is laid upon thee, but may share with thee in thy redemptive work. . . .

For the Church
    O God, we pray for thy Church, which is set today amid the perplexities of a changing order, and face to face with a great new task. . . . Oh, baptize her afresh in the life-giving spirit of Jesus! Grant her a new birth, though it be with the travail of repentance and humiliation. Bestow upon her a more imperious responsiveness to duty, a swifter compassion with suffering, and an utter loyalty to the will of God. Put upon her lips the ancient gospel of her Lord. . . .

For the Cooperative Commonwealth
    O God, save us, for our nation is at strife with its own soul and is sinning against the light which thou aforetime hast kindled in it. Thou has called our people to freedom, but we are withholding from men their share in the common heritage without which freedom becomes a hollow name. Thy Christ has kindled in us the passion for brotherhood, but the social life we have built, denies and slays brotherhood. . . .[11]

    The book triggered an appreciative response, though it was nothing like the wake left by *Christianity and the Social Crisis.* Josiah Strong, a pioneer of social Christianity in America, exclaimed, "Your volume is filled with the spirit of the Master, and apart from the Scriptures themselves, I have never read anything that so aroused in me the devotional spirit." Charles M. Sheldon, author of the best-selling *In His Steps,* wrote that his family used the prayers in their home mornings and evenings and found that they "voice our longing and our needs as we were not able to voice them." A reviewer predicted in a Baptist paper that the book "may well become the litany of the social awakening of the Christian Church." But again there were dissenters;

perhaps none hurt as much as the claim of an unnamed reviewer in a Rochester newspaper that many of the prayers were "lowered in their spiritual tone by the importation of socialistic language."

Pilgrim Press reprinted the book several times, and in 1912, at Rauschenbusch's request, gave it the simpler title, *Prayers of the Social Awakening*. The author delighted in sending gift copies to friends and to such notables as Senator Robert LaFollette and Prime Minister David Lloyd-George. A French translation appeared in 1913, and numerous groups undertook the printing and distribution of cards carrying their favorite prayers. Rauschenbusch was particularly pleased by reports that the little book inspired ministers to compose comparable prayers of their own. "I shall always regard it as one of the best gifts of God to me," Rauschenbusch said in 1913, "that he led my mind to these prayers."[12]

Pilgrim Press worked with him on two other small books in which he sketched the religious depths and social expression of love. The first, *Unto Me*, was published in 1912, and the second, *Dare We Be Christians?* in 1914. Neither book, however, was widely publicized or attracted a large readership. This was not the case with Rauschenbusch's next important volume, *Christianizing the Social Order*. The year following publication of *Christianity and the Social Crisis*, Rauschenbusch and Brett had agreed that Macmillan would bring out a sequel focused on historical and theological themes and called "The Church and the Kingdom." The manuscript was never written, however, because Rauschenbusch's mind was drawn toward the practical questions raised by audiences he addressed across the nation. He explained that people who had been persuaded of the need to reconstruct the social order now wanted marching orders, and their questions took on a decidedly practical cast: " 'What must we do? And what must we undo? What social ideal should guide us? What methods can we safely use in realizing it?' " He addressed such issues in two prestigious lectureships—the Earl Lectures, presented in April 1910, at the Pacific Theological Seminary in Berkeley, California, and the Merrick Lectures, delivered in April 1911, at Ohio Wesleyan University in Delaware, Ohio—and then arranged with Macmillan for his revision of this material to become the sequel to *Christianity and the Social Crisis*.[13]

A completed manuscript was due the summer of 1911, but the writing proved more difficult than he had anticipated, and it was not completed until the following summer. Part of the problem was finding time for the task, but even more it was a matter of finding a way to make his case fairly. Rauschenbusch knew he must submit capitalism to severe criticism, but he realized, too, that he must avoid unfair accusations against capitalists. "I shrink from condemning and wounding men who do not deserve it," he told his publisher. "The moral responsibility of the book often bears me down." He also feared the reaction that might be directed against himself. "I don't want to be persecuted if I can help it," he told a friend. "It makes me too unhappy." To another whom he asked to criticize the manuscript, he wondered if he had "overdone it, and trampled on capitalism so hard that my readers will take sides with it in sympathy with the under-dog?"[14]

Finally, as the summer break ended, he completed the manuscript, and in November 1912 Macmillan published *Christianizing the Social Order*. Readers familiar with his 1907 best-seller found Rauschenbusch's argument for Christianity's yoking of the religious and ethical realms repeated in more compact form than before. More now was said about the social awakening under way in both the church and the nation, and greater attention was given to the relationship of the two movements. He argued that in each of them God is acting through human instrumentalities to accomplish the divine will, leading the church to recenter its life and thought on Jesus and the Kingdom, and leading the nation to achieve a new social order that fulfills its highest ideals. Christians are called to participate in both reforms and to bring each what it needs from the other.

Far more than in the earlier book, Rauschenbusch now proposed a variety of actions for those ready to attempt reform. His diagnosis of the nation's ills and his proposals for cure reflected ideas from many sources—socialists, progressives, single-taxers, the Federal Council of Churches, and numerous individual reformers. At times, he overwhelmed his readers with a profusion of proposals. But embedded in the book was an underlying theological structure developed to guide Christians' reasoning about their involvement with social problems. This conceptual structure constitutes the most enduring legacy of *Christianizing the Social Order*.

The book's foundation was the foundation of his own religious life: the affirmation that because Jesus embodies the fullest revelation of God's will for humanity, Christians must seek the same ends that Jesus sought and value what he valued. Study of Jesus' life and teaching, said Rauschenbusch, shows that they were dominated by two fundamental convictions: the first, that the Creator has made every person a being of divine worth, so that whatever denies the worth of even the lowliest person is sinful and thus unacceptable; the second, that the Creator has linked all people in a single web of humanity, so that whatever pits one against another is sinful and unacceptable.

Rauschenbusch went on to contend (in a flush of optimism he later revised downward) that through efforts of the church in past centuries much of American life already reflects acceptance of the human dignity and fraternity taught by Jesus, and that the nation appears to be embarked on the journey toward realization of a "Christianized social order." This, explained Rauschenbusch, is not the Kingdom. It is an ordering of society that "makes bad people do good things"; its characteristic values and behaviors push mean, selfish people to a higher level of willing and acting. By contrast, an unchristian social order is one that "makes good people do bad things" (p. 127). It fosters behaviors and attitudes that make caring, sensitive individuals turn against others and seek their own aggrandizement at the neighbors' expense. At present, Rauschenbusch judged, American society is not purely one or the other. Instead, it is a "semi-Christian" social order, a combination of institutions that have been Christianized and of one institution—the economic system—that is dangerously un-Christian.

Rauschenbusch recognized that if Jesus' teachings about human worth and solidarity were to prevail in the debate about the future of American social institutions, they must be translated from religious jargon into the more accessible language of American democratic idealism. Thus, he contended that the economic system must be evaluated by standards of justice, liberty, and fraternity and that America's capitalist system falls woefully short of all three. The failure of justice is evident in the system's allowing the rich to grow richer through unearned profit coming from such practices as speculative holding of land, control of extortionist monopolies, and ownership of natural resources and utilities vital to the community. Workers, on the other hand, receive for their hard toil wages that are kept at the lowest level possible. Capitalism fails as badly when measured by the standard of liberty. Owners are ensnared in the dehumanizing grip of power and greed, while workers are captive to poverty and a system that allows them no control over their destiny. Finally, the system fails the test of brotherhood, for it gives owners autocratic power over workers and tempts workers to hatred of owners.

Rauschenbusch's indictment continued with the claim that the evils of unrestrained capitalism are spreading dangerously into other realms of American life. This "invasion of God's country" (p. 235) occurs, for example, when schools charged with teaching the young to think succumb to the pressure of training them for jobs, when the natural beauties of communities are ravaged for the sake of corporate profits, and when public servants trade single-minded devotion to duty for the rewards that come by advancing the interests of business.

His counsel to Christian seekers of justice, liberty, and fraternity included the admonitions that they recognize that reform of the economic system cannot occur without a determined and perhaps even violent effort of the working class, and that Christians must join hands with all who seek a more humane future. More than in his earlier writings, Rauschenbusch vigorously encouraged cooperation with American socialists. He admitted that some of them follow the lead of continental comrades in espousing a materialistic philosophy and rejecting the churches, but Christians must recognize that this is only one variant of the socialist style, a product of the particular circumstances in which socialism emerged in nineteenth-century Europe. If Christians demonstrate a commitment to social reform, American socialists may yet adopt the friendlier stance of British socialists and seek an alliance between socialism and Christianity. Rauschenbusch urged that every step in this direction be welcomed, for the passion of socialists for justice, liberty, and fraternity is essentially religious; despite their shortcomings, they are "tools in the hands of the Almighty" (p. 404). Christians should have no reservations about learning from their social analysis and developing collaborative action with them.

Rauschenbusch contended that Christians also must shed their reservations about the state. They too long have regarded it as an instrument of the devil and thought the best state the one that governs least. They now must learn to view it as the people in action, their vehicle for promoting the welfare of the total community. This noble end will be served when the state taxes unearned income, ends monopolies, regulates industry, assumes ownership of natural resources and vital public services, provides needed aid for the disadvantaged, and guarantees labor's right to organize, bargain, and strike.

Here was Rauschenbusch's major statement about Christians' work to promote a better social order. They do this best, he believed, when they strive with other citizens to develop new public policy. Their faith enables them to be clear about long-term goals, persistent in the face of obstacles, gentle with those threatened by change, and hopeful with those who long for a better future. They bring no distinctively Christian blueprint for reform, but resources of will and spirit that make them a potent leaven.

Like his book five years earlier, *Christianizing the Social Order* attracted immediate and continued attention. Two additional printings were made within a year, and a third in 1914. A Methodist reviewer who had predicted the volume would not do as well as its predecessor was answered by Rauschenbusch with the report that initial sales actually were better, and he complained happily, "I recently ordered five copies and the publishers could not fill the order." Again Rauschenbusch sought to have French and German translations made, but they did not appear until after the First World War. Within three years, however, a Norwegian scholar completed his project of translating the book and publishing it in three parts. Once again Rauschenbusch arranged for James E. Franklin to subsidize gift copies for two thousand students in theological seminaries across the nation.[15]

Letters from scores of appreciative students and other readers testified to the impact of the volume. "There has been so much well-intentioned, undigested, one-sided incoherence on behalf of social reform, that it is a comfort to get a book that is well-considered, thorough-going, fair and reasonable," said E. F. Merriam, a prominent Baptist editor. "It is a great book, and I am proud of you," wrote Augustus Hopkins Strong from retirement. Most reviews were favorable, though it was evident that this book was not a ground-breaker like the earlier one and did not provoke the same vigorous response. One writer in a New England seminary publication reflected a recurring note of the negative reviews: Rauschenbusch, he said, was insufficiently appreciative of the good done by capitalism. He added a point that was to recur in a later, less optimistic generation: The author overlooked the "evils belonging to human nature." Another reviewer complained that Rauschenbusch unfairly judged the practice of capitalism by the theory of socialism; who could say that socialist practice would be any better than capitalist practice?

A review that particularly pleased him was that of economist Scott Nearing. Professor Nearing wrote that although Rauschenbusch had underestimated "the spirit of service present in industry and overstated the idealism present in other realms . . . in the main, his picture is terribly true, and his diagnosis of the difficulty is infallibly correct." He concluded that "a thoughtful reading of this wonderful book will open the eyes of the vast majority of economists to truths in their own field of thought, which they at present barely suspect." Rauschenbusch replied to Nearing that his verdict was good news for one whose professional training and work lay outside the realm of economics. "I have suffered from the self-distrust of a self-made man, never knowing with certainty if I was within the main current of scientific economic thought, and always prepared to be told that I was all wrong. It required some fidelity to conviction in a naturally modest man to hold me up to the writing of two rather venturesome books."

This "modest man" was buoyed by the favorable words from Nearing and others, but he was realist enough to notice that other books on social themes were receiving a similar response and that all of this was, as he told James Franklin, "a very important sign of the times." Now the mood of America was ripe for muckrakers and reformers, but within another few years, a very different mood would prevail.[16]

With the fame Rauschenbusch won through his books came an avalanche of requests for his services. Leaders of numerous reform organizations sought him for membership in their agencies. He declined most of the invitations and told those whose organizations he did join that he would come to few meetings because his deafness prevented effective participation; he would try to make a contribution by correspondence. In 1908 he agreed to work with Frank Mason North and other social pioneers on the Committee on the Church and the Labor Problem, a key body within the recently formed Federal Council of Churches. Through letters to North he helped shape the document that soon became known as the "Social Creed of the Churches." In subsequent years Rauschenbusch continued to give his counsel generously to this ecumenical body built upon theological and social convictions close to his heart. At the request of Samuel Zane Batten, his friend from the Brotherhood of the Kingdom, Rauschenbusch in 1909 became a member of the Social Service Commission of the Baptist World Alliance. He also agreed to participate in the League for Social Service and in the Men and Religion Forward Movement. The only position of titular leadership he accepted was the presidency of the Religious Citizenship League, an organization established in 1913 by W. D. P. Bliss to link Protestants, Catholics, and Jews for legislative action on such goals as women's suffrage and the prohibition of child labor.[17]

Hundreds of groups sought him as a speaker. The most important invitation reaching him in Germany after publication of *Christianity and the Social Crisis* came from George W. Coleman, a Baptist layman in Boston who directed a popular Sunday evening lecture and discussion program on Beacon Hill. Rauschenbusch responded cautiously that he knew his book had upset some of the Rochester seminary's conservative constituency and that for this reason he would accept no major speaking invitations until he had a better reading of Baptists' response. "I do not propose to suppress God's message in me," he said, "but neither do I want to forfeit the position which enables me to pass it on most effectively." When it became evident that he had nothing to fear in Rochester, he accepted Coleman's invitation for a series of addresses in November 1908. In the aftermath, Coleman wrote to Dean Stewart with a glowing review of his professor's per-

formance: "There is no better advertisement the seminary could put
forth than to let Walter Rauschenbusch do the kind of work that he
did here in Boston. If I were a young man contemplating the ministry,
you couldn't drag me away from Rochester Theological Seminary."
Coleman's enthusiasm not only helped make Rauschenbusch's su-
periors more comfortable about his new apostolate; it also led to his
becoming a frequent speaker both at Coleman's Ford Hall forums and
at the Sagamore Sociological Conferences he convened each summer
near his Cape Cod cottage. The warm response and extensive newspaper coverage that came to Rauschenbusch in Massachusetts was a
key factor in bringing national attention to his skills as a platform
speaker.[18]

Rauschenbusch once told a group that during his first year back
in Rochester following publication of *Christianity and the Social Crisis*
he accepted so many invitations he had to work twice as hard as before. The first complete accounting he did of this new round of responsibilities was prepared for President Strong and covered the period between April 1910 and April 1911. Beyond his regular classroom
lectures and presentations at the People's Sunday Evening, he had
delivered a total of sixty-one addresses and sermons. Only one week
of classes had been missed. Some of the addresses were presented at
academic institutions: the Pacific Theological Seminary, Fiske University, Columbia University, the Yale School of Religion, the University of Wisconsin, and Ohio Wesleyan University. Two were in
Berlin at the World Congress of Free Christianity and Religious Progress. Two were before national Baptist gatherings. At least ninety
speaking invitations had been declined, plus five writing projects.

He appended to the report a disclaimer probably intended less for
President Strong than for trustees worried about the outside labors
of their newly famous professor. "Perhaps I ought to say that I have
no connection with any lecture bureau, have never put out any ad-
vertising matter, and have regarded the task of writing polite refusals
as one of my saddest burdens. My sincere wish is to be let alone." He
explained that as interest in his message grew he had felt duty-bound
to respond. "In all Christian humility I believe that the small amount
that I have actually been able to contribute toward this vast demand
has been of real use to the Christian life of our country, and I hope
that it has also directly benefitted the reputation, influence, and spirit
of our Seminary."[19]

Over the next several years, until the outbreak of the First World
War, Rauschenbusch kept up the same grueling pace. By 1912 demand
for his services became so great that he was obliged to contract with
a speakers' bureau to handle arrangements for most out-of-town

commitments. In 1913 he explained to an inquirer that two factors governed decisions regarding which invitations he would accept and which he must reject: "Whether the invitation stands for an unusual opportunity to impress ideas on some important body of people; and whether I can do the work with slight outlay of time and good financial income. Sometimes one point governs, sometimes the other, sometimes both." Many lecture trips brought pleasure, including sheer enjoyment of the adulation he received. Often, however, they did not, and letters home admitted the strain and fatigue. But with many lectures netting him at least $50, there was the satisfaction of knowing funds were accumulating for his family's needs.

By 1914, after numerous speaking engagements across the United States, Rauschenbusch realized he must cut back. The pace at which his hosts worked him often so sapped his energy that his addresses lacked the vigor he wanted them to have. Also, his hectic schedule denied him the time with his family and the outdoors that were essential for inner renewal, and it kept him from writing the books he realized were a more effective means of spreading his message.[20]

But the books already written and his hundreds of public appearances had made a mark, and the Rauschenbusch name was known widely across the nation, as well as among some church leaders in western Europe. He had met most American leaders of social reform and was admired by them. When *The Independent* magazine conducted a survey among readers in 1913 to determine whom they considered the most useful American, Thomas Edison was by far the first choice, but Walter Rauschenbusch's name ranked along with those of such religious leaders as Lyman Abbott, John R. Mott, Billy Sunday, Charles Sheldon, and Washington Gladden; rarely had an American seminary professor been so widely and favorably known. Honors came regularly. Several publications ran his picture and stories about him. Oberlin College (where daughter Winifred was a student) awarded him an honorary degree. Three books and two songs were dedicated to him.

Admiring friends sensed that Walter Rauschenbusch occupied a historic place in American life, and they searched for words to identify it properly. Some, knowing how much he valued prophetic figures of the past who spoke God's word of judgment and hope, called him a prophet. Rabbi Stephen Wise, leader of the Reform movement in American Judaism, wrote that he was "one of our few saintly prophets and prophetic saints." A Universalist editor called him "the chief apostle of the new order of religion and life." Baptist scholar Henry Vedder, who dedicated a book to him, hailed Rauschenbusch as the "Prophet of a New Reformation," and French pastor Wilfred Monod called him a great leader of "the Reformation within the Reformation."[21]

These appreciative words grasped two important truths about Walter Rauschenbusch. Like prophets before him, he courageously told the nation where it had strayed and how it must mend its ways. In the years ahead, particularly during Roosevelt's New Deal, much of what he and other Progressive reformers advocated was incorporated into American political and economic life. But the message of Rauschenbusch the prophet left those who heard or read it with a sense that something more was needed, that the demands of God's Kingdom had not yet been satisfied. He helped people know there was always an unfinished agenda of social reform.

Rauschenbusch played his prophetic social role as part of a more vast historical movement—a reformation that brought far-reaching change to the churches, renewing their theology and worship, challenging their divisions, expanding their geographical base, and refocusing their mission to the world. This reformation has not always proceeded in a Rauschenbuschian line, nor has it yet run its course. When at some future point Christians can look back upon this chapter of their long history, they will see that Walter Rauschenbusch stands as one of its giants for his part in awakening the churches to their social mission.

CHAPTER 11

DISSENTER

In the halcyon years of reform prior to the First World War, Walter Rauschenbusch's message won him such acclaim that it seemed a prophet could enjoy honor within his own country. However, he knew that what the flow of history had brought it could also take away. "Historical opportunities rarely last long," he told a New York audience in January 1914, and he pointed to signs portending a great reversal. If the world is embroiled in war, he warned, it will "absorb the attention of the people, consume their capacity for moral enthusiasm, and set free such forces of greed, debauchery and demoralization that all our religious aspirations would be cut down like young wheat in a hail-storm." Laborers for social reform must toil while it is still day, he concluded, "for in the life of nations as in that of individuals the night when no man can work often comes suddenly and in ways that none foresaw."[1]

Rauschenbusch's foreboding about war had recurred for more than a decade. His earlier hope for the Hague Tribunal had been dimmed by accelerating international tensions and the military buildup he witnessed in Germany during visits in 1907 and 1910. Several of his books warned of the conditions that breed war. "Ever the pride of kings and the covetousness of the strong," he wrote in 1910, "has driven peaceful nations to slaughter. Ever the songs of the past and the pomp of armies has been used to inflame the passions of the people." By 1914 his interest in international peace was sufficiently known that a team of American church leaders working with counterparts in Germany and England to ease tensions invited him to lead a group of Americans to a conference at Zurich in August.

The conference never met, for that very month Europe plunged into the maelstrom of the Great War. In September, Rauschenbusch received letters from German friends defending their nation's cause. Even his sister Frida, who earlier feared Germany's militaristic climate, now endorsed the Kaiser's march into Belgium and France. With the war spreading, Rauschenbusch's anxiety deepened, for this massive threat to humanity carried also a direct threat to his own family. The sons of relatives in Westphalia were fighting for Germany, and the sons of a cousin in Paris were enlisted in the French army. He feared, too, for his widowed sister and her daughters in Germany. Worst of all, he sensed that the United States could be sucked into the war and that his own three teenage sons might be called upon to fight.[2]

Students in Rauschenbusch's classes that autumn saw a marked change in their professor. One later wrote that the sparkle was gone from his eyes and there were fewer jokes. "He was a sad man." But Walter Rauschenbusch never was one to be paralyzed by fear. During September he took several steps to air his convictions and shape the response of Americans to the war. The first was the convening of a "Peace Group" among friends in Rochester for periodic discussions of what should be done about events in Europe. At the same time he began wearing a small piece of black crepe on his coat lapel and wrote a letter published in several national religious periodicals inviting others to join him in the practice. He explained that it expressed his "profound grief and depression of spirit" caused by the war, as well as his commitment to use "all possible efforts henceforth in the cause of peace." Next, as reports began to arrive from Europe of casualties and damage, he wrote letters to several Baptist periodicals urging that financial support be sent to Baptists suffering on both sides of the conflict.[3]

Rauschenbusch was pained to see that American newspaper accounts of the war favored England and the Allies. Both sides sought the support of American public opinion, and clearly Germany and the Central Powers were losing that battle. Many now portrayed the Allied effort as a righteous crusade against an evil aggressor, and thanks to England's control of news cables across the Atlantic, as well as its propaganda skills and long-standing ties with the United States, this view appeared plausible to more and more Americans. Rauschenbusch felt compelled to come to the defense of Germany. In "Be Fair to Germany," an article published in a national religious journal in October 1914, he contended that Americans must learn to weigh the claims of belligerents with jury-like impartiality, for their nation's role could be pivotal in an eventual peace settlement. He explained that because Americans had so few opportunities to hear Germany's side he would present its case, even though he had sympathy for the Allies also. His main point was that Germany is not so villainous as the press claims, nor England so virtuous. Several issues were addressed. German atrocities in Belgium and France, he said, were reprehensible but not surprising, for that is what war breeds: "When we reverse the law of morality and make it a duty to kill, the rest of the decalogue tumbles after it." Americans must recognize, too, that stories of enemy brutality are inevitably exaggerated in wartime and that any army fighting on foreign soil is more apt to engage in such behavior than one that is not; there are no stories of English atrocities because they have not fought in Germany.

Rauschenbusch went on to ask Americans also to recognize the way geography impinges upon events. Whereas England's insular position on the edge of Europe has given it security and required a strong navy for protection, Germany's location in central Europe, surrounded by powerful nations, has made it vulnerable and required the protection possible only with a strong army. Moreover, the current hostility between Germany and England must be seen in relation to their different starting points in the race for colonies and markets. England built a mighty colonial empire long ago, but Germany's belated rise to power allowed it to challenge that hegemony only recently. Why is German expansionism any more culpable than English expansionism? Rauschenbusch added that even though England was right to condemn Germany's violation of Belgium's neutrality, Americans must not be duped into thinking English intervention was prompted solely by righteous indignation. "Nations rarely fight for moral issues alone; always for material interest complicated with moral questions." In fact, he said, the English response reflected fear of Germany's controlling Belgian ports and thereby winning an economic advantage.[4]

Few Americans were speaking up for Germany, and Rauschenbusch later reported that some thoughtful people admitted his article had helped them appreciate Germany's case. But when the article was condensed and printed in the widely read *Literary Digest*, an outcry arose, especially in Canada, which as part of the British Commonwealth was being rapidly mobilized to support the Allied war effort. Several prominent Canadian newspapers carried portions of the abbreviated Rauschenbusch article and editorialized against him. The Canadian response brought a new experience for Rauschenbusch. In November 1914, Saskatchewan Methodists, who earlier had arranged for him to lecture at several conferences the following spring, angrily demanded cancellation of the invitation. "Methodists Do Not

Want to Hear Pro-German Divine," declared a newspaper headline. The story explained that Rauschenbusch had attacked "the British race" and defended "Prussian ethics." It was an unfair rebuke, but one with a lesson: "The old superstition that man is a reasonable being is dropped from my creed," he wrote his son Hilmar. With feeling running so strongly against him and the likelihood that it would intensify over the next months, Rauschenbusch asked the official responsible for inviting him to accept his withdrawal from the engagement.[5]

This was not the worst of the Canadian repercussions from his article, however. In December he learned that farmers living near his Ontario cottage were angry and might attempt to do him harm were he to return in the summer. Other warnings (including several anonymous letters) led him to conclude that the family must abandon its usual vacation plans until the anger abated. But there was to be no letup. Over the next several years the cottage was repeatedly vandalized, and the rumor even circulated among some in the area that Rauschenbusch was a German spy (leading him to joke privately about his submarine in Sturgeon Lake). Rauschenbusch never returned to this spot he loved more than any other, and in 1917 he finally managed to sell it at a substantial financial loss.[6]

Twenty-five years earlier, when Walter Rauschenbusch first undertook "God's special work," he felt hostility and loneliness, but never did they hit with the intensity he experienced in the first several months of the war. Even more upsetting than the cutting of ties with Canada was the estrangement he felt among people in Rochester who previously had applauded him so warmly. Longtime friend and ally in reform Joe Alling began to treat him coolly. Some professors at the seminary (especially several who were Canadians) now wondered about his judgment. There was no open defiance from local friends, only silence about the issue, and Rauschenbusch interpreted this in the worst light; it means, he said in November 1914, "they don't like to remind me that I belong to a disreputable family." It was not just that people disagreed with his position about the war. He told his former student secretary Dores Sharpe he had discovered that "anyone speaking for Germany, even in the most moderate way, excommunicates himself in a way and loses influence immediately." Some even treat him as a "fallen prophet who has now cast doubt on all his previous teaching by his present immoralities." They conclude that because he was wrong about the war he must also be wrong about other subjects important to him.

This sense of rejection was to grow in the years ahead, and it pained him enormously. "Unfortunately I am not thick-skinned," he told a friend. "I love my fellow-man and have tried to live without having enemies. It is physical misery to me to get mail loaded up with scornful and hateful letters, and I cannot do my work." But even more upsetting than the personal loss of standing was his reflection upon the suffering the war was inflicting upon the world. "It is on me night and day," he confided to Sharpe. "When I wake up at night, I fall to thinking of it, and I can't get to sleep again. It has never been so hard to be cheerful." Eight months later he was speaking autobiographically when he told a national Baptist convention, "Many of us feel that our spirits have been scarred forever and the very lines of our faces have deepened."[7]

The October 1914 article had elicited a harsh response, and Rauschenbusch knew that with American sentiment growing ever more pro-British, other public statements by him about the war would bring more anguish. But he could not keep silent. The following summer he discovered that Charles Aked, a prominent Congregational pastor in San Francisco who had come to the United States eight years earlier from England, shared many of his views. The two men decided to issue a joint statement expressing their views, and on 8 July 1915 they released it to the press.

Excerpts of "Private Profit and the Nation's Honor: A Protest and a Plea" appeared across the nation. The major thrust of the Rauschenbusch-Aked statement was to challenge Americans' support of the Allies through the sale of armaments. The nation has become "a workshop of death," they charged, in theory pledged to neutrality but in fact aiding one side against the other. By allowing this policy to go unchecked, the United States was encouraging the growth of powerful financial interests that profited from the expansion of war and that would not hesitate to push this nation directly into the conflict. The Rauschenbusch-Aked remedy: governmental prohibition of all arms shipments. This alone would preserve the honor of the United States and ensure that the nation would have a significant role as a global peacemaker.

Few Americans wanted to hear such words. Rauschenbusch reported that in their wake came a "hailstorm of anger," most of it distilled in dozens of letters that were separated from the rest of his mail by his son and read only when the day's work was completed. After this, nearly all invitations to write or speak about the war were declined. "Every instinct of truth in me prompts me to speak up," he explained to a friend, "but my experiences thus far have shown me that it does absolutely no good, and merely results in cutting into my health and lessening my influence." For the next three years his silence on the war was broken only occasionally by brief articles in the Baptist press and letters to local newspapers.[8]

The infrequent public utterances developed three themes. The real issues of the war, he insisted, lie beneath the pious and self-righteous talk on both sides. Any realistic analysis will recognize that neither side has a corner on virtue, that they are "all fighting for expansion and wealth. If they say they are not, it is cant." He argued, too, that Americans must keep their nation out of the war. Should it become a belligerent, the United States would soon become an autocratic, militaristic state and forfeit its role as a fair-minded peacemaker among the nations. The real enemy of the United States, he contended, is not Germany but war, along with the hatred and deception that war unleashes. Finally, he urged that American Christians resist efforts to use their religion in support of the war. Violence is done to the gospel when biblical images of God and Christ are invoked on behalf of an alleged holy war, and when the church is made a breeding ground for the passions and sacrifices of war. "It was hard enough to combine Christianity and capitalistic business. Now we are asked to combine Christianity and war." American Christians must learn— as he had learned from his own experience over the years—that their fundamental citizenship lies in a Kingdom that transcends national boundaries.[9]

As Rauschenbusch felt himself increasingly isolated in Rochester, he found welcomed support from two circles of fellow dissenters against the prevailing American climate. In April 1916 he discovered the newly established Fellowship of Reconciliation and rejoiced at its religiously based opposition to war and to the social injustices that breed war. Excited by the FOR, he wrote Dores Sharpe that it was "an electric shock to get together with people more radical than I am, that take the Sermon on the Mount seriously," and by the end of the year he had become an active member and a quiet advocate of the Fellowship's pacifist position. Rauschenbusch also felt drawn to the Quaker faith of FOR stalwarts; he once told a daughter that if the Baptists ever forced him out he would like to become a Quaker. At the same time, he found socialists' interpretation of the war as an economic struggle congenial with his own position. He nearly became a member of the Socialist party, but persisted in his long-standing conviction that membership would be viewed as a more complete endorsement of socialism than he was prepared to make. Though he declined to take that step, he did consent to be the major speaker at a large Socialist-sponsored rally against American entry into the war held in Rochester on 25 February 1917.[10]

The U.S. declaration of war six weeks later triggered a massive mobilization of spirit and resources. A new government agency worked skillfully to arouse the support of Americans for their nation's cause, and powerful psychological and legal pressures were mounted to make laggards conform. Most religious bodies declared their endorsement of this crusade to make the world safe for democracy. Rochester Theological Seminary was proud of its place in American life, and in May 1917 President Clarence Barbour announced his school's support of the war effort and its "absolute loyalty" to the nation. As in churches across the nation, an American flag flew conspicuously at the seminary, and, lest there be any doubts, an American flag went up outside the German Department's building. Soon Barbour took an emergency leave of absence to join the national YMCA's chaplaincy program among American troops.[11]

More than ever, Americans of German descent were pressured to declare their loyalty to the United States, and any wavering was viewed suspiciously. Leaders and friends of Rochester Theological Seminary watched anxiously for Walter Rauschenbusch's public profession of patriotism. Apprehension had been expressed earlier in the year by W. H. C. Faunce, a longtime friend who was president of Brown University. Remarkably, Faunce wrote Rauschenbusch that because he was "everywhere known as loyal to the reactionary and military powers now controlling Germany" he should publish an unequivocal rejection of German evils and an affirmation of America. Others began to urge such an utterance. One close friend, James Thomas, wrote in November 1917 that mutual friends had asked him to encourage Rauschenbusch to declare his loyalty publicly, but Thomas believed this was unnecessary because he thought anyone taking the time to investigate Rauschenbusch's statements would discover that the "perverse patriots" had no grounds for doubting his loyalty. Thomas rightly saw that however much Rauschenbusch wanted German militarism and autocracy ended, his pacifism forbade his advocating a military solution to the conflict; his sense of justice forbade his fueling partisan condemnations of Germany; and his realism forbade his endorsing the Allies' self-righteous war ideology.[12]

But other friends persisted and secured the support of President Barbour. The following April, when he was gravely ill, Rauschenbusch agreed to issue a public statement addressed to Cornelius Woelfkin, a former faculty colleague who succeeded Faunce as pastor of Fifth Avenue Baptist Church in New York City. With help from Paul Strayer, Rauschenbusch drafted a lengthy letter to Woelfkin. His apprehension about possible reactions to the letter caused him two sleepless nights. It was slightly edited by Barbour, given final approval by Rauschenbusch, then sent by Barbour for publication in local newspapers and several national religious journals.[13]

On 11 July 1918 the editor of the *Congregationalist and Advance* introduced the letter as Rauschenbusch's long-delayed declaration of "his desire to see German autocracy forever overthrown." This point was indeed made in the letter, more forthrightly than in any of his earlier public statements: "I heartily hope that out of all this suffering will come the downfall of all autocratic government in the central empires." Victory for Germany and its allies, he said, would be a "terrible calamity for the world," a mighty blow to the democratic ideals he had served all his life. But the Rauschenbusch letter did not give the Allied cause an unqualified endorsement. Germany surely has been wrong, he asserted, but so have others; what Germany has done recently other nations have done earlier. Hence he had no confidence that an Allied victory "would of itself free the world from imperialism." But there is hope for the future, he added, in the peace proposals of the British Labour party and of Woodrow Wilson. Americans should give the President their wholehearted support as he faces the difficult task of making his vision of a peaceable future prevail against selfish interests at home and abroad.

Clarence Barbour knew the letter would not satisfy extremists, but he agreed with Woelfkin that it should have the widest possible circulation, for it left no doubt about the loyalty of the school's most illustrious professor. Barbour realized, however, that the tone of the letter was not as militant as he had wished, for Rauschenbusch had rejected his suggestion that he advocate that "the German government be crushed." Upon reading the letter in the press, Augustus Hopkins Strong wrote his son that although it was a rather mild statement by Rauschenbusch, "it will do something to reinstate him in the good opinion of Rochester." As for Rauschenbusch's own feeling about the letter, he knew it would not satisfy all. But as had happened often in the past, he sought to occupy ground that both put him in talking distance of those he wished to reach and allowed him to make the point they needed to hear. So even as he gave patriots the assurance of loyalty they sought (which for him was never in doubt), he also reasserted the case for which he had contended all along: that Americans must avoid simplistic judgments about guilt and innocence and must maintain the discriminating realism without which they would be ill-equipped to pursue the tasks of peace and reconstruction.[14]

Preoccupation with the war increased Rauschenbusch's conviction that he must conserve his energy and accept fewer speaking invitations on reformist themes than had been customary for him in the prewar years. A speakers' bureau near Boston, staffed by friends, began now to oversee his speaking engagements, and from 1914 on the majority of his lecture trips were confined to New England. With a different mood settling over the nation, he realized that he would have the greatest effect where he had more than a single session with his audience. This strategic decision led to a succession of lectureships: in 1914 the Gates Lectures at Grinnell College in Iowa; in 1915 the Enoch Pond Lectures at Bangor Theological Seminary in Maine; and in 1917 the Nathaniel W. Taylor Lectures at the Yale School of Religion in Connecticut.

These engagements brought needed income, but with two children in college and a third nearing the end of high school, financial pressures led Rauschenbusch to accept three other lucrative and grueling assignments. For six weeks in 1915 he taught two courses for the summer session at the Pacific Theological Seminary. The following year he spent three weeks with a Chautauqua group traveling through North Carolina. Most of his companions were young men and women in the cast of *The Mikado*, and he admitted to his family that with his speeches never filling the tent "I am only a side-issue." Finally, for two months during the autumn of 1917 he undertook the most wearying assignment of all, a visiting professorship at Oberlin College in Ohio. He lectured there four times on Mondays and Tuesdays, then took an overnight train to Rochester, arriving in time to meet two classes on Wednesday morning. Even for someone much younger than his fifty-six years, it would have been an exhausting schedule.[15]

Invitations to write continued to arrive, but most were declined. He agreed in 1914 to submit a manuscript to Macmillan on "Social Redemption" (developing the themes of his course on "The History of Social Redemption"), but he delayed the project and finally failed to complete it. Mind and spirit were simply too drained by the war to allow successful management of his typically heavy work load.

Another reason for not completing the Macmillan assignment was his immersion in a writing project for Association Press. In 1915 he began a short book for use by college seniors as part of a four-year voluntary study program organized by a coalition of national Christian student organizations. Its theme was the social teachings of Jesus. Rauschenbusch explained to one of his editors that the invitation was irresistible, for many years earlier he had vowed to do all in his power "to make the thoughts of Jesus operative in the Church," and this book would give him the opportunity to pursue that task among young men and women who soon would occupy positions of lay and professional leadership within many denominations.

Most of his writing of *The Social Principles of Jesus* had to be squeezed into weekends during the 1915–16 academic year, and he presented the manuscript to the publisher in June 1916. As before, Rauschenbusch enjoyed writing about Jesus, but the experience of working collaboratively with an editorial committee was new to him, and he found the process uncomfortable and taxing. Nevertheless, he was pleased with the book when it appeared later in the year, for it was the most comprehensive exposition he had attempted of a theme important to him nearly all his ministry. Moreover, he saw the book as an opportunity to help counter attempts to co-opt Christianity in support of the war.

Few college students had read this kind of book about Jesus. Those who desire to follow him, said Rauschenbusch, will work tirelessly for the downtrodden, affirming their sacred worth, seeking to make every social institution an instrument of God's gracious purposes for humanity, and persisting in the struggle through every adversity. So popular was the book that a new printing quickly appeared, and by 1918 more than 27,000 copies had been sold. An important segment of young American leaders now knew Rauschenbusch's message and carried its challenge with them into the tasks of the postwar period.[16]

Rauschenbusch's desire to reform the church by recentering it upon Jesus and the Kingdom was advanced also in his next book. When historian Williston Walker wrote on behalf of the faculty at the Yale School of Religion inviting him to deliver the Nathaniel William Taylor Lectures in April 1917, Rauschenbusch felt honored but hesitant. The men occupying the distinguished lectureship in past years had addressed doctrinal issues beyond the range of his interest and competence, but he decided to accept the invitation when he realized he could remain within the Taylor tradition by probing the theological dimensions of the church's social task. Since the beginning of his ministry in New York City this had been a major concern, and for the last several years it again had captured his mind. He saw that many Christians were cooling toward reform, and he wanted to challenge the resurgence of conservative patterns. But it also was true that the ranks of younger leaders gripped by the movement of thought and action called the Social Gospel (a term Rauschenbusch used sparingly until this book) had grown rapidly, and he sensed some of them were unsure of their relationship to traditional Christianity. They must be helped, he told Leighton Williams, to ground their thought "more fully on the foundations of the Christian faith." Moreover, the gap between Social Gospelers and conservatives was widening, and he realized many ministers were pulled between the two camps. They labored under the burden of what he called a "dumbbell system of thought, with the social gospel at one end and individual salvation at the other end, and an attenuated connection between them."[17]

All his adult life he had struggled to unite the individual and the social, the old and the new, and now he saw he must attempt to show each side that its perception of Christianity was incomplete until it respected and learned from what was best in the other. The old theology must develop social relevance, the new social movement must discover religious depth. Though not a professional theologian, Rauschenbusch began the task and hoped others soon would take it up. Actually there was an advantage in his being the trailblazer. His spiritual journey had made him indebted to both the older and the newer theologies, and he had learned from a variety of the great voices of the period—Neander, Bushnell, Maurice, Robertson, Tolstoi, Harnack. He spoke not as a theological partisan but as one who had gleaned light from many sources in order to illumine the path of Christian thought and discipleship for his age.

Most of Rauschenbusch's preparation for the Taylor Lectures occurred during a sabbatical leave in the autumn quarter of 1916, and arrangements were made for Macmillan to publish an expanded version under the same title as the lectures—"A Theology for the Social Gospel." The four lectures elicited such a favorable reception from Yale faculty and students that Rauschenbusch initially felt the book would make a positive contribution. As the time neared for publication, however, misgivings arose. There were no second thoughts about the message of the book, but he feared that growing hostility toward German-Americans would prevent the book from receiving a fair hearing. Might it not be better to delay publication until after the war? The counsel of friends and family was divided, but when the publisher urged that they proceed as planned, Rauschenbusch gave the go-ahead, and the book appeared in November 1917.[18]

Neither the book nor the author received the abuse Rauschenbusch had anticipated. The minds of most Americans were far from the issues he addressed, and the book sold considerably fewer copies than his earlier works published by Macmillan. Reviewers were divided. Those already favorably disposed toward the Social Gospel praised the book, and those not favorably disposed panned it. Rauschenbusch's Episcopal friend James Bishop Thomas hailed it as an important contribution to the "new Reformation." Baptist theologian Gerald Birney Smith welcomed it as "a breath of fresh air" sweeping through "the

musty halls of the conventional theological edifice." Disciples editor
Charles Clayton Morrison saw it as a critical step in the church's
search for "a whole gospel." Augustus Hopkins Strong (to whom Rauschenbusch had dedicated the book) acknowledged privately that its
social outlook was "a contribution to the old theology of lasting value,"
but he regretted Rauschenbusch's failure properly to affirm the tran-
scendence and righteousness of God, the deity of Christ, and the authority of Scripture. A Lutheran editor charged that Rauschenbusch
had relied more on rhetoric than on argument and that he "evidently
does not know the content and purpose of theology." A Presbyterian
reviewer echoed this sentiment and recommended that the author
study Calvinism.[19]

Readers familiar with Rauschenbusch's earlier volumes found a
less luminous argument here, but they also found fresh development
of familiar Rauschenbusch themes as well as a cautious probing of
new ground. The Kingdom of God, he again contended, was the central
teaching of Jesus, and restoration of this doctrine is the critical first
step to the church's reform. He went on to argue that until Christians
let the Kingdom shape their thinking they will not perceive either
the magnificence of God's gift of salvation or, by contrast, the mas-
siveness of the evil opposing it. Drawing upon the writings of German
and American thinkers, Rauschenbusch took his long-standing convictions about social solidarity a step further with the claim that in-
sofar as institutions and collective behavior patterns wield their power
to thwart God's purposes they constitute a Kingdom of Evil. This
kingdom reinforces the individual's disposition toward sin and re-
ceives renewed force from every sinning individual. Here is a better
way, he said, to understand the reality of what previous generations
of Christians affirmed with the help of such categories as the fall,
original sin, and the devil. It is this massive system of sin and evil
that God condemns and that the church combats in favor of God's
Kingdom of justice, freedom, and love.

The concept of social sin, continued Rauschenbusch, helps explain
Christ's action to free humanity from sin. Christians have long affirmed that all people bear responsibility for the death of Christ and
that his death makes redemption possible for all. The first affirmation,
explained Rauschenbusch, means that Christ was cruelly killed by
people acting under the sway of behavior patterns that recur in every
generation. Hence, people today who are guilty of the same behavior
as Christ's killers—political oligarchy, judicial corruption, religious
bigotry, militarism, mob pressure, and class contempt—share responsibility for putting him to death. Those who admit their complicity also discover that the Kingdom of Evil did not conquer Jesus,

for it failed to impose its behavior upon him. Jesus persisted to the end in his self-sacrificing love for God and humanity, rather than yield to the temptation of fighting his opponents with their own weapons. In doing so he revealed the character of the love that is the fundamental quality of God's life as well as the essence of truly human life. Those today who follow Jesus in struggling for the triumph of such love can expect opposition and persecution, but they also can have the great comfort of knowing that their struggle effects a powerful union with the crucified and resurrected Christ.

The experiences of Walter Rauschenbusch in the last several years had reinforced his conviction that although God's cause will ultimately triumph, there can be no steady progress to victory. Followers of Christ know conflict and only partial realizations of the Kingdom. But they know, too, he said in *A Theology for the Social Gospel*, that death does not end one's life and growth toward the Kingdom. He believed that traditional Christian thought about the afterlife had wrongly stressed the static union of the individual soul with God. Is it not more in keeping with the gospel, he asked, to picture the mystery of life after death as a process of continuing growth toward God and service to other souls? He also suggested a comparably provocative way for Christians to view the sacraments based upon what he took to be New Testament understandings of baptism and the Lord's Supper. He asked: Should not Christians understand baptism as marking one's renunciation of the Kingdom of Evil and commitment to the Kingdom of God? And should not the Lord's Supper be understood both as a participation in the new community created by Christ and a pledge to follow him in self-sacrificing struggle for God's Kingdom? Ironically, in sketching outlines for a theology of the "communion of saints" and the two sacraments, Rauschenbusch the radical Protestant took his first cautious steps toward the more Catholic view of the church that was to spread widely among Protestants in the next decades and to provide an important theological foundation for the ecumenical movement. He believed such steps could not be avoided if "solidaristic" conceptions of sin and salvation were restored to their rightful place in Christian thought.

Most of Rauschenbusch's agony after 1914 was generated by the war, but other pressures also beat upon his spirit. One source was the new militancy of theological conservatives. He was accustomed to barbs from premillennialists, but now they came with greater frequency and from others as well. The new turn was signaled in April

1914, when Methodists in New Jersey announced that *Christianity and the Social Crisis* was not a proper book for Methodist families to read. He did not respond to the Methodists, but he did feel obliged to answer his Baptist critics. Rauschenbusch wrote fundamentalist leader W. B. Riley that Riley's public denunciation of him for teaching a heretical view of Christ neither fairly reflected his writings nor demonstrated an adequate knowledge of classical Christology. Moreover, the accusation wounded him as a Christian brother. "When you charge me with 'denying the Lord that bought me' you hurt me just as if you charged me with being false to my wife or cruel to my children." Rauschenbusch added that he had no intention of replying to Riley publicly, for he had no stomach for controversy, but he hoped his Baptist brother would desist from such recklessness in the future.

Similar charges and responses recurred. When the editor of a Baptist paper in Kentucky seconded the *Journal and Messenger's* complaint that a Rauschenbusch prayer for Tuberculosis Sunday had "neither Christ nor God in it," Rauschenbusch replied at length. He explained he had composed the prayer for use by Christians and Jews alike and did not think it right to insist that all invoke the name of Christ. "It seemed to me in harmony with the Master's own spirit if I addressed the prayer simply to God, just as he taught the Lord's Prayer to be addressed to 'our Father in heaven.' " He concluded by asking the editor to print the offending prayer so his readers could determine for themselves whether it was animated by love for the God revealed in Jesus Christ.[20]

With critics multiplying in Rochester and beyond, Rauschenbusch turned increasingly to his family for support and consolation. Pauline remained his chief confidante and stay. At times she believed he had magnified slights and slurs and told him so. But she realized that what upset him usually upset her as well; consequently she regretted that at times she was too hurt to be able to comfort him. With the children nearing adulthood, they now understood his ministry better than before and enjoyed assisting him, mainly by helping with secretarial chores. The two older children also made strong and articulate endorsements of his social views. At Oberlin, Winifred headed the student socialist organization, and following graduation in 1916 she traveled for a year across Ohio promoting women's suffrage. At Amherst, Hilmar edited the college literary magazine and became a national officer of the student organization opposing compulsory military training. In later years it was evident that all five children had been deeply influenced by their father's social vision.

But the children's adolescent years also brought worry for Rauschenbusch. Some of it resulted from their refusal to accept the model

behavior he expected. Although he did not want to be as strict a dis-
ciplinarian as August Rauschenbusch, occasionally he found himself
repeating some of his father's ways. In a letter to Hilmar in 1917,
following a period of tension between father and son, Rauschenbusch
confessed he found parenting a young adult difficult and expressed
the hope that his son would help him learn to "make the transition
from parenthood to friendship." Hilmar's path the following year was
particularly troubling to his father, for Hilmar's decision to become
an Army ambulance driver (which Rauschenbusch approved) led to
duty on bloody French battlefields.

A major uneasiness as the children grew to adulthood arose from
their reluctance to receive the baptism regarded by Baptists as the
mark of spiritual maturity. For their father the church's social failure
was the occasion for a lover's quarrel and attempts at reform, but for
the children it constituted a barrier to membership.[21]

The major source of friction at home continued to be his sister. In
1914 Walter helped Emma write the story of her husband's innovative
work in India, but she chafed at his unwillingness to accept her claim
that the Indian mission had been a formative influence upon his
thinking during the years in New York City. Her dislike of Pauline
became more transparent than ever, to the extent that in April 1915,
after Emma had spent several hours with one of her nephews berating
Pauline, Walter angrily asked what right she had to talk to his child
that way and insisted upon "a very searching apology." They arranged
a truce, but it proved to be tenuous.[22]

Twice during the war years, Walter and Pauline considered leaving
Rochester for a community where they would feel less isolated and
harassed. When he was teaching in California during the summer of
1915, the possibility of a permanent position there was raised, but
the Rauschenbusches decided not to pursue it. A similar question came
up about Chicago two years later. Winifred (who had begun work
there) enthusiastically endorsed the idea and told her father that he
would find numerous like-minded people, but nothing came of it.
Pauline and Walter did decide, however, that they would move to a
different part of Rochester, into a smaller house or apartment where
they would no longer have the expense required by a large, old house.
But the onset of Walter's final illness led them to conclude in 1918
that a move would be an intolerable disruption of their beleaguered
lives.[23]

The first blow struck in November 1917. Suddenly there was a
variety of symptoms: troublesome teeth, numb fingers, extreme fatigue, convulsive movements, and a low blood count. Rauschenbusch
surmised that "mental depression is both effect and cause." His doc-

tors prescribed rest, and he canceled all outside engagements. With several faculty associates away that year, he had to carry an unusually heavy teaching load, and there seemed to be no way of cutting it back. "Work and effort come hard and cost will power," he admitted to President Barbour. "The fear of further trouble weighs on me and family cares and questions do not grow less in these dark times."

On 13 March 1918, after a new round of tests, Rauschenbusch was told that he had "pernicious anemia" and must immediately stop teaching. Even after this was done, the earlier symptoms persisted, and in addition there was an abnormally fast heart rate, increased sleeplessness, and pain in the abdominal region. At the recommendation of local doctors, he went with Pauline in early May to Johns Hopkins Hospital in Baltimore for extensive diagnostic tests. After two weeks there, doctors reported that the cause of his anemia had not been identified and that though he might be able to teach part-time the following winter, there was "practically no hope of complete and permanent restoration."[24]

It was a bleak prognosis, and Walter sensed death might be near. The sadness was mixed with a kind of resignation and even anticipation. The day before leaving Johns Hopkins he bared his soul in a letter to Dores Sharpe:

> I dread nothing more than a dreary old age. I have often prayed God to grant me an honorable discharge when my work is done. Is this what he now offers me? I feel under obligation to do all I can to recover, but I am not enthusiastic about it. I can see no solution which would make this an easy world for a man with my kind of name.
>
> I have several books I should like to write; I should find it hard to part from my family and a few friends like you. But otherwise I keep wondering if God is not intending to be very kind to one of his servants who, for reasons known to Him, has carried a heavy load for 30 years and yet has done the day's work as well as the next man.[25]

Seventeen months earlier, when fellow Baptist historian Henry Vedder faced a similar prospect, Rauschenbusch encouraged him to write a short summary of his deepest convictions, a final word interpreting "the inner significance of your own life to your friends." Now, in the twilight of life, Rauschenbusch summoned his energy for such a leave-taking. He wrote a variety of statements. One was a creedlike affirmation of faith in God and hope for the final triumph of the Kingdom. Another was a pair of poetic musings upon his own soul and its union with God. The opening words of one of them showed his kinship with mystics across the centuries.

In the castle of my soul
Is a little postern gate,
Whereat when I enter,
I am in the presence of God.
In a moment, in the turning of a thought,
I am where God is. . . .
The world of men is made of jangling noises.
With God is a great silence.
But that silence is a melody,
Sweet as the contentment of love,
Thrilling as a touch of flame.

Rauschenbusch's public farewell also included two letters written in response to requests for statements from friends. The letter to Cornelius Woelfkin about the war was the first. The second was to Baptist home missions executive L. C. Barnes, affirming the importance of a personal religious life and his belief that his own ministry had been a form of evangelism. "My life would seem an empty shell if my personal religion were left out of it. It has been my deepest satisfaction to get evidence now and then that I have been able to help men to a new spiritual birth." Walter Rauschenbusch wanted everyone to know he belonged to the company of those who believe religion begins and ends in personal communion with God. His ministry had been eloquent testimony to the correlative conviction that one discovers the neighbor in the midst of that communion.[26]

Soon after returning to Rochester in late May, Rauschenbusch noted that pain had intensified in the abdominal area. His physicians detected an abnormal growth there and concluded he must undergo immediate surgery. On 14 June 1918 surgeons removed the tumor and part of his large intestine. They discovered the tumor was malignant and judged that he had no more than six months to live. But the prognosis was withheld from the Rauschenbusches, who were led to believe his chances of partial recovery were good.

The final weeks were cheered by letters from Hilmar. A birthday greeting to Pauline told of a new sense of purpose that gripped Hilmar as he tended the wounded in France. The other contained a fairy tale in which the young man poetically affirmed his determination to follow the path blazed by his father. The two letters, together with a picture of Hilmar, were the only personal items Rauschenbusch asked to have with him in the hospital. The four other children now were able to visit him. Pauline spent each day near his bedside. Close friends came for brief visits. Edmund and Carolyn Lyon canceled their vacation and gave great assistance to the whole family.

By the third week of July it appeared Walter had rallied sufficiently to leave the hospital. "When you come home, dearest," wrote Pauline, "every morning you and I will have a little time together to read and pray and ask God to help us through the day, and to give you just what you need for that day." She arranged for the downstairs study to be converted into a bedroom and for awnings to be installed over the windows. Walter connived with a nurse for flowers to be delivered to 4 Portsmouth Terrace as a surprise for Pauline. But his body was too weakened by cancer for such a homecoming, and on 22 July—Pauline's birthday—he slipped into unconsciousness. Two days later Pauline wrote Hilmar that his father was "peacefully slumbering ever deeper and deeper, until he wakes up with God." The following afternoon, at 4:22 on Thursday, 25 July 1918, he died.

To fifteen of Walter's closest friends, Pauline immediately telegraphed the news of his death. To her son in France, she wrote that his father at last was free—"free from care and worry and sickness and can hear. Think of it, he can hear, Hilmar."[27]

A private memorial service, held two days later at the Rauschenbusch home, was led by Clarence Barbour. Lisa Rauschenbusch remembered sitting on the stairs with her brother Carl, holding his hand. Several weeks earlier Walter Rauschenbusch had altered his instructions for the funeral. It would be better, he told Pauline, in view of people's feelings about Germany, not to sing the old German hymns he had loved since his youth. He also had instructed that his body be cremated, and a year later, when Hilmar returned, he and the other Rauschenbusch children spread the ashes on a Canadian lake.

In October a memorial service was held at the seminary, and for the first time an issue of the school's journal was devoted to a deceased faculty member. Included in it were statements of friends who sought words adequate to evaluate the man and his work. Excerpts from these tributes provide a fitting last glimpse of this remarkable person.

Ray Stannard Baker spoke mainly of his influence upon the nation. "The country owes him a debt of gratitude greater than it yet realizes for the pioneering he did in applying old and deep religious truth to disturbing modern problems. He opened the way for many younger thinkers and workers, and his influence will long be potent in American life."

Looking at Rauschenbusch's impact upon the churches, Harry F. Ward declared that no one "had a larger part in shaping the course of organized Christianity than did he."

Several former students spoke more personally. Dores Sharpe said, "I have lost in Walter Rauschenbusch the most constant, the most helpful, the most Christlike friend I have ever known. . . . He saw afar because he daily walked with God."

Edwin T. Dahlberg remembered that when Rauschenbusch "used to come out from behind his desk and pray at the beginning of each class hour, we were all of us led so near to Christ that we shall always be better men for it."

Justin Wroe Nixon affirmed his belief that "somewhere, in God's own time and way, we shall hear again that hearty, chuckling laugh and shall grasp again that warm hand we have loved to hold fast in our own."

> He lives because such a soul in the universe of a Fatherly God cannot die. It is the privilege of those of us who remain to work in the new age whose peculiar problems he defined so clearly—it is our privilege to transmute his teaching into deeds, to bring into actuality a worthy measure of the ideal of which he dreamed.[28]

The memories and aspirations of such young men—together with the Rauschenbusch writings that taught thousands of others—constituted a rich legacy to the future.

NOTES

Works, institutions, and persons frequently cited in the notes are identified by the following abbreviations.

AB-SCHL	American Baptist–Samuel Colgate Historical Library, Rochester, New York
AR	August Rauschenbusch
ASL	Ambrose Swasey Library of Colgate Rochester Divinity School/Bexley Hall/Crozer Theological Seminary/Saint Bernard's Institute, Rochester, New York
CI	*Christian Inquirer* (New York)
CSC	Walter Rauschenbusch, *Christianity and the Social Crisis*. New York, 1907.
CSO	Walter Rauschenbusch, *Christianizing the Social Order*. New York, 1912.
DS	*Der Sendbote* (Cleveland)
ERC	Emma Rauschenbusch Clough
HBS	Hamburg Baptist Seminary, Hamburg, Federal Republic of Germany
HR	Hilmar Rauschenbusch
LuW	August Rauschenbusch, *Leben und Wirken von August Rauschenbusch*. Completed and edited by Walter Rauschenbusch. Cleveland, 1901.
LW	Leighton Williams
MF	Munson Ford

NABC   Archives, North American Baptist Conference, Sioux
            Falls, South Dakota
NYBUME   *Annual Report, New York Baptist Union for Ministerial
            Education*
PR   Pauline Rauschenbusch
RTS   Rochester Theological Seminary, Rochester, New York
RTSBR   *Rochester Theological Seminary Bulletin: The Record*
WR   Walter Rauschenbusch
WRR   Winifred Raushenbush Rorty (spelling deliberately al-
            tered by WRR)

Unless otherwise indicated, all manuscript materials are in the Rauschenbusch Family Collection of the American Baptist–Samuel Colgate Historical Library, Rochester, New York.

Preface

1. H. Richard Niebuhr, *The Kingdom of God in America* (New York, 1937), p.
   194.

2. Martin Luther King, Jr., "Pilgrimage to Nonviolence," *Christian Century*,
   13 April 1960, p. 439.

Chapter 1: Son of August Rauschenbusch

1. On the events surrounding Walter Rauschenbusch's birth, see *LuW*, pp.
   217–19; "flippant remarks" quote, undated letter from AR to WR, probably written in September 1892; "God will make . . ." quote, AR to Wilhelm Rauschenbusch, 6 October 1861. The story of AR's naming of his
   son appears in a private autobiographical fragment written by WR for
   his wife in December 1900.

2. The chief source of information about AR's life and ministry is *LuW*. It
   was begun as an autobiography by AR shortly before his death, but he
   completed only half of it; WR finished and edited it. WR also prepared
   several shorter sketches of AR. His account of the 1850 baptism is from
   "Augustus Rauschenbusch, D.D.," *Baptist Home Missions Monthly*, September 1898, pp. 323–24.

3. "Worldliness and indifference . . ." quote, from a circular letter by AR,
   1853, HBS; Ricke Leimkuehler, "Why the Rev. August Rauschenbusch
   Took a Special Interest in the Missionary Work in Missouri," manuscript,
   1964, NABC. Two of Leimkuehler's grandparents were baptized by AR.

4. Excerpts from the constitution of the German Baptist Church on Pin Oak Creek in Charles F. Zummach, "A Bright Star in God's Firmament," *Baptist Herald*, 1 June 1942, p. 6.

5. WR's account of the baptism in *LuW*, p. 181. The baptism also is discussed by Reinhold J. Kerstan, "Historical Factors in the Formation of the Ethnically Oriented North American Baptist General Conference," Ph.D. diss., Northwestern University, 1971, pp. 110–13. "The war is the judgment . . ." quote, in Frank H. Woyke, *Heritage and Ministry of the North American Baptist Conference* (Oakbrook Terrace, Ill., 1979), p. 91.

6. Ricke Leimkuehler, "Rev. August Rauschenbusch: Some of His Peculiarities," manuscript, 1966, p. 3, NABC.

7. Robert G. Torbet, *A History of the Baptists* (Valley Forge, Pa., 1973), p. 312; *NYBUME, 1850* and *1851;* Winthrop Hudson, *Religion in America*, 3rd ed. (New York, 1981), pp. 109–204.

8. "By far . . ." quote, in Philip Schaff, *America*, ed. Perry Miller (Cambridge, Mass., 1961), p. 11; Freeman quote, *NYBUME, 1855*, p. 24.

9. Charles F. Zummach, "Our School of the Prophets," in *These Glorious Years: The Centenary of the German Baptists in North America* (Cleveland, 1943), pp. 64–69; Albert John Ramaker, "The Story of the German Department," *RTSBR*, October 1927, pp. 30–34; Robert T. Handy, *A Christian America: Protestant Hopes and Historical Realities* (New York, 1971), pp. 27–94.

10. Blake McKelvey, *Rochester: The Flower City, 1855–1890* (Cambridge, Mass., 1949), pp. 1–60; Doris M. Savage, "The Rochester Theological Seminary in the Old United States Hotel," *Rochester History* 31 (July 1969).

11. *LuW*, pp. 183–84, 190–91. When WR closed his parents' Rochester home, he found the pot of soil and buried it in the family garden (WR, 1888–91 Diary).

12. *NYBUME, 1860*, p. 18; Albert John Ramaker, "An Historical Sketch of the Seminary: The Period of Early Struggles, 1850–1872," *RTSBR*, May 1925, pp. 10–12; Zummach, "Our School," pp. 69–71; A. H. Newman, *A History of the Baptist Churches in the United States of America*, American Church History, vol. 2 (New York, 1894), pp. 378–83, 433–36.

13. *LuW*, pp. 185–92.

14. The original of WR's autobiographical fragment is in ASL; copies in NABC and AB-SCHL. A shorter account appears in *LuW*, pp. 219–22. Near the end of his life, WR again considered writing an autobiography, but he did not embark upon it. Like his father, he saved most of his voluminous papers, and early in his ministry he also began keeping clippings about himself and the causes he served. Most of this material is at AB-SCHL.

15. McKelvey, *Rochester*, p. 117; *LuW*, pp. 222–23, 233; "helping Papa . . ." quote, WR to "Tante," n.d. (probably to Lina Döring in August 1872), NABC.

16. WR to Lina Döring, 6 October 1873, NABC; WR to PR, 17 May 1898; "I often milked . . ." quote, WR to Lina Döring, 24 October 1872; "On market days . . ." quote, in *CSO*, p. 159.

17. "The best of my children . . ." quote, AR to Maria Ehrhardt, 24 July 1873, NABC; "very rewarding profession" quote, AR to Maria Ehrhardt, 13 October 1873, NABC.

18. *LuW*, pp. 213–24; AR to Maria Ehrhardt, 13 October 1873 and 10 April 1877, NABC; "He educated me . . ." quote, WR to D. C. Vandercook, 23 February 1917.

19. Pertinent facets of the religious scene in Germany are sketched in Robert M. Bigler, *The Politics of German Protestantism: The Rise of the Protestant Church Elite in Prussia, 1815–1848* (Berkeley and Los Angeles, 1972); John E. Groh, *Nineteenth-Century German Protestantism: The Church as Social Model* (Washington, D.C., 1982), pp. 22–23, 110–18, 371–86; Kenneth Scott Latourette, *Christianity in the Nineteenth and Twentieth Centuries*, vol. 2, *The Nineteenth Century in Europe* (New York, 1959), p. 113; and John E. Groh, "Architects of the Kingdom: A History of Public Appeals to God's Kingdom in Nineteenth-Century German Protestantism," Ph.D. diss., University of Chicago, 1972. Neander's Kingdom concept appears in Augustus [Johann August] Neander, *The Life of Jesus Christ in Its Historical Connexion*, trans. John McClintock and C. E. Blumenthal (London, 1869), pp. 81–89. AR's views appear in *LuW*, pp. 90, 142, 209–16, 226, 246–47, and in Carl E. Schneider, "The Americanization of Karl August Rauschenbusch, 1816–1899," *Church History* 24 (1955): 6.

20. "He kept me . . ." quote, WR to Vandercook, 23 February 1917. Three documents dating from WR's early school experience are at AB-SCHL: Censur, Rochester Real-Schule, 6 June 1871; Certificate of Promotion, School No. 14, June 1874; Certificate, Grammar School No. 15, June 1876. Information about the Free Academy appears in McKelvey, *Rochester*, pp. 135, 287–89, and in J. M. O'Grady, "In the Early Days of Pi Phi," *Pi Phi Quarterly*, December 1904.

21. WR's essay, entitled "The United States and Great Britain," was probably written during the 1878–79 school year. "The young gentleman . . ." quote, in *Rochester Daily Union and Advertiser*, 27 June 1879; "Benny's Grand Baby Show" brochure is preserved in Local History Archives, Rochester Public Library.

22. WRR to D. R. Sharpe, 17 December 1938; interview with Lisa Rauschenbusch, 16 May 1981.

23. Woyke, *Heritage*, pp. 47–48; "Poor Mrs. Rauschenbusch . . ." quote, in *Autobiography of Augustus Hopkins Strong*, ed. Crerar Douglas (Valley Forge, Pa., 1981), p. 231.

24. AR to Maria Ehrhardt, 17 November 1871, NABC (also cited in Woyke, *Heritage*, p. 50).

25. AR to Ehrhardt, 24 July 1873, NABC.

26. AR to Ehrhardt, 13 October 1873, NABC.

27. AR to Ehrhardt, 9 August 1877, 12 September 1878, NABC; Woyke, *Heritage*, p. 51.

28. "I come in . . ." quote, Autobiographical fragment, 1900; "I stood up . . ." quote, WR to ERC, 29 March 1915. I should add that nothing has been found to support D. R. Sharpe's claim that August Rauschenbusch had a "drinking" problem; see Sharpe, *Walter Rauschenbusch* (New York, 1942), p. 42.

29. "Ran with a gang . . ." quote, in Robert T. Handy, ed., *The Social Gospel in America, 1870–1920* (New York, 1966), p. 264; "quite unruly . . ." quote, in Martin Leuschner, "Walter Rauschenbusch and Our Day," manuscript, 1934, NABC; "unbelief" story, F. W. C. Meyer to WRR, 17 September 1929.

30. WRR, "Beginnings" (notes by WR's daughter about his life); Baptismal records, Latta Road Baptist Church, Rochester (the successor to First German Baptist Church); "by a long struggle . . ." quote, WR to L. C. Barnes, 10 May 1918.

31. Handy, *Social Gospel*, pp. 264–65.

32. WRR to D. R. Sharpe, 8 October 1941.

Chapter 2: Primus Omnium

1. *LuW*, pp. 16, 115–28; WR, 1879 Diary.

2. Hajo Holborn, *A History of Modern Germany, 1840–1945* (New York, 1969), pp. 223–97; Gordon A. Craig, *Germany, 1866–1945* (New York, 1978), pp. 27–223; K. Baedeker, *Northern Germany* (London, 1877), p. 61; WR, "Life at a German Gymnasium," notes for a speech at RTS, 25 November 1904; "a great variety . . ." quote, WR to MF, 13 February 1881; "dear little town" quote, WR to AR, 7 July 1883.

3. The Gütersloh Gymnasium's founding is discussed in Friedrich Bruns, "Von der Gründung bis zum 1. Weltkrieg," *Festschrift zur Hundertjahrfeier des Evangelisch-stiftischen Gymnasiums zu Gütersloh* (Gütersloh, 1951), pp. 13–56; Klaus J. Laube, "Volkening und seine Freunde in Gütersloh," pp. 7–21, and Hans Hilbk, "Die Idee des Evangelisch-Stiftischen Gymnasiums und ihre Verwirklichung im Gütersloh des 19. Jahrhunderts," in *Jahrbuch für Westfälische Kirchengeschichte, 1979*, pp. 39–61. "Wicked doctrines . . ." quote, in R. H. Samuel and R. Hinton Thomas, *Education and Society in Modern Germany* (London, 1949), p. 63; "Love for God . . ."

quote, in Erwin Steinmeier, *Der evangelische Religionsunterricht an den Gymnasien in Gütersloh und Minden-Ravensberg* (Bunde, 1980), p. 90.

4. James E. Russell, *German Higher Schools* (New York, 1899), pp. 121–351; James C. Albisetti, *Secondary School Reform in Imperial Germany* (Princeton, 1983), pp. 3–56; WR, 1879 Diary; "I translated German . . ." and "I nearly stood on my head" quotes, WR to MF, 30 November 1879.

5. Quotes in WR to MF, 30 November 1879. Other reports of the early months at Gütersloh appear in WR to MF, 13 February 1881; 1879 Diary; WR to Mama and Emma, 5 October 1879; Notebook, Gütersloh, 1879; AR to Maria Ehrhardt, 24 April 1880, HBS.

6. WR to MF, 13 February 1881, 18 June 1881; WR to AR, 3 April 1881, 12 June 1881; "good preparation" quote, WR to MF, 19 July 1881.

7. WR to parents, 18 June 1881; "Summary from Minutes" of meetings of the Gütersloh Prima, 1881; interview with Gütersloh faculty members, March 1982; "first man of the establishment" quote, WR to MF, 19 March 1882.

8. WR to AR, 22 August 1881, 10 December 1881, 11 September 1882; "quickness and acuteness . . ." quote, WR to MF, 19 March 1882; "very much in love" quote, WR to MF, 12 November 1881. Two small booklets of poems written by WR during the Gütersloh years are at AB-SCHL.

9. "No! Ne'er would I surrender . . ." quote, in Gütersloh Poetry, book 2, 16 August 1880; "You see . . ." quote, WR to MF, 18 March 1883.

10. WR to AR, 28 September 1880, 23 April 1881, 10 July 1881, 23 October 1881, 13 January 1883; WR to parents, 3 December 1882; WR to Maria Döring, 14 November 1880; Steinmeier, *Religionsunterricht*, pp. 25–26; "Bericht über das Schuljahr 1879–1880," Gymnasium Archives.

11. *LuW*, p. 129; Robert Stupperich, "Die kirchliche und theologische Wirkung der Erweckungsbewegung im Spiegel des Gütersloher Verlagswesens," *Jahrbuch für Westfälische Kirchengeschichte, 1979*, pp. 23–37; WR to AR, 5 November 1881, 7 July 1882; WR, 1888–91 Diary; "very wooden socially" quote, WR to AR, 10 December 1882.

12. "I hardly get a glimpse . . ." quote, WR to MF, 19 June 1881; "How I long . . ." quote, Gütersloh Poetry, book 1, 31 October 1880; "that I turn all green . . ." quote, WR to MF, 19 June 1881.

13. Steinmeier, *Religionsunterricht*, pp. 82, 157; *Zum Gedächtnis, D. Theodor Braun* (Gütersloh, 1911); "a loyal servant . . ." quote, in "Zeugnis der Reise," 7 February 1883.

14. WR to AR, 14 November 1880, 23 July 1882, 3 December 1882; "the Chaplain was a man . . ." and "He dealt . . ." quotes, in WR, "Religion in Germany," *Brick Church Life* (Rochester), January 1915; "I get more . . ." quote, WR to AR, 23 April 1881.

15. "Do you resist . . ." quote, in *Prüfe dich selbst!* (Gütersloh, 1880); "sometimes I have . . ." quote, WR to AR, 12 October 1880; "I cannot help it . . ." quote, WR to AR, 14 November 1880; "I thank and love . . ." quote, Hanna to WR, 23 November 1882, NABC.

16. WR to AR, 10 July 1881, 16 October 1881; Douglas, *Autobiography of Strong*, p. 260; "to feel the guiding hand . . ." quote, Hanna to WR, 23 November 1882, NABC. Note that WR's letters to Hanna are not extant; occasionally Hanna quoted from letters he received from WR.

17. WR, 1879 Diary; Latourette, *Nineteenth Century in Europe*, pp. 107–8; "great and heavy pain" quote, WR to AR, 10 December 1882.

18. Bruns, *Festschrift*, pp. 14–18; William O. Shanahan, *German Protestants Face the Social Question* (Notre Dame, 1954); Groh, *Nineteenth-Century German Protestantism*, pp. 225–485; Heinrich Hermelink, *Das Christentum in der Menschheitsgeschichte von der französischen Revolution bis zur Gegenwart* (Tübingen, 1955), 2:525–49.

19. Steinmeier, *Religionsunterricht*, pp. 18, 53–55, 77–79, 144–45; WR to MF, 30 November 1879; "Commit whatever grieves thee . . ." quote, from *North American Hymnal* (1956), p. 386; "the best expression . . ." quote, in "Instructions in Case of My Death," 31 March 1918.

20. WR to Maria Döring, 14 November 1880, NABC; WR to AR, 6 November 1881, 12 February 1882, 5 November 1882; WR to MF, 12 November 1882; "The Gospels are the best . . ." quote, WR to Lina Döring, 24 March 1883, NABC.

21. Steinmeier, *Religionsunterricht*, pp. 107–10; WR to AR, 23 April 1881, 23 July 1882, 15 October 1882; "no green sprig . . ." and other lines in WR to AR, 11 September 1882. A similar view of the Kingdom appears in Neander, *General History of the Christian Religion and Church*, vol. 1, 12th American ed., trans. Joseph Torrey (Boston, 1871), p. 1; also Neander, *Life of Jesus Christ*, p. 346.

22. WR, "Baptist Mission Work in Germany," *National Baptist*, 31 July 1884; WR, "Travels," Notes of speech, n.d.; WR to AR, 1 February 1883; "The proclaiming of God's word . . ." quote, WR to AR, 3 May 1883. WR's first published article had appeared on 11 June 1879 in *Der Sendbote (DS)*, the weekly paper of the German Baptists in North America. It encouraged family attendance at Sunday school.

23. Andrew L. Drummond, *German Protestantism since Luther* (London, 1951), p. 233; WR to AR, 20 August 1882; "I always feel . . ." quote, Hanna to WR, 27 May 1883, NABC; "I wish I could take . . ." quote, WR to MF, 27 May 1883.

24. "You ask me . . ." quote, in Gilbert to WR, 5 June 1881; WR to AR, 31 December 1881.

25. WR to AR, 15 August 1880, 19 November 1881; "It is good . . ." quote, WR to AR, 8 April 1882.

26. Poem of 12 July 1881 in WR, Gütersloh Poetry, book 1; "both grateful ..." quote, WR to AR, 28 September 1882.

27. WR to AR, 24 December 1880, 21 July 1881, 22 August 1881, 11 September 1882; "You must permit me ..." quote, WR to AR, 1 February 1883; "Look here, Papa ..." quote, WR to AR, 15 October 1882; "the third party ..." quote, WR to parents, 2 December 1882.

28. The work of Pastor Döring and other Elberfeldians is noted in Friedrich W. Krummacher, *An Autobiography*, trans. M. G. Easton (New York, 1869), pp. 153, 158, 222, and in *LuW*, p. 6.

29. WR to AR, 12 July 1881, 10 December 1881, 8 April 1882, 1 February 1883, 21 February 1883. Accounts of the activities of his German cousins are preserved in WR's 1908 Scrapbook. A typescript of WR's copy of the "Chronicles" is at AB-SCHL.

30. The most complete study of the family history is by a German cousin of Rauschenbusch, Ann-Katrin Bauknecht, whom I interviewed in Stuttgart on 15 February 1982. WR referred to his family's past in "Augustus Rauschenbusch." Some of that story is related in *LuW*.

31. "A distinctive family character" and "make a more confident prognosis ..." quotes, WR to AR, 12 December 1882; "live up to the traditions ..." quote, WR to Vandercook, 23 February 1917; "aristocrat" quote, in Paul Moore Strayer, "Walter Rauschenbusch: An Apostle of the Kingdom," *Homiletical Review*, 19 February 1919, p. 92. WR's proud sense of family tradition was communicated to me in an interview with his daughter, Lisa Rauschenbusch, on 16 May 1981.

32. WR to MF, 19 June 1881; AR to Maria Ehrhardt, 29 June 1881, HBS; Hanna to WR, 7 November 1880, NABC; WR to AR, 19 May 1883; "intensely happy ..." quote, WR to MF, 20 August 1882.

33. WR to MF, 18 March 1883, 22 September 1883; WR to AR, 18 March 1883, 4 April 1883, 18 April 1883, 27 April 1883, 31 May 1883, 7 July 1883; "I drank in their words ..." quote, WR to MF, 27 May 1883; "a learned theologian ..." quote, WR to MF, 31 December 1884.

34. WR, "The Ideals of Social Reformers," *American Journal of Sociology* 2 (September 1896): 211; WR to AR, 10 July 1881, 22 August 1881; "my fatherland" quote, WR to AR, 9 October 1881; "My country hail to thee ..." poem, 4 July 1881, in Gütersloh Poetry, book 2. The undated printed poem is preserved in WR's first scrapbook.

Chapter 3: Seminarian

1. WR to MF, 19 March 1882; "In Political Economy ..." quote, WR to MF, 27 May 1883; "quite lazy" quote, WR to MF, 12 November 1882.

2. Arthur J. May, *A History of the University of Rochester, 1850–1962* (Rochester, 1977), pp. 3–90; Asahel C. Kendrick, *Martin B. Anderson, LL.D.: A Biography* (Philadelphia, 1895); *LuW*, p. 224; "It is the aim . . ." quote, in *Thirty-fourth Annual Catalogue of the Officers and Students of the University of Rochester, 1883–4*, p. 30.

3. *Catalogue, 1883–4*, p. 8; "became an object . . ." quote, in Mitchell Brunk, "Walter Rauschenbusch," *Adult Leader*, October 1934. One set of records is in the University of Rochester Registrar's Office; the other is in the University Archives.

4. Webster's achievements are discussed in *Interpres*, University of Rochester, 1888, pp. 99–100, and *Rochester Post-Express*, 18 June 1906. "To hear Professor Webster . . ." quote, WR to MF, 26 February 1884; WR's remarks on Webster are in his eulogy in "Obituary," *Union University Quarterly*, August 1906, pp. 124, 122, 126.

5. Henry May, *Protestant Churches and Industrial America* (New York, 1949), pp. 31–90; *Union University Quarterly*, August 1906, p. 125; "first awakening of interest" quote, WR to G. H. Roller, 12 March 1915. George's *Progress and Poverty* appeared in 1879.

6. Francis P. Weisenburger, *Ordeal of Faith: The Crisis of Church-going America, 1865–1900* (New York, 1959), pp. 50–79; Dennis R. Davis, "The Impact of Evolutionary Thought on Walter Rauschenbusch," *Foundations* 11 (1968): 260–61. The only published statement of Webster's philosophical outlook is his *Life Spiritual: A Baccalaureate Address* (New York, 1890).

7. RTS Catalogues, 1883–86, and RTS Statistics on Entering Students and Examination Records, ASL; *American Baptist Yearbook, 1883*, p. 72; WR to Lina Döring, 21 March 1884, NABC; "grandly interesting" quote, WR to MF, 22 September 1883; "in these days" quote, *NYBUME, 1885*, p. 44.

8. Howard Osgood, "Modern Biblical Criticism," *Proceedings of the Baptist Congress, 1883*, p. 58; Norman H. Maring, "Baptists and Changing Views of the Bible (Part 1)," *Foundations* 1 (1958): 58, 67; "deeply read . . ." quote, in WR, "Address," *RTSBR*, May 1916, p. 19; Osgood quotations are from his booklet *The Old Testament: What It Is and What It Teaches* (Rochester, 1879), pp. 6, 15. I discuss Osgood's later involvement with WR in chapter 4.

9. "I enjoy . . ." quote, WR to MF, 26 February 1884; Stevens quotations are from his "Inspiration of the Apostles," *Baptist Quarterly Review* 8 (1886): 80, 81; "He taught us an important code . . ." quote, in WR, "Obituary," *RTSBR*, February 1910, p. 6; WR, "The Synagogue," written during the 1883–84 school year.

10. Sydney E. Ahlstrom, *A Religious History of the American People* (New Haven, 1972), pp. 763–84; F. M. Szasz, *Divided Mind of Protestant America, 1880–1930* (University, Ala., 1982), pp. 1–41; "no outlook except . . ."

quote, WR to John S. Phillips, 24 May 1909; "the travail . . ." and other quotes, WR to C. E. Smith, 21 March 1912. WR's study of parallel New Testament texts, "Harmony of the Gospels," February 1884, is preserved at NABC.

11. True's interests are reflected in his "Church of England: Its Conditions and Its Recent History," *Baptist Quarterly Review* 11 (1889): 178–206; in *NYBUME, 1882*, p. 44; and in an obituary article in WR's 1902 Scrapbook. WR's student papers for True were "The Donatists," 1884–85, and "The Waldensees," 27 November 1885; his review of Reusch's *Der Index der Verbotenen Bücher* was published in *Baptist Quarterly Review* 8 (1886): 564–67. Accounts of Neander's historical approach appear in C. Ullmann, "Preface" in Neander, *General History*, vol. 1, pp. ix–xxxii, and in Philip Schaff's essay in *Reformed and Catholic: Selected Historical and Theological Writings of Philip Schaff*, ed. Charles Yrigoyen, Jr., and George M. Bricker (Pittsburgh, 1979), pp. 268–83.

12. WR, "Lectures on Preaching," 1884; Thomas Harwood Pattison, *The History of Christian Preaching* (Philadelphia, 1903), pp. 310–15; WR to Lina Döring, 20 March 1886, NABC.

13. Augustus Hopkins Strong, *Philosophy and Religion* (New York, 1888), pp. 461–67; Douglas, *Autobiography of Strong*; Grant Wacker, *Augustus H. Strong and the Dilemma of Historical Consciousness* (Macon, Ga., 1985). In 1886 Strong's *Lectures* were superseded by the first edition of his *Systematic Theology*, which for decades was one of the most widely used theological textbooks among conservative Protestants in the United States.

14. WR, "Sabellius and Sabellianism," 1884–85 academic year; WR, "The Bushnellian Theory of the Atonement," 17 November 1885.

15. Robertson's thought and influence are discussed in Owen Chadwick, *The Victorian Church* (New York, 1970), part 2, pp. 135–36, and William R. Hutchison, *The Modernist Impulse in American Protestantism* (Cambridge, Mass., 1976), pp. 80–84. "To have more time . . ." quote, WR to MF, 22 September 1883; "I owe more . . ." quote, WR to Maria Döring, 13 July 1886, NABC; "absorbed the idea . . ." quote, WR to J. S. Phillips, 24 May 1909.

16. *Life, Letters, Lectures, and Addresses of Frederick W. Robertson, M.A.*, ed. Stopford E. Brooke (New York, 1865), pp. 278, 293, 308, 356. Robertson's name recurs in WR's Sermon Notebooks, e.g., 18 June 1888, 12 May 1889, 13 April 1890, 10 May 1896.

17. *Rochester Democrat and Chronicle*, 21 May 1884 and 28 April 1885; W. S. Rainsford, *Story of a Varied Life* (New York, 1924); RTS Scrapbooks, 1884, 1885, ASL.

18. WR to MF, 14 June 1884; WR, "First Sermon," NABC; "I rejoiced . . ." quote, WR to MF, 31 December 1884.

19. WR to MF, 30 May 1885.

20. WR to MF, 26 February 1884; WR to F. W. C. Meyer, 16 August 1884; AR to Maria Ehrhardt, 25 September 1886, NABC; *Democrat and Chronicle*, 20 May 1886; "You write me so full of love" quote, WR to Lina Döring, 6 November 1884, NABC; WR, "The Ethics of Thinking," May 1886.

Chapter 4: Pastor

1. WR to Lina Döring, 20 March 1886, NABC; Woyke, *Heritage*, pp. 81, 176; F. M. Müller to WR, 11 February 1886; WR to MF, 30 June 1886.

2. Glimpses of New York at this time in *King's Handbook of New York* (New York, 1892); Richard O'Connor, *Hell's Kitchen* (Philadelphia, 1958), pp. 11–98; *WPA Guide to New York City* (New York, 1982), pp. 144–56; Jacob Riis, *How the Other Half Lives*, ed. Sam B. Warner, Jr. (Cambridge, Mass., 1970), pp. 105–6; Robert D. Cross, ed., *The Church and the City, 1865–1910* (Indianapolis, 1967), pp. 29–39.

3. The sketch of Second Church is based on WR to MF, 30 June 1886; WR to Maria Döring, 13 July 1886, NABC; WR, "History of Second German Baptist Church," notes, n.d.; *CI*, 15 November 1888, 13 December 1888, 31 October 1889. "A miracle before our eyes" quote, in *DS*, 23 June 1886.

4. WR to Maria Döring, 13 July 1886, NABC; WR, Sermon Notebook 2, 1886; WR to F. W. C. Meyer, 28 June 1886 and 23 September 1886, NABC; WR to MF, 30 June 1886.

5. WR, 1888–91 Diary; WR to Lina Döring, 14 July 1886, NABC; WR to Caroline Rauschenbusch, 24 September 1886, NABC; WR to AR, 12 October 1880. It is clear from these documents that WR's hearing problem began several years before the time indicated by D. R. Sharpe, *Walter Rauschenbusch* (New York, 1942), pp. 65–66, and in less dramatic circumstances.

6. "Bringing them . . ." quote, WR to MF, 30 June 1886; "I enjoyed everything . . ." and subsequent quotes, WR to Maria Döring, 13 July 1886, NABC.

7. E. F. Merriam to WR, 12 August 1886, 7 September 1886; "for a few years . . ." quote, 18 September 1886, 29 September 1886; J. N. Murdock to WR, 19 April 1887. Osgood's role is disclosed in C. H. Moehlmann, "The Life and Writings of Walter Rauschenbusch," *Colgate Rochester Divinity School Bulletin*, October 1928, p. 33, and repeated in F. W. C. Meyer to WRR, 17 September 1929. "I know what is to be done . . ." quote, WR to J. N. Murdock, n.d. (undoubtedly 1887).

8. "Doubts and deviant attitudes" quote, AR to Sister, 25 September 1886, NABC; "I have no desire more serious . . ." quote, WR to Caroline Rauschenbusch, 24 September 1886, NABC.

9. George H. Charles, Jr., to WR, 14 October 1886; *DS*, 10 November 1886.

10. WR to Lina Döring, 14 July 1886, 14 December 1886, NABC; WR, 1888–91 Diary; interview with Lisa Rauschenbusch, 16 May 1981.

11. Quotes in WR, "City Mission Work among the Germans," Address to Southern New York Baptist Association, 6 October 1887. Records of the Second German Baptist Church Youth Association, dating from November 1889, give the names and addresses of many church members. All official documents were carefully kept by WR; they are now the property of the Valley Stream Baptist Church, Valley Stream, New York, successor to the Second German Baptist Church.

12. Complete notes of some 370 sermons survive from the 1886–91 period. Before 1888 most were written in German; later, though WR composed them in English, he continued normally to deliver them in German, for he believed strongly in the need for German immigrants to be able to worship in their native tongue. His most frequently used New Testament sources in this period are John (texts for 53 sermons), Matthew (48), Luke (25), Romans (22), Acts (18), Revelation (17), 1 Corinthians (16), 1 John (14), and Hebrews (12).

13. "The gospel simple . . ." quote, Ed Hanna to WR, 9 April 1887, NABC; "My idea then . . ." quote, in WR, "Genesis of 'Christianity and the Social Crisis,' " *RTSBR*, November 1918, p. 51.

14. "Salvation of society . . ." quote, in WR's first sermon on a social theme, preached 9 August 1889, on Revelation 21:2, in Sermon Notebooks, 1889.

15. "Be not so busy . . ." quote, in Sermon Notebooks, 22 March 1888; "I gave myself to God . . ." quote, in 1888–91 Diary. Two of the clippings were WR's own reports of the Moody Conference, published in *CI*, 16 August and 13 September 1888.

16. The first hymnal was *Neue Lieder* (1889), edited by WR and W. Appel. Numerous letters between WR and Sankey are preserved at AB-SCHL. Their hymnals went through several editions; eleven different titles are listed in E. H. Starr, *A Baptist Bibliography*, vol. 19 (Rochester, 1973), pp. 121–22. The four major publications were *Evangeliums-Lieder* (1890), *Evangeliums-Lieder No. 2* (1894), *Evangeliums-Lieder Nos. 1 and 2* (1897), and *Evangeliums-Sänger* (1910). WR also helped prepare the official German Baptist Hymnal, *Neue Glaubensharfe* (1917).

17. *CI*, 29 March 1888, 4 October 1888, 7 March 1889, 23 May 1889, 4 October 1889. Information about Schmidt in *Cornell University Necrology of the Faculty, 1938–39* (Ithaca, N.Y., 1939), p. 33, and about Williams in *Marlborough Record*, 26 July 1935. "Warm friendship . . ." quote, in LW, "The Brotherhood of the Kingdom and Its Work," *The Kingdom*, August 1907.

18. E. F. Merriam, "The Brotherhood of the Kingdom," *The Watchman*, 13 August 1908; "Only an afternoon . . ." quote, in Plas Llecheiddior Visitors Book. My 1889 dating of Williams's proposal is based upon a letter of

Nathaniel Schmidt to WR, 18 April 1889, and upon WR's notes for a talk in 1903, "Explanation of the Brotherhood." Some scholars have thought the society emerged earlier.

19. "All sorts of practical . . ." quote, WR to Maria Döring, 14 January 1887, NABC; "there are many silent prayers . . ." quote, Mrs. E. Kaiser to WR, 2 July 1888.

20. *Southern New York Baptist Association Annual Report, 1886, 1887, 1888;* *CI*, 1 March 1888, 6 December 1888; "excellent pastor" quote, *CI* 20 December 1888; 1888–91 Diary; A. H. Strong to WR, 25 April 1888; "hothouse atmosphere . . ." quote, in *DS*, 11 June 1888.

21. "Second German Church," *CI*, 30 May 1889; R. S. MacArthur, "This and That," *CI*, 31 October 1889; Richard Harley, "Baptist City Mission Notes," *CI*, 5 December 1889; "Second German Church," *CI*, 3 April 1890; WR, "The Second German Church, New York City," *National Baptist*, April 1890.

22. WR to J. D. Rockefeller, 5 July 1886 (Rockefeller Family Archives, Record Group D); Bessie R. Strong to WR, 6 May 1889; J. D. Rockefeller to WR, 20 May 1889, 26 November 1889, 29 November 1889, 3 March 1890.

23. WR, "A Word for the Little Churches," *Examiner*, 10 March 1892; "workshop . . ." quote, in Sermon Notebooks, 23 February 1890.

24. "Oh, the children's funerals . . ." quote, WR, "The Kingdom of God," Address at the Cleveland YMCA, 1913, in Handy, *Social Gospel*, pp. 265–66; "The world is hard . . ." quote, WR to Maria Döring, 14 January 1887, NABC.

25. "And by reason . . ." quote, in *Baptist Congress, 1889*, p. 55; "I had no idea . . ." quote, in "Genesis of 'Christianity and the Social Crisis,'" *RTSBR*, November 1918, p. 51.

26. WR's fervent support of Cleveland's candidacy is evident in Joe Gilbert to WR, 23 October 1884. On McGlynn, George, and the 1886 election, see Stephen Bell, *Rebel, Priest, and Prophet: A Biography of Dr. Edward McGlynn* (New York, 1937), pp. 33–38; Thomas J. Condon, "Political Reform and the New York City Election of 1886," *New York Historical Society Quarterly* 44 (1960): 363–94; Charles A. Barker, *Henry George* (New York, 1955), pp. 453–81. "How Father McGlynn . . ." quote, in *CSO*, p. 91; "I owe my . . ." quote, in *CSO*, p. 394. A graduate student studying George reported to me that WR's name appears on a list of ward captains in the 1886 campaign. Although I have not been able to locate the list and have found no mention by WR of such involvement, he might well have served in this capacity.

27. This summary of George's position is based chiefly upon his *Progress and Poverty* (1879) and *Social Problems* (1883). See also Eileen W. Lindner, "The Redemptive Politic of Henry George: Legacy to the Social Gospel," Ph.D. diss., Union Theological Seminary, 1985; Fred Nicklason, "Henry

George, Social Gospeller," *American Quarterly* 22 (1970): 649–64; Robert V. Andelson, *Critics of Henry George* (East Brunswick, N.J., 1979); John L. Thomas, *Alternative America: Henry George, Edward Bellamy, Henry Demarest Lloyd, and the Advocacy Tradition* (Cambridge, Mass., 1983).

28. This account of Richard Ely's thought and career is based chiefly on his *French and German Socialism in Modern Times* (1883), *The Past and Present of Political Economy* (1884), and *Ground under My Feet* (1938); Benjamin G. Rader, *The Academic Mind and Reform* (Lexington, Ky., 1966); Handy, *Social Gospel*, pp. 173–83.

29. "What we need . . ." quote, in Ely, *Social Aspects of Christianity*, new and enl. ed. (New York, 1889), pp. 148–49; "It is as truly . . ." quote, in ibid., p. 73.

30. "A personal friend . . ." quote, in WR, "Noch einmal die sociale Frage," *DS*, 28 January 1891; "hard study . . ." quote, in Ely, *Social Aspects*, p. 17; Ely to WR, 8 April 1891.

31. "Wails of the mangled . . ." quote, in Sharpe, *Rauschenbusch*, p. 80 (unfortunately this paper has been lost); "Beneath the Glitter," *CI*, 2 August 1888; "felt scared . . ." quote, WR to John S. Phillips, 24 May 1909.

32. WR to Maria Döring, 13 July 1886, NABC; "Boston Meetings," *CI*, 30 May 1889; LW, "One Thing Thou Lackest," *CI*, 11 April 1889; "to show that the aim . . ." quote, in C. Howard Hopkins, *The Rise of the Social Gospel in American Protestantism* (New Haven, 1940), p. 175. WR pasted a statement of the Society's aims in his first scrapbook.

33. "If there are men . . ." quote, in WR, "That Boston Fad," *CI*, 15 August 1889; "made the most . . ." quote, 1888–91 Diary; *Annual Report of the Baptist Congress, 1889*, pp. 58–60.

34. "From the standpoint . . ." quote, in *For the Right*, November 1889; "ideas are more powerful . . ." quote, in *For the Right*, June 1890; "radical yet Christian" quote, *New York Times*, 8 November 1890; "the moneyed men . . ." quote, 1888–91 Diary.

35. "The older brethren . . ." quote, in *CSO*, p. 92.

36. "But I claim . . ." quote, *Baptist Congress, 1889*, pp. 55–56; "The State must be built . . ." quote, ibid., p. 140. WR made a similar case for social mission the following year in *For the Right* and in *Der Sendbote;* for the first, see Winthrop S. Hudson, ed., *Walter Rauschenbusch: Selected Writings*, Sources of American Spirituality (New York 1984), pp. 60–63; for the second, see Klaus Jaehn, *Rauschenbusch: The Formative Years* (Valley Forge, Pa., 1976), pp. 30–40.

37. "Revolutionary movement" and subsequent quote, in WR's lesson on Luke 18:15–30, *CI*, 21 August 1890; "radical obedience" quote in lesson on Luke 6:27–38, *CI*, 27 March 1890.

38. "There is nothing . . ." quote, in lesson on Luke 18:15–30, *CI*, 21 August 1890. The Tolstoi influence was acknowledged in the Luke 6:27–38 lesson,

in the 1888–91 Diary and in WR to G. H. Roller, 12 March 1915. The two Tolstoi works cited were *My Religion* and *War and Peace*.

39. A. H. Strong to WR, 6 March 1889; "My hearing . . ." and "their affection . . ." quotes, 1888–91 Diary.

Chapter 5: Seeker

1. WR recommended the *Fabian Essays in Socialism* (London, 1891) for German Baptists in "Noch einmal die sociale Frage," *DS*, 28 January 1891; "men whose minds . . ." quote, in WR, "That Boston Fad," *CI*, 15 August 1889.

2. Birmingham's reforms are discussed in Robert A. Woods, *English Social Movements* (1891; Freeport, N.Y., 1972), p. 71, and Peter d'A. Jones, *The Christian Socialist Revival, 1877–1914* (Princeton, 1968), p. 42. WR's Liverpool statements in 1888–91 Diary; his remarks about Birmingham in WR, "Municipal Socialism," *The Voice*, 3 September 1891 (this and other published reports from Europe are included in the 1892 Scrapbook).

3. ERC's dissertation was published as *A Study of Mary Wollstonecraft and the Rights of Woman* (London, 1898).

4. The Salvation Army and related developments are treated in K. S. Inglis, *Churches and the Working Classes in Victorian England* (London and Toronto, 1963). "Soul saving . . ." quote, in WR, "In Darkest America," n.d., 1890 Scrapbook; "looks more like . . ." quote, in 1888–91 Diary; WR on the shortcomings of charity in *The Righteousness of the Kingdom*, ed. Max Stackhouse (Nashville, 1968), pp. 175–76, 188–92.

5. The varieties of English socialist thought are discussed in G. D. H. Cole, *Socialist Thought: Marxism and Anarchism, 1850–1890* (London, 1954), vol. 2 of *A History of Socialist Thought*, pp. 379–424; 1888–91 Diary; WR's Hyde Park comments in *Righteousness of the Kingdom*, pp. 233–34.

6. "Bowing, kneeling . . ." quote, in *Righteousness of the Kingdom*, p. 234; "For centuries . . ." quote, in ibid., p. 145.

7. 1888–91 Diary.

8. Ibid.; Politzer to WR, 7 July 1891; LW to WR, 3 July 1891.

9. Problems such as those experienced by WR are addressed in Edna S. Levine, *The Psychology of Deafness* (New York, 1960). Rare clues of WR's attitude about his deafness appear in PR to Professor Bernard, 29 December 1929; WR to Franklin, 3 March 1916; WR, Sermon Notebooks, 2 May 1897.

10. WR's musings about a move are expressed in the 1888–91 Diary.

11. W. R. Ward, *Theology, Sociology and Politics: The German Protestant Social Conscience, 1890–1933* (Berne, 1979), pp. 11–77; 1888–91 Diary; "The

Party breeds fanatics . . ." and "The whole weight . . ." quotes, in WR, "The Socialists of Europe," *The Voice*, 5 November 1891.

12. Quotes (including the title "Revolutionary Christianity") from 1888–91 Diary.

13. WR to Nathaniel Schmidt, 22 January 1892. The library call slips that WR used in Berlin and Greifswald are preserved in the Rauschenbusch Family Collection, as are his reading notes and the critiques of Schmidt and Williams. WR's most copious notes were taken of sociological studies by Albert Schäffle and Alexander von Oettingen.

14. Quotations from "Revolutionary Christianity" are from the version edited by Max L. Stackhouse, *Righteousness of the Kingdom;* page numbers for most quotations are given in the text.

15. "Striking epochs" and "perhaps the most important one" quotes, WR to G. H. Roller, 12 March 1915; "History turns . . ." quote, in *Righteousness of the Kingdom,* p. 161.

16. "Like an ellipse . . ." quote, in WR, "Noch einmal die sociale Frage," *DS,* 28 January 1891; "responded to all . . ." quote, in WR, "The Kingdom of God," in Handy, *Social Gospel,* p. 266.

17. Keller's role and views are discussed in *The Recovery of the Anabaptist Vision,* ed. Guy F. Hershberger (Scottsdale, Pa., 1957). WR's first public affirmation of the Anabaptists occurred two years later at a session of the Baptist Congress (*Annual Report of the Baptist Congress, 1893,* p. 13). "Decidedly more historical" and "the Anabaptists contain . . ." quotes, in 1888–91 Diary.

Chapter 6: Servant of the Kingdom

1. Glimpses of WR during his first months back in New York are in *CI*, 17 and 31 December 1891, 7 and 14 January, 12 May and 27 October 1892; "the building of a Christianity . . ." quote, WR to Lina Döring, 20 August 1892, NABC.

2. *CI*, 26 May 1892; "The whole aim . . ." quote, in *Annual Report of the Baptist Congress, 1892,* p. 127. A similar message is in WR, "A Conquering Idea," *Examiner,* 21 July 1892.

3. "It has been a hard year . . ." quote, WR to Rockefeller, 9 May 1892 (Rockefeller Family Archives, Record Group 1); "out of work . . ." quote, in *CSC,* p. 305.

4. All quotations from Batten's "Minutes of the Brotherhood of the Kingdom." Further glimpses of the organization's early years are contained in Batten, "The Brotherhood of the Kingdom," Brotherhood Tract, 1902; Leighton Williams, "The Brotherhood of the Kingdom and Its Work,"

The Kingdom, August 1907; WR, "Explanation on the Brotherhood," notes for a speech, 1903; WR, "The Brotherhood of the Kingdom," Brotherhood Leaflet No. 2, 1893; *CSO*, pp. 23, 94; and some ten letters to and from WR in 1892 and 1893. Important later works on the Brotherhood are Mitchell Bronk, "An Adventure in the Kingdom of God," *The Crozer Quarterly*, January 1937, pp. 21–28; C. Howard Hopkins, "Walter Rauschenbusch and the Brotherhood of the Kingdom," *Church History* 7 (June 1938): 138–56; Frederic M. Hudson, "The Reign of the New Humanity: A Study of the Background, History, and Influence of the Brotherhood of the Kingdom," Ph.D. diss., Columbia University, 1968.

5. AB-SCHL preserves WR's meticulous "Journal of the Corresponding Secretary of the Brotherhood of the Kingdom."

6. Plas Llecheiddior guest book at AB-SCHL. "I am still . . ." quote, WR to Will Munger, 24 May 1894; "come in for . . ." quote, WR to Munger, 11 July 1896.

7. "Because the Kingdom . . ." quote, in WR, "The Brotherhood of the Kingdom," Brotherhood Leaflet No. 2, 1893; "embraces all pure aspirations . . ." quote, in WR, "The Kingdom of God," Brotherhood Leaflet No. 4, 1894; "a perfect humanity . . ." quote, WR, "History of the Idea of the Kingdom of God," *DS*, 26 November 1902 (first delivered as a speech in 1894). WR's major biblical exposition of this theme was "The Kingdom of God in the Parables of Jesus," manuscript, 1895. Some of WR's views about the Kingdom were anticipated and perhaps stimulated by Josiah Strong, *Our Country* (New York, 1885), p. 182.

8. "We desire . . ." quote, in "The Brotherhood," 1893.

9. Willmarth's remarks were reported in *National Baptist*, 23 November 1893. Letters between WR and Willmarth appeared in ibid., 14 and 28 December 1893 and 4 January 1894.

10. WR, "Our Attitude Toward Millenarianism," *Examiner*, 24 September and 1 October 1896.

11. J. G. Schurman, president of Cornell University, was among those who expressed uneasiness about the Brotherhood's position on socialism (Schurman to WR, 16 September 1893); WR discussed this and other questions about the Brotherhood with a reporter whose article appeared in the *New York Press*, 3 June 1894. WR's first public statement about socialism was an address at the German YMCA in Philadelphia in 1893; it was published in pamphlet form as "Kann ein Christ auch ein Socialist sein?" "A river flowing . . ." and "For working purposes . . ." quotes, in WR, "The Ideals of Social Reformers," *American Journal of Sociology* 2 (September 1896): 202, 211.

12. "Members of the classes . . ." quote, in WR, "The Ideals of Social Reformers," p. 217; WR's civic federation speech reported in *Detroit Free Press*, 17 November 1894.

13. The playground movement is studied in Dominick Cavallo, *Muscles and Morals: Organized Playgrounds and Urban Reform, 1880–1920* (Philadelphia, 1981). WR first broached the issue of playgrounds and sandpiles in "Playgrounds for the Children," *Examiner*, 18 August 1892. Summaries of his efforts for sandpiles in 1896 recur in the journal he kept as corresponding secretary; more than a dozen letters on the topic are preserved at AB-SCHL. "The worthiest . . ." quote, in WR, *The Outlook*, 14 March 1896; the *New York Herald* article (n.d.) is in WR's 1896 Scrapbook.

14. Pauline's early years are discussed in two letters she wrote to Carolyn Lyon (n.d.) and in her daughter Winifred's memorandum "Pauline Rother Rauschenbusch," n.d. "Proud and independent . . ." quote, WR to RTS classmates, n.d. (probably March 1893); "the usual effects . . ." and "with your help . . ." quoted in PR to ERC, 19 January 1893.

15. "What a heaven . . ." quote, PR to WR, 23 September 1893; "help-meet" quote, PR to WR, 18 August 1894; "Pauline helps . . ." quote, WR to Lina Döring, 20 December 1893, NABC; "hearing ear" quote, in O. E. Krueger, "A Memorial to Pauline Rauschenbusch," *Baptist Herald*, 30 March 1950, p. 23; "I delight . . ." quote, PR to WR, 8 September 1894; "reproductive faculty . . ." quote, in WR, Sermon Notebooks, 22 July 1895; "I am so thankful . . ." quote, PR to WR, 22 July 1895.

16. "I always feel . . ." quote, WR to PR, 12 September 1895; "restful side . . ." quote, WR to PR, n.d. (1893); "I need more meditation . . ." and "I do not feel . . ." quote, WR to PR, 8 September 1895; "Our finances . . ." quote, WR to PR, 7 September 1895.

17. "The soul of a child . . ." quote, Sermon Notebooks, 30 September 1894; "a small Kingdom . . ." quote, Sermon Notebooks, 24 April 1892; "She is engaged . . ." quote, in WR, "Compensations in Being a Woman," *The Watchman*, 18 July 1895.

18. WR to Will Munger, 24 May 1894; WR to PR, 13 September 1894; Krueger, "Memorial"; "pious ministers . . ." quote, WR to Munger, 11 July 1896; "favorite daydream" quote, PR to WR, 12 September 1894.

19. Allan Nevins, *Study in Power: John D. Rockefeller*, vol. 2 (New York, 1953), pp. 89–94, 159–60; Laura Rockefeller to PR, 20 December 1900.

20. "Small Kingdom . . ." quote, in Sermon Notebooks, 27 September 1893; "preach Christ . . ." quote, in ibid., 4 July 1897; "if you have not mastered . . ." quote, in ibid., 29 May 1892; "the greatest prize . . ." quote, in ibid., 2 April 1893.

21. The book was entitled *Die politische Verfassung unseres Landes: Ein Handbuch zum Unterrichte für die deutsch-amerikanische Jugend* (Cleveland, 1902). "Control . . ." quote, in Sermon Notebooks, 5 November 1892.

22. The sketch of Second Church activities is based on congregational records, WR's Scrapbooks, and sermons (esp. 4 June 1893 and 4 July 1897); also on Hudson, "Reign of the New Humanity," pp. 35–38, 164–80; O. C. Al-

brecht to WR, 6 July 1895; and WR, "The Stake of the Church in the Social Movement," *American Journal of Sociology* 3 (July 1897): 25–26.

23. Tenth-anniversary mementos are preserved in 1896 Scrapbook. WR's study book was *Das Leben Jesu: Ein systematischer Studiengang für Jugendvereine und Bibelklassen* (Cleveland, 1895).

24. A. H. Strong to WR, 31 August 1892; WR to Will Munger, 24 May 1894; WR to PR, 13 May 1897; WR to School Committee, DS, 30 June 1897; "forefront of radical Christianity" quote, Sermon Notebooks, 8 September 1895.

25. Strong to WR, 29 May 1897; "We have one or two . . ." quote, 10 June 1897; see also Strong to WR, 12 June 1897, 14 June 1897, 15 June 1897; "we shall yet . . ." quote, Strong to WR, 19 June 1897.

26. The Schmidt episode is summarized in Hudson, "Reign of the New Humanity," pp. 190–203; "This is one of the saddest . . ." quote, in WR, "Kingdom of God," in Handy *Social Gospel*, p. 266. Minutes of the NY-BUME executive committee show that Rockefeller was one of the two trustees consulted. It is also recorded there that "neither endorse the appointment and both expressed themselves satisfied to abide by the choice of the committee" (14 June 1897, ASL).

Chapter 7: German Baptist

1. *NYBUME, 1897, 1902; American Baptist Yearbook, 1897;* A. H. Strong, *Historical Discourse . . . the Fiftieth Anniversary of the Rochester Theological Seminary, May 9, 1900* (Rochester, 1900); "pre-eminently a Baptist century" quote by J. B. Gambrell, in *A Century of Baptist Achievement*, ed. A. H. Newman (Philadelphia, 1901), p. 448.

2. Woyke, *Heritage*, pp. 238–47; WR, "What Shall We Do with the Germans?" pamphlet, 1895.

3. "Industrious, intelligent . . ." and "a German converted . . ." quotes, in A. P. Mihm, "German Immigration," *Baptist Home Missions Monthly*, September, 1898, pp. 307, 308; Batten's comment in Lawrence B. Davis, *Immigrants, Baptists, and the Protestant Mind in America* (Urbana, Ill., 1973), p. 141.

4. "I believe in . . ." quote, *Annual Report of the Baptist Congress, 1888*, p. 87; "Is the American stock so fertile . . ." quote, in WR, "What Shall We Do with the Germans?" pamphlet, 1895; "The Germans . . ." quote, in "The German Seminary in Rochester," pamphlet, 1897. No author was listed for either pamphlet, but in his 1897 Scrapbook WR put his name on the first one, and the appearance there of the second suggests that he was the primary author of that one also.

5. "We have loyally accepted . . ." quote, in "What Shall We Do with the Germans?"

6. This cluster of problems facing German Baptists is analyzed by Davis, *Immigrants*, pp. 101–4; Woyke, *Heritage*, pp. 182–84, 201–2, 281–82; and Eric H. Ohlmann, "The American Baptist Mission to German-Americans: A Case Study of Attempted Assimilation," Th.D. diss., Graduate Theological Union, 1973. The larger immigration picture is presented by John Higham, *Strangers in the Land: Patterns of American Nativism, 1860–1925* (New York, 1963). WR's chief affirmation of the superiority of the German Baptist churches was his "Shall I Join an English Church?" in *Der Jugend Herold*, July 1896, p. 147.

7. James M. Berquist, "German-America in the 1890s: Illusions and Realities," in *Germans in America: Aspects of German-American Relations in the Nineteenth Century*, ed. E. Allen McCormick (New York, 1983); WR, "Allerlei aus Deutschland," *DS*, 6, 13, and 20 September 1899; "sense of mystery . . ." and "Let the Teutons . . ." quotes, in *Rochester Democrat and Chronicle*, 8 May 1902.

8. *Frankfurter Zeitung*, 10 June 1898; *DS*, 13 September 1899; "Is it strange . . ." quote, in "England and Germany," *The Watchman*, 16 November 1899, p. 11, reprinted in Handy, *Social Gospel*, pp. 300–307.

9. The entire Thanksgiving sermon appeared in the *Rochester Post-Express*, 25 November 1898.

10. The effect of the czar's initiative on the peace movement in the United States as a whole is discussed in C. Roland Marchand, *The American Peace Movement and Social Reform, 1898–1918* (Princeton, 1972), pp. 29–31. WR's sermon appeared in both the *Democrat and Chronicle* and the *Post-Express* on 13 February 1899. Newspaper and magazine accounts of "the Rochester Movement," letters, and reminiscences are preserved in WR's 1899 Scrapbook. "The faint beginning . . ." quote, in *CSC*, p. 379.

11. Most of WR's reviews in these years appeared in the *American Journal of Theology* and *Deutsch-Amerikanische Zeitschrift für Theologie und Kirche;* they covered a wide range of books, including some by Theodor Zahn and Johannes Weiss. "I am thankful . . ." quote, in *Report of the Brotherhood of the Kingdom, 1895*, p. 61; Zart, *The Charm of Jesus* (New York, 1899).

12. "We take our brother . . ." and "draws us . . ." quotes, in WR, "Revelation: An Exposition," *The Biblical World* 10 (August 1897): 102, 103; "Jesus Christ is the standard . . ." and "Each Christian has . . ." quotes, in WR, "The Spiritual Criticism of the Bible," *Examiner*, 5 November 1905.

13. "Contain a real . . ." quote, in WR, "Social Ideas in the Old Testament," *Pulpit Treasury*, April 1899; "the ring . . ." quote, in WR, "Social Ideas in the New Testament," ibid., June 1899.

14. Reminiscences in W. S. Argow, "The Centennial of Walter Rauschenbusch," *Baptist Herald*, 28 September 1961, p. 14.

15. WR presented these thoughts on prayer and on personal religious commitment in an address entitled "Religion the Life of God in the Soul of Man" to the New York State Conference of Religion on 20 November 1900. This is one of numerous WR essays reprinted in *Walter Rauschenbusch: Selected Writings*, pp. 122–33.

16. "Whether we have fallen . . ." quote, in WR, "The Culture of the Spiritual Life," *Rochester Baptist Monthly*, November 1897; WR, "Thoughts on Prayer," ibid., January 1901.

17. Laura Rockefeller to PR, 18 May 1899; R. Höfflin, "Prof. August Rauschenbusch als theologischer Lehrer," *DS*, 27 December 1899; WR, "Allerlei aus Deutschland," *DS*, 31 August 1899; "He was so loveable . . ." quote, ERC to PR, 30 May 1899.

18. F. W. C. Meyer, review of *Leben und Wirken von August Rauschenbusch* in *Baptist Standard*, 23 March 1901; "the father of the German Baptists" quote, in review by A. H. Newman, *Examiner*, 11 April 1901; "no perfect saint" quote, in *LuW*, p. v. The papers, diaries, and letters that WR used in completing the book are preserved in HBS Archives.

19. WR, "The German Work at Rochester and Its Endowment," *Baptist Standard*, 9 July 1898; "in an emotional address . . ." quote, in Woyke, *Heritage*, p. 230.

20. WR to PR, 27 and 29 May 1901; Reinhold Kerstan, "Historical Factors," pp. 168–85; "because of my convictions" quote, WR to Class of 1902, 12 May 1904.

21. "While you can . . ." quote, PR to WR, 4 August 1902; "Memorandum of a Conversation with Dr. Strong, Sept. 6th, 1902."

22. *Democrat and Chronicle*, 23 September 1902; Woyke, *Heritage*, pp. 243, 290; "In the most important . . ." quote, *DS*, October 1902; "duty with such fidelity . . ." quote, Clarke to WR, 27 September 1902; "What will become . . ." quote, Samuel Haemel to WR, 6 October 1902; "I for one . . ." quote, Frank Kaiser to WR, 14 October 1902.

Chapter 8: Rochesterian

1. "All Rochester knows . . ." quote, D. D. MacLaurin, "Rochester Theological Seminary Commencement," *The Watchman*, 5 May 1902; "I love this city . . ." quote, in speech for James Johnston, 15 October 1903 (manuscript in AB-SCHL); "one of the fairest . . ." quote, in *Rochester Post-Express*, 25 November 1898.

2. Blake McKelvey, *Rochester: The Quest for Quality, 1890–1925* (Cambridge, Mass., 1956); Blake McKelvey, "Walter Rauschenbusch's Rochester," *Rochester History*, 14 (October 1952); "many of them . . ." quote, in Baker, "Do It for Rochester," *American Magazine*, September 1910, p. 684.

3. "Settle down to the task . . ." quote, in WR, "The Service of the Church to Society," *Treasury of Religious Thought*, September 1899. Other statements of his outlook include "Proposed Cures for Social Wrongs," ibid., February 1900; "Dogmatic and Pragmatic Socialism," *Rochester Democrat and Chronicle*, 25 February 1901; "Wanted—A New Type of Layman," ibid., 21 February 1906; "The Superior Social Efficiency of Modern Christianity," *Homiletic Review*, May 1906; "A Generous Explanation," *National Baptist Review*, 12 February 1910; "Some Moral Aspects of the 'Woman Movement,' " *Biblical World* 42 (October 1913): 195–99; "The Belated Races and the Social Problems," American Missionary Association pamphlet, January 1914; "The Problem of the Black Man," *American Missionary* 5, n.s. (March 1914), pp. 732–33.

4. WR, "Does Rochester Want Competing Gas? Points Submitted for Discussion to the Economic Club, February 27, 1902," pamphlet; *Democrat and Chronicle*, 20 January 1902; "one of the most effective . . ." quote, WR, *Post-Express*, letter to the editor, 17 March 1902; *Democrat and Chronicle*, 9 April 1902.

5. WR, "Speech for James Johnston," manuscript; *Democrat and Chronicle*, 16 October 1901; Strong to WR, 13 October 1913; Clarence Barbour to WR, 13 October 1903; George Forbes to WR, 14 October 1903; J. H. Gilmore to WR, 16 October 1903; W. Bausch to WR, 29 October 1903.

6. WR, "Report of the Investigating Committee of the Y.M.C.A.," 29 May 1904; *Rochester Union and Advertiser*, 30 May 1904; *Democrat and Chronicle*, 16 and 18 February 1904.

7. WR's speech was reported in the *Democrat and Chronicle*, 3 September 1904. His continued activity on this issue is evident in WR, "What Is the Matter with Rochester?" Address at Labor Lyceum, 3 April 1904; *Rochester Evening Times*, 6 September 1904; *Democrat and Chronicle*, 21 March 1905, 23 January 1906, 24 February 1906; *Post-Express*, 27 January 1906.

8. "Certainly the habits . . ." quote, *Rochester Herald*, 10 July 1904; *Democrat and Chronicle*, 11 and 23 July 1904, 12 May 1905.

9. *Democrat and Chronicle*, 3 February 1902; *Union and Advertiser*, 4 April 1904; American Anti-Saloon League Field Secretary to WR, 7 February 1905; "If working people . . ." quote, in *Union and Advertiser*, 29 March 1909.

10. Herbert S. Weet, "The Development of Public Education in Rochester, 1900–1910," *Rochester Historical Society Publications* (ed. B. McKelvey) 17 (1939): 183–232. Key articles in the extensive newspaper coverage of this episode are *Democrat and Chronicle*, 11 September 1908, 14 November

1908, 4 May 1910; *Rochester Herald,* 14 November 1908; and *Post-Express,* 14 November 1908. "I know how you shrink . . ." quote, PR to WR, 20 October 1908.

11. Report excerpts are from WR, "Draft of the Report of the Committee on Public Schools," manuscript; "Every teacher . . ." quote, WR to PR, 9 January 1909; "strong, shrewd . . ." quote, John Strong to PR, 26 December 1908. A view critical of WR's role is developed by John R. Aiken, "Walter Rauschenbusch and Education for Reform," *Church History* 36 (December 1967): 456–69.

12. Edwin A. Rumball, announcing a City Club meeting on a postal card, n.d.; the meeting was reported in the *Rochester Evening Times,* 11 March 1915.

13. WR to "Dear Brother," 8 September 1904.

14. WR, "The New Evangelism," *The Independent* 56 (1904): 1055–61. Thanks to a gift from a sympathetic businessman, Rufus W. Weeks, three thousand copies of the article were reprinted. Excerpts appeared in English and French publications.

15. "We propose . . ." quote, in *Evening Times,* 21 October 1908; "audiences were most profoundly interested . . ." quote, in *Democrat and Chronicle,* 15 March 1909.

16. WR's Scrapbooks contain numerous clippings about P.S.E. activities. Strayer's collection of clippings is preserved in the Rochester Public Library's Local History Room. Parts of the P.S.E. story are told in McKelvey, *Rochester,* pp. 138–44; Paul Moore Strayer, *Reconstruction of the Church* (New York, 1915), pp. 215–17; and Paul Moore Strayer, *A Sheaf of Prayers* (Rochester, n.d.). "Change of temper . . ." quote, WR to Lyon, 10 December 1915.

17. WR, "Suggestions for the Organization of Local Chapters of the Brotherhood of the Kingdom," brochure, n.d.; "boldest and most important . . ." quote, LW to WR, 4 December 1903; "We do not intend . . ." quote, WR to Edwin Rumball, 26 November 1910 (Rumball Collection, Cornell University Library).

18. "Everything is now coming our way" quote, WR to Brotherhood, 20 July 1907, published in *The Kingdom,* September 1907; "my dear friend . . ." and following quotes, WR to Brotherhood, 20 August 1912.

19. "That quality . . ." quote, J. R. Williams to Doctor Beaven, Mrs. Rauschenbusch, and friends of Walter Rauschenbusch, 3 April 1934; "one reason why . . ." quote, WR to Dores Sharpe, 15 November 1915; "that these were . . ." quote, in Paul Moore Strayer, "Walter Rauschenbusch," *Homiletical Review,* February 1919.

20. "Rigid self-discipline . . ." quote, in D. R. Sharpe, "Walter Rauschenbusch as I Knew Him," *The City Church,* May–June 1956, p. 13; "His ability to

love people . . ." quote, WRR to D. R. Sharpe, 17 December 1938; "We try to love . . ." quote, WR to J. D. Rockefeller, 1 January 1912. Other assessments appear in WR to Hubbell, 2 March 1912; W. M. Metz to W. Logan, 28 January 1913; WR to W. H. Tinker, 19 April 1913; WR to A. Arnold, 6 November 1916.

21. The lives of Edmund and Carolyn Lyon are sketched in Carolyn Lyon Remington, *Vibrant Silence* (Rochester, 1965). "During the time . . ." quote, Strayer to WR, 26 April 1909; WR to Lyon, 3 February 1916.

22. "We enjoy our rest . . ." quote, Laura Rockefeller to PR, 13 June 1902; "We rejoice in all . . ." quote, John Rockefeller to WR, 19 July 1904; "long, continued and most . . ." quote, Rockefeller to WR, 8 July 1910 (the last two letters in the Rockefeller Family Archives, Record Group 2).

23. This account of the Rauschenbusches' home life is based chiefly on interviews with Stephen Raushenbush (who changed his first name and the spelling of his surname in the 1920s), 24 and 25 March 1981; with Carl Raushenbush, 14 May 1981; and with Lisa Rauschenbusch (the only one of the children to preserve the traditional spelling of the family name), 16 and 17 May 1981.

24. "It always grieves . . ." quote, WR to PR, 3 January 1910; "No one realizes . . ." quote, PR to WR, 26 January 1911; "I have an amazed . . ." quote, in WR, "For the Social Conception of the Kingdom of God," *The Congregationalist and Christian World*, 19 November 1910.

Chapter 9: History Professor

1. "Let others teach . . ." quote, in *NYBUME, 1906*, p. 42; other quotes in Douglas, *Autobiography of Strong*, p. 340.

2. This description of RTS developments is based on catalogs and reports to trustees *(NYBUME)*; "mingle with ease . . ." quote, in *NYBUME, 1907*, p. 31.

3. WR to Strong, 24 December 1909.

4. Strong to WR, 28 December 1909; *NYBUME, 1910*, p. 38; WR to RTS faculty, 13 January 1910; Conrad Moehlman to WR, 10 September 1908; Cornelius Woelfkin to WR, 11 October 1910; W. S. Hubbell to WR, 5 July 1910.

5. "Augustus Hopkins Strong: An Appreciation by Walter Rauschenbusch," n.d.

6. RTS's transition is covered well in Leroy Moore, Jr., "The Rise of American Religious Liberalism at the Rochester Theological Seminary, 1872–1928," Ph.D. diss., Claremont Graduate School, 1966. "What work . . ." quote, in *NYBUME, 1911*, p. 38. The question of a Rauschenbusch presidency

was raised in Walter Betteridge to WR, 8 August 1911; Lisa Rauschenbusch also recalled it in an interview, May 1981.

7. A. H. Strong to John Strong, 6 December 1913 (Augustus H. Strong Papers, AB-SCHL); WR to Cross, 5 June 1912; Cross to WR, 7 June 1912; WR to Barbour, 3 July 1914; WR to Nixon, 21 March 1916.

8. "Dr. Rauschenbusch . . ." quote, *NYBUME, 1915*, p. 20; Barbour to WR, 24 February 1916; "history live . . ." quote, in *Rochester Post-Express*, 21 January 1903; "Professor Rauschenbusch . . ." quote, in "The '1900' Record" (Report to the Class of 1900); "all alike seem to have given themselves . . ." quote, in *NYBUME, 1906*, p. 59.

9. Glimpses of WR's teaching style are found in *NYBUME, 1905*, pp. 40–41, and WR to RTS trustees, 30 April 1912. "Could go into his office . . ." quote, in J. E. Skoglund, "Edwin Dahlberg in Conversation: Memories of Walter Rauschenbusch," *Foundations* 18 (1975): 217; "never forget . . ." quote, C. W. Atwater to WR, 6 April 1910; "to right a saleslady's mistake . . ." quote, J. M. Evans to WR, 11 January 1913; "Students all loved him" and "He was really . . ." quotes, in "Dahlberg," pp. 217, 211. Other former students' recollections occur in H. M. Frost to P. Minus, 11 August 1982; Paul S. Burdick to P. Minus, 11 September 1982; and R. W. Thomson to P. Minus, 9 August 1982.

10. WR to RTS trustees, 24 April 1906; WR to "My good friends at the Seminary," *RTS Record, 1907*, p. 12.

11. *Post-Express*, 26 August 1908; "Evangelisch-sozialer Kongress in Dessau, 9 bis 11 Juni," in *Chronik der Christlichen Welt*, vol. 18, 1908 (Marburg University Library); WR, "Impressions of Germany," manuscript of lecture delivered 8 October 1908 and five subsequent times; *CSO*, pp. 36, 91; Claude Welch, *Protestant Thought in the Nineteenth Century* (New Haven and London, 1985), 2:1–30. In 1911 WR was one of only three American scholars included in a public tribute to Harnack on his sixtieth birthday. The Ritschlian influence was especially evident in his final book, *A Theology for the Social Gospel*, but there WR also expressed regret that Ritschl's theological perspective had been developed without benefit of the insight generated by sociological analysis (pp. 138–39). In 1913 WR complained to a friend, "The Christian social thinkers in Germany . . . are rather tame and do not get beyond mild reform talk. Most of them are made conservative by their government positions" (WR to J. E. Franklin, 16 June 1913). In view of the non-Ritschlian origins of Rauschenbusch's thought and his continued ambivalence toward the German scholar and his disciples, it is misleading to label him a "Ritschlian."

12. "Report of Professor Stewart," *NYBUME, 1904*, p. 43; "Report of the Committee of Examination," *NYBUME, 1910*, p. 54; "Report of the Dean," *NYBUME, 1911*, pp. 42–43; *RTSBR*, May 1913, pp. 3–6; *NYBUME, 1913*, p. 36.

13. "I miss it all . . ." quote, in *RTS Record, 1907;* "I rejoice . . ." quote, Letter to 1903 Alumni, 1909.

14. "Dry bones . . ." quote, Henry Robbins to WR, 24 August 1903; "We have very little . . ." and "the way people looked . . ." quotes, in *Rochester Union-Advertiser*, 14 May 1914.

15. WR's chief explanations of his approach to historical study are "The Influence of Historical Studies on Theology," *American Journal of Theology* 11 (1907): 111–27; "The Value and Use of History," *RTSBR*, November 1914, pp. 31–41; and "Introduction to the Study of Church History," lecture notes, 1905. The estimate mentioned of the uniqueness of WR's historiographical scholarship is by Henry Warner Bowden, *Church History in the Age of Science: Historiographical Patterns in the United States, 1876–1918* (Chapel Hill, N.C., 1971), pp. 175, 179.

16. All quotations save the last two are from "Introduction to the Study of Church History," 1905, pp. 1–4; "it carries . . ." and "every reformatory . . ." quotes, from WR, "The Development of the Catholic Church," lecture notes, February 1907.

17. WR, "Baptists in History," *The Baptist Observer*, October 1906.

18. Quotes in "Why I Am a Baptist," *Rochester Baptist Monthly*, December 1905; WR, "The Social Mission of Baptists," *The Christian Socialist*, 1 November 1907.

19. "Kept alive artificially" quote, in WR, "Christian Union as an Historical Problem," *RTSBR*, May 1917, p. 60; "formal union" quote, in WR, "The True American Church," *The Congregationalist*, 23 October 1913, p. 562.

20. The 1913 statement appears in WR, "Genesis," *RTSBR*, November 1918, p. 52; "to do for Church History . . ." quote, WR to Frederick Harris, 23 June 1917.

21. WR, "The Development of the Catholic Church," lecture notes, February 1907, pp. 1, 4, 7.

22. WR, "The Reformation: The Condition of Europe before the Reformation," lecture notes, 1905; "The Anabaptists took Jesus Christ . . ." quote, in *Rochester Democrat and Chronicle*, 15 September 1903. WR's translating and editing of two letters by Conrad Grebel was an important early instance of American Anabaptist scholarship: "The Zurich Anabaptists and Thomas Münzer," *American Journal of Theology* 9 (January 1905): 91–106. A brief appreciation of the Anabaptists also appears in WR, "The Baptist Contribution to Religious and Civil Liberty," in *Freedom and the Churches*, ed. C. W. Wendte (Boston, 1910), pp. 1–5. An important influence on WR's interpretation of the Anabaptists was English Baptist Richard Heath, who published both on the Anabaptist movement and on the social awakening.

23. "An unexampled . . ." quote, in WR, "Baptists and Church History," *RTSBR*, May 1913, p. 31; "right of private judgment . . ." quote, in WR, "The Freedom of Spiritual Religion," Sermon preached before the Northern Baptist Convention, 8 May 1910. WR's major writing in Amer-

ican church history was done for *Handbuch der Kirchengeschichte*, ed. Gustav Krüger (Tübingen, 1909); his contribution to this "handbook" has not been published in English.

24. WR's brief explanation of his "History of Social Redemption" course appeared in *RTSBR*, May 1916, p. 41. This subject was the theme of the fourth chapter of *CSC* and was restated in shorter form in the third chapter of part 2 of *CSO*. WR remarked in the introduction to *CSC* that he had "never met with any previous attempt to give a satisfactory historical explanation of this failure" and that he regarded this chapter as one of the most important in the book (p. xiii).

25. WR's analysis of this theme appeared often in his speeches; it was stated both in *CSC* (pp. 201–10) and in *CSO* (pp. 83–95).

Chapter 10: "Apostle of a Mighty Gospel"

1. "Dangerous book," "a good deal of anger . . . ," and "for the Lord Christ . . ." quotes, in WR, "Genesis of 'Christianity and the Social Crisis,' " *RTSBR*, November 1918, pp. 51–53; "I often was overwhelmed . . ." quote, WR to Professor Genocchi, 24 June 1908. In an unpublished "Bibliography for the Book," WR prepared an outline of reading he had done for each chapter, as well as brief notes about when each was written and rewritten.

2. WR to Macmillan Company, 17 September 1906; WR to Brett, 30 October 1906; WR to Macmillan, 27 November 1906; WR to Brett, 5 December 1906; Brett to WR, 7 December 1906; WR to Macmillan, 20 March 1907; E. C. Marsh to WR, 22 March 1907.

3. "Seldom have I . . ." quote, in Dean Stewart, "Professor Rauschenbusch's 'Christianity and the Social Crisis,' " *Rochester Baptist Monthly*, June 1907, p. 212. Page numbers in parentheses in the text here and below are for quotations from *CSC*.

4. Stewart to WR, 29 April 1907; "all act and speak . . ." quote, F. C. A. Jones to WR, 13 May 1907; "as epoch-making . . ." quote, Strong to WR, 27 June 1907.

5. Sales and royalty figures are estimated on the basis of reports from Macmillan saved by WR. He also preserved numerous letters and reviews that came in response to *CSC*. The Baker article, "A Vision of the New Christianity: An Account of Professor Walter Rauschenbusch and His Work," was first published in *The American Magazine*, December 1909; the following year it appeared as the concluding chapter of Baker's book, *The Spiritual Unrest*. "Has been used as a textbook . . ." quote, WR to Pitt F. Parker, 30 September 1912; Fosdick's statement appears in *A Rauschenbusch Reader*, ed. Benson Y. Landis (New York, 1957), p. xiii.

6. *Living Church*, 27 July 1907; *New York Herald*, 28 July 1907; Albion W. Small, Review of *CSC*, *Unity*, 12 December 1907; Charles Henderson, Review of *CSC*, *American Journal of Theology*, January 1908, pp. 172–74.

7. WR to George Coleman, 17 June 1908; Stewart to WR, 9 March 1908; *Journal and Messenger*, 14 November 1907; *Examiner*, 18 July 1907; I. M. Haldeman, "Rauschenbusch's Christianity and the Social Crisis," pamphlet, 1911.

8. WR to J. E. Franklin, 11 July 1911 and 20 July 1912; "an apostle of a mighty Gospel ..." quote, WR to students, 18 May 1911. Only a French translation of *CSC* appeared (in 1919).

9. "Psychological moment" and "that it gave them ..." quotes in "Genesis," 1918, p. 53.

10. Phillips to WR, 8 February 1909, 12 March 1909, and 14 July 1910. The "favorite book" statement and other information about the prayers appear in an undated and untitled set of outline notes, probably written in 1913 for the Gates Lectures at Grinnell College.

11. All the prayers are in *For God and the People:* "For the Fatherhood of God," p. 45; "For This World," p. 47; "For Children Who Work," pp. 51–52; "For Employers," p. 61; "For a Share in the Work of Redemption," p. 117; "For the Church," p. 119; "For the Cooperative Commonwealth," p. 125.

12. Strong to WR, 30 November 1910; Sheldon to WR, 30 January 1914; *Examiner*, 5 December 1910; *Rochester Post-Express*, 7 December 1910; "I shall always ..." quote, in untitled notes cited above (n. 10). German, Spanish, and Japanese editions appeared after WR's death.

13. WR to Brett, 26 December 1910, 30 January 1911, 21 April 1911; " 'What must we do? ...' " quote, in *CSO*, p. viii.

14. "I shrink from condemning ..." quote, WR to Brett, 30 September 1911; "I don't want to be persecuted ..." quote, WR to Weeks, 2 August 1912; "overdone it ..." quote, WR to Phillips, 27 July 1912.

15. Information about translations of this and other WR books is summarized in *Righteousness of the Kingdom*, pp. 289–91. "I recently ordered ..." quote, in *Methodist Quarterly Review*, 1914, p. 390.

16. Merriam to WR, 1 December 1912; Strong to WR, 30 December 1912; "evils belonging to human nature" quote, in *Hartford Seminary Record*, January 1913; Nearing review, in *Annals of the American Academy of Political and Social Sciences*, n.d.; WR to Nearing, 21 April 1913; WR to Franklin, 16 June 1913.

17. WR's involvement with the Federal Council of Churches is reflected in F. M. North to WR, 3 August 1908; WR to North, 28 August 1908; North to WR, 10 December 1908; WR to James Cannon, 7 December 1911; WR to Charles Macfarland, 14 October 1912; E. B. Sanford to WR, 4 November 1912. His involvement with the other organizations is reflected in WR to C. A. Nesbit, 4 July 1911; Josiah Strong to WR, 21 April 1913; Batten to WR, 4 October 1911; Bliss to WR, 17 November 1913; WR to Bliss, 9 December 1913.

18. "I do not propose . . ." quote, WR to Coleman, 17 June 1908; "There is no better . . ." quote, Coleman to Stewart, 7 December 1908.

19. The report of his doubled work load in "Genesis of 'Christianity and the Social Crisis,' " 1918; "Perhaps I ought . . ." quote, WR to Strong, 25 April 1911.

20. "Whether the invitation . . ." quote, WR to Horace W. Cole, 31 October 1913. The shifts of mood and conviction are reflected in dozens of letters—e.g., WR to PR, 29 July 1909, 6 July 1911, 5 June 1912, 16 February 1913; WR to Phillips, 13 January 1911; WR to C. V. Vickrey, 5 February 1913; WR to E. B. Scheve, 13 February 1914; WR to J. W. Nixon, 26 March 1914; WR to S. G. Bland, 5 February 1914.

21. *The Independent*, 1 May 1913, p. 963. Book dedications: Henry Vedder, *The Reformation in Germany* (New York, 1914); John Spargo, *The Substance of Socialism* (New York, 1909); Charles D. Williams, *The Christian Ministry and Social Problems* (New York, 1917). Hymn dedications by Charles E. Perkins and William G. Ballantine. The Wise comment is in Wise to E. S. Wiers, 30 November 1914; "the chief apostle . . ." quote, in *The Universalist Leader*, 18 January 1913; Wilfred Monod, Review of *Pour Dieu et pour le peuple* in *Semaine Litteraire*, December 1913.

Chapter 11: Dissenter

1. "Historical opportunities . . ." quote, in Address to Religious Citizenship League, 30 January 1914, manuscript.

2. "Ever the pride . . ." quote, in *For God and the People*, p. 109. The Zurich conference is discussed in E. E. Pratt to WR, 16 April 1914, and Frederick Lynch to WR, 27 May 1914. Concerns for family discussed in ERC to WR, 6 September 1914; WR to Hilmar Rauschenbusch, 23 September 1914; WR to David Curtis, 24 November 1914; WR to Robert Fareilly, 30 December 1914.

3. "He was a sad man" quote, W. S. Webb to Gene Bartlett, 2 June 1964; W. G. Gannett to WR, 30 September 1914; "profound grief and depression of spirit" quote, WR to Editor, *Congregationalist*, 24 September 1914; *Journal and Messenger*, 29 October 1914.

4. "Be Fair to Germany: A Plea for Open-mindedness," *Congregationalist*, 15 October 1914.

5. *Regina Morning Leader*, 5 November 1914; WR to C. E. Bland, 9 November 1914; WR to D. R. Sharpe, 9 November 1914 and 2 January 1915; "The old superstition . . ." quote, WR to HR, 19 November 1914.

6. George Coleman to WR, 19 December 1914; David Curtis to WR, 7 December 1914; WR to Sharpe, 15 November 1915; WR to Curtis, 24 March 1915; C. B. Naismith to WR, 21 May 1915; WR to John J. Petrie, 29 May 1916; W. C. Moore to WR, 5 May 1917.

7. WR to Alling, 7 March 1917 ("The substance of a letter written to a friend by WR"); "they don't like to remind me . . ." quote, WR to Thomas C. Hall, 10 November 1914, Union Theological Seminary Archives; "anyone speaking for Germany . . ." and "It is on me . . ." quotes, WR to Sharpe, 9 November 1914; "Unfortunately I am not thick-skinned" quote, WR to A. A. Boyden, 24 September 1915; "Many of us feel . . ." quote, in *Los Angeles Sunday Times*, 23 May 1915.

8. WR to PR, 24 June 1915, 4 July 1915; "hailstorm of anger" quote, WR to Sharpe, 15 November 1915; "Every instinct of truth . . ." quote, WR to G. H. Ekins, 20 January 1916.

9. "All fighting for expansion and wealth" quote, in "War and Hate: A Reply," *Standard*, 18 November 1916; "It was hard enough . . ." quote, WR to J. S. Phillips, 16 May 1917. Other WR statements about the war appeared in *Standard*, 26 August 1916 and 30 September 1916 and in newspaper reports of local events: *Rochester Times*, 5 September 1916, and *Rochester Herald*, 23 August 1915, 20 January 1917, 26 February 1917. Also in letters to the editor: ibid., 28 April 1916, 17 July 1916, 20 July 1916; *Unity*, 7 December 1916; *Rochester Evening Times*, 10 January 1917, 14 February 1917, 23 February 1917, and in an interview, ibid., 2 February 1917.

10. Helpful background on WR's struggles is supplied in Marchand, *The American Peace Movement*, and in Ray H. Abrams, *Preachers Present Arms* (Scottsdale, Pa., 1967). His increasing sympathy for the FOR and for American socialists is seen in Rufus M. Jones to WR, 28 April 1916; E. W. Evans to WR, 28 July 1916; WR to Sharpe, 13 December 1916; Jesse H. Holmes to WR, 19 February 1917; WR to Upton Sinclair, 12 October 1915; WR to A. J. Muste, 13 March 1917. "An electric shock . . ." quote, WR to Sharpe, 21 April 1916. FOR files in Nyack, New York, show that WR became a member on 6 December 1916. The comment about his possibly becoming a Quaker was recalled by Lisa Rauschenbusch in an interview, May 1981. A report of his Rochester rally speech appeared in the *Rochester Herald*, 26 February 1917.

11. *NYBUME, 1917*, pp. 32, 37.

12. "Everywhere known as loyal . . ." quote, Faunce to WR, 22 January 1917; "perverse patriots" quote, Thomas to WR, 12 November 1917.

13. Preparation and dissemination of the letter are discussed in Strayer to WR, 25 April 1918; WR to Woelfkin, 25 April 1918 and 1 May 1918; Woelfkin to WR, 1 May 1918; Barbour to WR, 1 May, 23 May, and 7 June 1918.

14. "The German government be crushed" quote, Barbour to WR, 1 May 1918; "it will do something . . ." quote, A. H. Strong to John Strong, 2 July 1918 (Augustus H. Strong Papers, AB-SCHL). Different interpreta-

tions of WR's letter to Woelfkin are discussed in Sharpe, *Rauschenbusch*, pp. 388–92, and WRR to Sharpe, 30 January 1942.

15. WR to Harold Marshall, 20 March 1914, 1 May 1916; "I am only a side-issue" quote, WR to Family, 16 June 1916.

16. E. C. Marsh to WR, 19 January 1916, 16 May 1916; WR to Frederick Harris, 17 January 1916, 21 July 1916; WR to Edwards, 21 July 1916; WR to Sharpe, 4 December 1916, 17 November 1917; Association Press to WR, 1 March 1918; "to make the thoughts . . ." quote, WR to R. H. Edwards, 21 August 1915.

17. Walker to WR, 9 December 1915; WR to Walker, 31 December 1915, 15 January 1916; "more fully on the foundations . . ." quote, WR to LW, 18 June 1917; "dumb-bell system . . ." quote, in *Theology of the Social Gospel* (New York, 1917), p. 9.

18. WR to Macmillan, 3 September 1917; WR to H. S. Latham, 1 November 1917; W. Gladden to WR, 13 November 1917; Strayer to WR, 6 November 1917; E. C. Marsh to WR, 5 November, 8 November, and 12 November, 1917; C. H. Frank to WR, 7 November 1917; WR to C. H. Frank, 8 November 1917; WR to Marsh, 9 November 1917.

19. James Bishop Thomas, in *The Social Preparation*, July 1918, p. 23; Gerald Birney Smith, in *American Journal of Theology* 22 (October 1918), p. 583; Charles Clayton Morrison, in *The Christian Century*, 14 February 1918; Strong to WR, 28 December 1917; "evidently does not know . . ." quote, *Lutheran Quarterly*, January 1918, p. 142; *The Presbyterian*, n.d.

20. The New Jersey caution was reported by *Journal and Messenger*, 16 April 1914; "When you charge me . . ." quote, WR to Riley, 24 March 1914; "It seemed to me . . ." quote, WR to editor of *Western Recorder*, 30 September 1916. A similar pattern is seen in WR to editor of *Western Recorder*, 20 March 1915; WR to editor of *Herald and Presbyter*, 12 October 1916; WR to George Sutherland, 1 January 1915; Fred J. Sauer to WR, 26 January 1915; WR to G. D. Brookes, 6 December 1916.

21. PR to WR, 28 April 1916; WR to HR, 22 March 1917; "make the transition . . ." quote, WR to HR, 1 May 1917; Paul Rauschenbusch to WR, 17 December 1916; WR to HR, 4 October 1916, 22 March 1917; PR to Lincoln Steffens, 28 January 1921.

22. H. S. Latham to WR, 23 June 1914; WR to H. A. Bridgman, 12 October 1914; ERC to WR, 13 May 1914 and 5 August 1916; WR to ERC, 30 November 1914 and 24 April 1915; "very searching apology" quote, WR to ERC, 26 March 1915; WR's notes on his argument with ERC, 29 March 1915.

23. PR to WR, 20 June 1915; WRR to PR, 13 March 1917; WR to Paul Rauschenbusch, 7 November 1916.

24. "Mental depression . . ." quote, WR to Sharpe, 17 November 1917; G. W. Gould (name uncertain) to WR, 3 December 1917; WR to Sharpe, 2 February 1918; "Work and effort come hard . . ." quote, WR to Barbour, 25 February 1918; "practically no hope . . ." quote, in WR, "Summary by Dr. Hamman," 15 May, 1918; WR, 1918 Diary (kept for several weeks during the late winter).

25. "I dread nothing . . ." quote, WR to Sharpe, 19 May 1918.

26. "The inner significance . . ." quote, WR to Vedder, 7 December 1916. The "Affirmation of Faith" apparently accompanied a memorandum WR wrote for his family, 31 March 1918, that later was given the title "Instructions in Case of My Death." The lines of poetry cited are from a poem WR called "God"; the other poem he called "The Castle of My Soul." After WR's death, Pauline gave the poem excerpted here the title "The Little Gate to God" and circulated it widely. The letter to Barnes was published in *RTSBR*, November 1918, pp. 38–39.

27. Information about WR's last weeks in PR to Sharpe, 18 May and 27 August 1918; WR to HR, 27 May, 5 June, and 11 June 1918; A. H. Strong to John Strong, 22 July 1918 (Augustus H. Strong Papers); "When you come home . . ." quote, PR to WR, 14 July 1918; "peacefully slumbering . . ." quote, PR to HR, 24 July 1918; "free from care . . ." quote, 27 July 1918.

28. *RTSBR*, November 1918, contains the tributes: Baker, p. 73; Ward, p. 68; Sharpe, p. 79; Dahlberg, p. 77; Nixon, p. 79.

BIBLIOGRAPHY

Ahlstrom, Sydney E., ed. *Theology in America: The Major Protestant Voices from Puritanism to Neo-Orthodoxy.* American Heritage Series. Indianapolis: Bobbs-Merrill Company, 1967. Chapter 12 is on Rauschenbusch.

Aiken, John R. "Walter Rauschenbusch and Education for Reform." *Church History* 36 (1967): 456–69.

Allen, Jimmy Raymond. "Comparative Study of the Concept of the Kingdom of God in the Writings of Walter Rauschenbusch and Reinhold Niebuhr." Th.D. dissertation, Southwestern Baptist Theological Seminary, 1958.

Altschuler, Glenn C. "Walter Rauschenbusch: Theology, the Church, and the Social Gospel." *Foundations* 22 (1979): 140–51.

Argow, W. S. "The Centennial of Walter Rauschenbusch." *Baptist Herald*, 28 September 1961, pp. 14–15.

Baker, Ray Stannard. *The Spiritual Unrest.* New York: Frederick H. Stokes Company, 1910. Chapter 7 reproduces Baker's 1909 article in *The American Magazine* on Rauschenbusch, entitled "The Spiritual Unrest: A Vision of the New Christianity."

Barnes, Sherman B. "Walter Rauschenbusch as Historian." *Foundations* 12 (1969): 254–62.

Barnette, Henlee Huxlit. "The Ethical Thought of Walter Rauschenbusch." Ph.D. dissertation, Southern Baptist Theological Seminary, 1948.

Bartlett, Gene E. "Rauschenbusch: A Portrait in Perspective." *Missions*, October 1961, pp. 23–25.

Batten, Samuel Zane. "Walter Rauschenbusch." *The Social Service Bulletin* (Methodist Federation for Social Service), September 1918, p. 2.

Bodein, Vernon Parker. *The Social Gospel of Walter Rauschenbusch and Its Relation to Religious Education.* Yale Studies in Religious Education, vol. 16. New Haven: Yale University Press, 1944.

229

Bowden, Henry Warner. *Church History in the Age of Science: Historiographical Patterns in the United States, 1876–1918*. Chapel Hill: University of North Carolina Press, 1971. Chapter 7 is on Rauschenbusch.

Bowden, Henry Warner. "Walter Rauschenbusch and American Church History." *Foundations* 9 (1966): 234–50.

Bronk, Mitchell. "Walter Rauschenbusch." *Adult Leader,* October 1934.

Brunson, Drexel Timothy. "The Quest for Social Justice: A Study of Walter Rauschenbusch and His Influence on Reinhold Niebuhr and Martin Luther King, Jr." Ph.D. dissertation, Florida State University, 1980.

Cauthen, Kenneth. *The Impact of American Religious Liberalism*. New York: Harper and Row, 1962. See especially chapter 5, "The Social Gospel: Walter Rauschenbusch."

Cross, Robert D. Introduction to *Christianity and the Social Crisis* by Walter Rauschenbusch. New York: Harper Torchbooks, 1964.

Dale, Verhey Allen. "The Use of Scripture in Moral Discourse: A Case Study of Walter Rauschenbusch." Ph.D. dissertation, Yale University, 1975.

Daniel, C. A. "Walter Rauschenbusch as I Knew Him." *Michigan Christian Advocate,* 24 November and 1 December 1938.

David, William E. "A Comparative Study of the Social Ethics of Walter Rauschenbusch and Reinhold Niebuhr." Ph.D. dissertation, Vanderbilt University, 1958.

Davies, Horton. "The Expression of the Social Gospel in Worship." *Studia Liturgica* 2 (1963): 174–92.

Davis, R. Dennis. "The Impact of Evolutionary Thought on Walter Rauschenbusch." *Foundations* 21 (1978): 254–71.

Dickinson, Richard. "The Church's Responsibility for Society. Rauschenbusch and Niebuhr: Brothers under the Skin?" *Religion in Life* 27 (1957–58): 163–71.

Ede, Alfred J. "The Social Theologies of Walter Rauschenbusch and Vatican II in Dialogue." *Foundations* 18 (1975): 198–208.

Fricke, Ernest E. "Socialism and Christianity in Walter Rauschenbusch." D.Theol. dissertation, Basel University, 1965.

"Funeral Service," "Memorial Service," "Tributes from Friends, Alumni, Students," "Reviews of Major Books." *Rochester Theological Seminary Bulletin: The Record* 69 (1918): 2–80.

Gabriel, Ralph Henry. *The Course of American Democratic Thought*. 2d ed. New York: Ronald Press Company, 1956. Chapter 20 deals partly with Rauschenbusch.

Gustafson, James M. "From Scripture to Social Policy and Social Action." *Andover-Newton Bulletin* 9 (1969): 160–69.

Haldeman, I. M. *Rauschenbusch's "Christianity and the Social Crisis."* New York: Charles C. Cook, n.d.

Handy, Robert T., ed. *The Social Gospel in America, 1870–1920*. Library of Protestant Thought. New York: Oxford University Press, 1966. Part 3 deals with Rauschenbusch.

Handy, Robert T. "Walter Rauschenbusch." In *Ten Makers of Modern Protestant Thought,* edited by G. L. Hunt. New York: Association Press, 1958.

Handy, Robert T. "Walter Rauschenbusch in Historical Perspective." *Baptist Quarterly* 20 (1964): 313–21.

Hopkins, C. Howard. *The Rise of the Social Gospel in American Protestantism, 1865–1915.* Yale Studies in Religious Education, vol. 14. New Haven: Yale University Press, 1940. See especially chapter 13, "Walter Rauschenbusch Formulates the Social Gospel."

Hopkins, C. Howard. "Walter Rauschenbusch and the Brotherhood of the Kingdom." *Church History* 7 (1938): 138–56.

Hudson, Frederic M. "The Reign of the New Humanity: A Study of the Background, History, and Influence of the Brotherhood of the Kingdom." Ph.D. dissertation, Columbia University, 1968.

Hudson, Winthrop S. *The Great Tradition of the American Churches.* New York: Harper and Row, 1953. See especially chapter 10, "A Lonely Prophet: The Continuity of the Great Tradition."

Hudson, Winthrop S. "Rauschenbusch—Evangelical Prophet." *The Christian Century,* 24 June 1953, pp. 740–42.

Hudson, Winthrop S. "Walter Rauschenbusch and the New Evangelism." *Religion in Life* 30 (1961): 412–30.

Hudson, Winthrop S., ed. *Walter Rauschenbusch: Selected Writings.* Sources of American Spirituality. New York: Paulist Press, 1984.

Hutchison, William R., ed. *American Protestant Thought: The Liberal Era.* New York: Harper and Row, 1968. Chapter 10 includes an essay by Rauschenbusch.

Hutchison, William R. *The Modernist Impulse in American Protestantism.* Cambridge, Mass.: Harvard University Press, 1976. Chapter 5 includes consideration of Rauschenbusch.

Jaehn, Klaus Jurgen. *Rauschenbusch: The Formative Years.* Valley Forge, Pa.: Judson Press, 1976.

Johnson, Carl Ebert. "Walter Rauschenbusch as Historian." Ph.D. dissertation, Duke University, 1976.

King, William McGuire. "The Biblical Base of the Social Gospel." In *The Bible and Social Reform,* edited by Ernest R. Sandeen. The Bible in American Culture. Philadelphia: Fortress Press, 1982.

Landis, Benson Y., comp. *A Rauschenbusch Reader: The Kingdom of God and the Social Gospel.* With an Interpretation of the Life and Work of Walter Rauschenbusch by Harry Emerson Fosdick. New York: Harper and Brothers, 1957.

Langford, S. Fraser. "The Gospel of Augustus H. Strong and Walter Rauschenbusch." *The Chronicle* 14 (1951): 3–18.

Locke, Harvey James. "Rauschenbusch." Ph.D. dissertation, University of Chicago, 1930.

McClintock, David Alan. "Walter Rauschenbusch: The Kingdom of God and the American Experience." Ph.D. dissertation, Case Western Reserve University, 1975.

McGiffert, Arthur C. "Walter Rauschenbusch: Twenty Years After." *Christendom* 3 (1938): 96–109.

McInerny, William F., Jr. "Scripture and Christian Ethics: An Evaluative Analysis of the Uses of Scripture in the Works of Walter Rauschenbusch." Ph.D. dissertation, Marquette University, 1984.

McKelvey, Blake. "Walter Rauschenbusch's Rochester." *Rochester History* 14 (1952): 1–27.

Marney, Carlyle. "The Significance of Walter Rauschenbusch for Today." *Foundations* 2 (1959): 13–26.

Massanari, Ronald Lee. "The Sacred Workshop of God: Reflections on the Historical Perspective of Walter Rauschenbusch." *Religion in Life* 40 (1971): 257–66.

Mays, Benjamin E., comp. *A Gospel for the Social Awakening: Selections from the Writings of Walter Rauschenbusch.* New York: Association Press, 1950.

Meyer, F. W. C. "Rauschenbusch Aflame for God!" *The Baptist Herald,* 1 October 1936, pp. 304–5.

Meyer, F. W. C. "Walter Rauschenbusch: Preacher, Professor, and Prophet." *The Standard* (3 February 1911): 662–63.

Moehlman, Conrad H. "The Life and Writings of Walter Rauschenbusch." *Colgate Rochester Divinity School Bulletin* 1 (1928): 32–37.

Moehlman, Conrad H. "Walter Rauschenbusch and His Interpreters." *The Crozer Quarterly* 23 (1946): 34–49.

Moellering, R. L. "Rauschenbusch in Retrospect." *Concordia Theological Monthly* 27 (1956): 613–33.

Moore, James R. "Walter Rauschenbusch and the Religious Education of Youth." *Religious Education* 68 (1973): 435–53.

Moore, Leroy, Jr. "The Rise of American Religious Liberalism at the Rochester Theological Seminary, 1872–1928." Ph.D. dissertation, Claremont Graduate School, 1966.

Muelder, Walter G. "Walter Rauschenbusch and the Contemporary Scene." *The City Church,* March–April 1957, pp. 10–12.

Müller, Reinhart. *Walter Rauschenbusch: Ein Beitrag zur Begegnung des deutschen und des amerikanischen Protestantismus.* Leiden: E. J. Brill, 1957.

Niebuhr, Reinhold. "Walter Rauschenbusch in Historical Perspective." *Religion in Life* 27 (1958): 527–36.

Nixon, Justin Wroe. "The Realism of Rauschenbusch." *The City Church,* November–December 1956, pp. 5–7.

Nixon, Justin Wroe. "The Social Philosophy of Walter Rauschenbusch." *Colgate Rochester Divinity School Bulletin* 1 (1928): 103–9.

Nixon, Justin Wroe. "Walter Rauschenbusch: The Man and His Work." *Colgate Rochester Divinity School Bulletin* 30 (1958): 21–32.

Nixon, Justin Wroe. "Walter Rauschenbusch after Forty Years." *Christendom* 12 (1947): 476–85.

Nixon, Justin Wroe. "Walter Rauschenbusch—Ten Years After." *The Christian Century,* 8 November 1928, pp. 1359–61.

Noble, David W. *The Paradox of Progressive Thought.* Minneapolis: University of Minnesota Press, 1958. Chapter 10 deals with Rauschenbusch.

Noble, David W. *The Progressive Mind, 1890–1917*. Rev. ed. Minneapolis: Burgess Publishing Company, 1981. See especially chapter 4.

Oxnam, G. Bromley. *Personalities in Social Reform*. New York: Abingdon-Cokesbury Press, 1950. See chapter 2: "The Minister as Social Reformer: Walter Rauschenbusch."

Robins, Henry Burke. "The Contribution of Walter Rauschenbusch to World Peace." *Colgate Rochester Divinity School Bulletin* 12 (1940): 149–54.

Robins, Henry Burke. "The Religion of Walter Rauschenbusch." *Colgate Rochester Divinity School Bulletin* 1 (1928): 37–43.

Sharpe, Dores R. *Walter Rauschenbusch*. New York: Macmillan Company, 1942.

Sharpe, Dores R. "Walter Rauschenbusch as I Knew Him." *The City Church*, May–June 1956, pp. 12–14.

Singer, Anna M. *Walter Rauschenbusch and His Contribution to Social Christianity*. Boston: Gorham Press, 1926.

Skoglund, John E. "Edwin Dahlberg in Conversation: Memories of Walter Rauschenbusch." *Foundations* 18 (1975): 209–18.

Smith, H. Shelton. *Changing Conceptions of Original Sin*. New York: Charles Scribner's Sons, 1955. Chapter 9 includes consideration of Rauschenbusch.

Smucker, Donovan E. "Multiple Motifs in the Thought of Rauschenbusch: A Study in the Origins of the Social Gospel." *Encounter* 19 (1958): 14–20.

Smucker, Donovan E. "The Origins of Walter Rauschenbusch's Social Ethics." Ph.D. dissertation, University of Chicago, 1957.

Smucker, Donovan E. "The Rauschenbusch Story." *Foundations* 2 (1959): 4–12.

Smucker, Donovan E. "Rauschenbusch's View of the Church as a Dynamic Voluntary Association." In *Voluntary Associations: A Study of Groups in Free Societies*, edited by D. B. Robertson, pp. 159–70. Richmond, Va.: John Knox Press, 1966.

Smucker, Donovan E. "Walter Rauschenbusch: Anabaptist, Pietist, and Social Prophet." *Mennonite Life* 36 (1981): 21–23.

Smucker, Donovan E. "Walter Rauschenbusch and Anabaptist Historiography." In *The Recovery of the Anabaptist Vision*, edited by Guy F. Hershberger, pp. 291–304. Scottsdale, Pa.: Herald Press, 1957.

Stackhouse, Max L. "Eschatology and Ethical Method: A Structural Analysis of Contemporary Christian Social Ethics in America with Primary Reference to Walter Rauschenbusch and Reinhold Niebuhr." Ph.D. dissertation, Harvard University, 1964.

Stackhouse, Max L. "The Formation of a Prophet. Reflections on the Early Sermons of Walter Rauschenbusch." *Andover-Newton Quarterly* 9 (1969): 137–59.

Stackhouse, Max L. Introduction to *The Righteousness of the Kingdom* by Walter Rauschenbusch. Nashville: Abingdon Press, 1968. Contains the most complete bibliography of works by Rauschenbusch (pp. 289–307).

Stormer, John A. *None Dare Call It Treason*. Florissant, Mo.: Liberty Bell Press, 1964. Chapter 7, "Subverting Our Religious Heritage," includes a quick look at Rauschenbusch.

Strain, Charles R. "Toward a Generic Analysis of a Classic of the Social Gospel: An Essay Review of Walter Rauschenbusch, *Christianity and the Social Gospel.*" *Journal of the American Academy of Religion* 46 (1978): 525–43.

Strain, Charles R. "Walter Rauschenbusch: A Resource for Public Theology." *Union Seminary Quarterly Review* 34 (1978): 23–34.

Strayer, Paul Moore. "Walter Rauschenbusch: An Apostle of the Kingdom." *Homiletical Review*, February 1919, pp. 91–94.

Thompson, Ernest Trice. *Changing Emphases in American Preaching: The Stone Lectures for 1943.* Philadelphia: Westminster Press, 1943. See chapter 5, "Walter Rauschenbusch and the Challenge of the Social Gospel."

Vulgamore, Melvin L. "The Social Gospel Old and New: Walter Rauschenbusch and Harvey Cox." *Religion in Life* 36 (1967): 516–33.

White, Ronald C., Jr., and C. Howard Hopkins. *The Social Gospel: Religion and Reform in Changing America.* Philadelphia: Temple University Press, 1976. Chapter 5, "An American Prophet," is about Rauschenbusch.

Woyke, Frank H. *Heritage and Ministry of the North American Baptist Conference.* Oakbrook Terrace, Ill.: North American Baptist Conference, 1979.

INDEX